The Macintosh
iLife '04

by Jim Heid

Peachpit
Press

Avondale
MEDIA

The Macintosh iLife '04
Jim Heid

Peachpit Press
1249 Eighth Street
Berkeley, CA 94710
800/283-9444
510/524-2178
510/524-2221 (fax)
Find us on the World Wide Web at: www.peachpit.com
To report errors, please send a note to errata@peachpit.com

Peachpit Press is a division of Pearson Education

Published by Peachpit Press in association with Avondale Media.
Copyright © 2004 by Jim Heid
Editor: Barbara Assadi, BayCreative
Book Design and Illustration: Arne Hurty, BayCreative
Compositor and Layout Design: Jonathan Woolson
Production Coordinator: Myrna Vladic, Baddog Graphics
Indexer: Emily Glossbrenner, FireCrystal Communications
Cover design: Arne Hurty, BayCreative

Trademarks
Trademarks are used throughout this book

ISBN 0-321-24671-3
9 8 7 6 5 4 3 2 1
Printed and bound in the United States of America.

For Maryellen,
for my mother,
and in loving memory
of George Heid, my dad.
A master of the analog
hub, he would have
loved this stuff.

George Heid (right), recording direct to disc
on a moving train, in the early 1950s.

About the Author

Jim Heid has been working with and writing about personal computers since 1980, when he computerized his home-built ham radio station with a Radio Shack TRS-80 Model I. As Senior Technical Editor of one of the first computer magazines, *Kilobaud Microcomputing*, he began working with Macintosh prototypes in 1983. He began writing for *Macworld* magazine in 1984, and has been a Contributing Editor ever since. He currently writes its monthly "Digital Hub" column, which covers iLife and related topics. He has also written for *PC World, Internet World,* and *Newsweek* magazines, and until recently wrote a weekly, nationally syndicated Macintosh column for the *Los Angeles Times*.

Jim frequently teaches courses in digital video, DVD authoring, and related topics. He has taught at the Kodak Center for Creative Imaging in Camden, Maine, at the University of Hawaii, and at dozens of technology conferences in between. He's also the host and editorial director of iDay, a series of one-day seminars covering iLife and digital-media topics (www.avondalemedia.com).

Jim's interest in music, photography, and movie-making preceded his passion for personal computers. He began playing piano at age 6 and got his first reel-to-reel tape recorder—a hand-me-down from his father's recording studio—when he was 10. He began taking pictures at age 12, and set up a basement darkroom and began making home movies at 14.

To satisfy his craving for the latest digital cameras, Jim is a frequent seller on eBay. His interest in eBay led to a book, *Sell it On eBay: TechTV's Guide to Successful Online Auctions*, which he coauthored with his friend and business partner, Toby Malina.

In 2002, Jim, Toby, and long-time colleague Steve Broback co-founded Avondale Media, a video- and event-production company that produces instructional DVDs, seminars, and other training resources. As editorial director, he oversees the editorial development and production of DVDs and events.

Jim lives with his wife and colleague, Maryellen Kelly, and their standard poodle and mascot, Sophie, on a windswept headland near Mendocino, California. On most Wednesday evenings, he co-hosts "Point & Click Radio," a weekly computer radio show, which you can listen to at www.kzyx.org/pc.

Acknowledgements

The *Macintosh iLife '04* is the result of the heroic efforts of an exceptional group of people, all of whom have my thanks and admiration.

One of them also has my love. My deepest thanks go to Maryellen Kelly, my wife, colleague, and best friend. You are absolutely everything to me. What do you call 22 years? A good start. I love you!

Next up are the dream teams that helped produce the DVD and book. On the book front, there's the dynamic duo of Barbara Assadi and Arne Hurty, principals of San Francisco's BayCreative. Three editions later, your talent never ceases to amaze me. We've made magic together, and I look forward to doing so again. After some rest.

Jonathan Woolson crafted every layout in Adobe InDesign, polishing every page until it sparkled. Along the way, he provided tips and insightful content recommendations. He even wrote a couple of the AppleScripts on the DVD. You've helped make this book what it is, and I can't thank you enough.

Thanks also go to everyone at Peachpit Press: to Marjorie Baer and Nancy Ruenzel, for having the vision to recognize just how special this project could be; to Rebecca Ross, who deftly carried the third edition torch; and to Myrna Vladic, Scott Cowlin, Kim Lombardi, Mimi Heft, and indeed, to everyone who labors on Eighth Street. You make the others look like amateurs.

Then there's the other dream team. The DVD wouldn't have happened without Steve Broback and Toby Malina, my partners at Avondale Media and my friends. Steve's support and savvy make my Avondale endeavors a pleasure. Toby directed the video shoot with her usual skill, keeping everything humming and always knowing when to make me do something over again. You're a great friend, colleague, and coauthor.

The video owes its look to director of photography Eric Stromberger, who makes magic with tracing paper; to Fred Schuller, who manned camera and audio gear and drove to Cloverdale once more than anyone should have to; to production technical Michael Zilber; and to makeup artist Vicky Helstrom. A big thanks and a virtual Kinkade also go to Paul Anderson, who provided technical advice with his usual staggering degree of thoroughness.

My thanks and respect go to the Apple engineers and product managers behind iLife '04. Fred Johnson answered questions despite a crushing schedule, and always with a smile. You're a pro and a prince, sir, and I thank you. Thanks also to Xander Soren, Quincy Carroll, Grace Kvamme, Paul Towner, Greg Scallon, Peter Lowe, and Steve Jobs. I love your products and am profoundly gratified that you liked mine.

On the home front, a pack of friends, canine and otherwise, helped preserve my sanity with beach trips and intravenous coffee drips. Judy, Terry, Mimi, Robin, Violet—what fun we have! Sound the alert!

And finally, the last-but-definitely-not-least department: thanks to Bura Virgil and to Laura Ingram; to Keri Walker; to Rennie and everyone at MCN; to Scott Southard, Bob Laughton, and Chuck Wilcher; and to Sophie, my sweet softie, my safety valve, my silver lining.

Jim Heid

Contents

iMovie: Editing Video

iDVD: Putting it All Together

GarageBand: Making Your Own Music

DVD

Table of Contents

Preface to the iLife '04 Edition

iLife goes on. In January 2004, Apple delivered the iLife '04, a new version of its personal digital media studio. iLife '04 brought new versions of iPhoto, iMovie, and iDVD, plus something completely different: GarageBand, a personal recording studio and much more.

It was time to get to work, and the book you're reading is the result.

The Macintosh iLife '04 is the third edition of a book and DVD that were originally called *The Macintosh Digital Hub.* The original edition debuted in 2002—before Apple brought iTunes, iPhoto, iMovie, and iDVD under the iLife umbrella. When that happened, in January 2003, the second edition, renamed *The Macintosh iLife*, appeared.

Years pass and book titles change, but one thing has remained the same: my belief that the printed page and the video screen make a powerful combination for learning. That's why this is the only computer book on the market that has a companion instructional DVD.

If you're among the thousands of Mac users who have bought previous editions of this book and DVD, thank you and welcome back. If this is your first time here, welcome to a very different kind of computer book—a book that uses color and an innovative design to teach programs that are colorful and innovative, and a book that works together with its DVD to allow you to experience digital media instead of just reading about it.

Welcome to *The Macintosh iLife '04.*

What's New in iLife '04?

Here's a quick recap of the enhancements that Apple added to iLife '04. If you're new to iLife and are unfamiliar with its jargon, don't worry—you'll find everything you need to know in the pages that follow.

iTunes. The latest version of Apple's digital music jukebox is the gateway to a groundbreaking online music store, where you can listen to 30-second previews of nearly a million songs, buy tunes for 99 cents apiece, and even share your musical tastes with others.

iPhoto. Version 4 of iLife's digital shutterbug is much faster than its predecessors. (There was no iPhoto 3, by the way.) iPhoto 4 also provides some new organizational aids that make it easier to paw through a fully stocked photo shoebox, as well as some lovely new slide show effects.

iMovie. iMovie 4 is also faster, and it provides new editing features that make it easier to time edits with precision— a subject to which I devote the iMovie segment of the DVD.

iDVD. iDVD 4 has some great new slide show features, allows for visual transitions between menus, and adds other advanced authoring features. And a new set of menu themes gives you more design options than ever.

GarageBand. Amateur and professional musicians alike are slack-jawed at the power of this music-making program. I can't tell you how many hours I've spent with GarageBand. My wife probably can.

What's New in the Book

Besides adding a new section on GarageBand, I've revised every page of this book for iLife '04. I've spent much of the last couple of years teaching iLife and digital media—at user groups, at the University of Hawaii, at Macworld Expos, and at the iDay digital media seminars that my company produces. I've learned a lot about how people use these programs. I've revamped many sections accordingly, fleshing out steps and adding new tutorials and tips.

I've also added new coverage of topics that I've covered in the monthly "Digital Hub" column that I write for *Macworld* magazine. And I've incorporated updated versions of some of the tips and articles that have appeared on this book's companion Web site, www.macilife.com.

What's New on the DVD

When you revise a book, you can insert new text and remove old stuff where necessary. Video is different. There's no way to shoot 14 seconds of new video and insert it in something that you shot a year earlier. You can't match the look of the set or the lighting, nor can you hide the fact that I'm wearing fewer strands of hair and a few more pounds than in 2002.

The DVD in this book is completely new. Some of the introductory content in each segment is the same, but every segment also contains new tips as well as details on new iLife '04 features. And, of course, the GarageBand segment—where I make my televised debut as a very amateur musician—is brand new.

Something else is new about this DVD: it's a hybrid. If your Mac has a DVD drive, you can access a bounty of add-ons for iLife '04—music loops for GarageBand, new design themes for iDVD, scripts that automate iTunes, and much more.

Enthusiasts Wanted

The new hybrid DVD is just one more way that I've tried to make *The Macintosh iLife '04* the best iLife learning resource available. Producing this book and DVD is a big job, but it's also a labor of love. I've been involved with music, photography, and movie-making since I was a kid, and I consider myself lucky to be able to play with and teach these media.

I'm an unabashed enthusiast—not only for the Mac, but also for the power and beauty of music, photography, and moving pictures. I tried to convey this enthusiasm in these pages and on the DVD. It thrills me to see people discover the ear appeal of a well-crafted music playlist, the ease and immediacy of digital photography, and the gratification of turning raw video into a polished presentation.

I love this stuff, and this book and DVD are for everyone else who does. Have a nice iLife.

An Important Note for Mac OS X 10.2 (Jaguar) Users

You can play back the video portion of *The Macintosh iLife '04* DVD using a set-top DVD player or a Mac (or PC) equipped with a DVD drive.

If you watch the DVD using Mac OS X 10.2 (also called Jaguar), you may notice some jittery-looking "interference" when the DVD is showing what's happening on my Mac's screen.

These visual glitches are caused by a problem in Jaguar's DVD playback software. We at Avondale Media were among the first to discover this problem, and we worked with Apple to make sure it was fixed in Mac OS X 10.3 Panther. And indeed, it is—Panther plays back this book's DVD beautifully.

If you're still using Jaguar, consider upgrading to Panther. It's a much better cat—faster, more reliable, and packed with great features. And remember that, regardless of which operating system you use, this DVD will look its very best if you watch it on a TV set.

Read Me First: Using the Book and DVD

Why combine a book and a DVD? Because each has its own strengths. The printed word conveys depth and detail, but many people learn best by watching over someone's shoulder. Video lets you see for yourself, and video on a DVD lets you watch in any order you want.

Print and video complement each other, and that's why you will find references to the DVD throughout this book. It's also why you will find references to the book throughout the DVD.

Where should you begin? You decide. If you're new to the iLife, you might want to break open a Mountain Dew and watch the DVD from start to finish. Or, watch the introduction, then use the DVD's main menu to jump to the segment you're most interested in. Or, keep the book near your Mac as a reference, and check out chapters of the DVD when you want to see something in action.

How you master iLife is up to you; just have fun doing it.

How the Book Works

This book devotes a separate section to each of the iLife '04 programs: iTunes and iPod for listening to music; iPhoto for photography; iMovie for video editing; iDVD for creating DVD-Video discs, and GarageBand for making music. Each section is a series of two-page spreads, and each spread is a self-contained reference that covers one topic.

Most spreads begin with an introduction that sets the stage with an over-view of the topic.

Most spreads refer you to relevant chapters on the DVD to help you locate video that relates to the current topic.

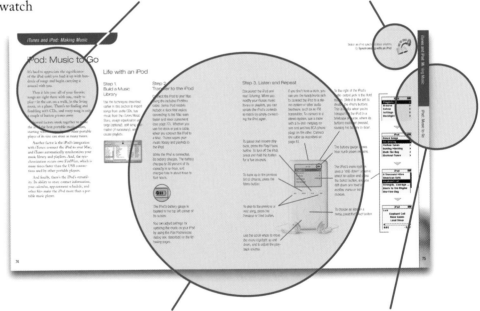

Here's the main course of each spread, where you'll find instructions, background information, and tips.

The section and spread names appear on the edges of the pages to allow you to quickly flip to specific topics.

How the DVD Works

The Macintosh iLife '04 DVD plays on any standard DVD player, as well as on Macs (and PCs) equipped with DVD drives. Because of the nature of video, picture quality is a bit better if you play the DVD on a TV set instead of on your computer. Still, you may find it fun to have the DVD playing in a small window on your computer monitor as you learn about an iLife program.

To return to the Main Menu, press your DVD remote's Title key (which instead may be called Top Menu or Disc).

To watch a segment, choose its menu item. When that segment ends, playback continues on to the next segment. Use your DVD player's Menu button to return to the main menu.

Most DVD player remote controls have number keypads. You can jump straight to a topic by pressing its number. See your DVD player's user manual for details on entering numbers using your remote control.

To browse the DVD by topic, choose Jump to Topic. To return to the topic menu, press your DVD remote's Menu key.

Special Features of the DVD

The DVD contains some special features; here's how to use them.

Jump to topic. The Jump to Topic menu option lets you quickly access any of the DVD's chapters. To view a specific GarageBand topic, for example, choose Jump to Topic, then choose the GarageBand menu option. Another menu appears listing each of the GarageBand chapters.

What's new? If you're an iLife veteran, you might want to choose the Main Menu option named What's New in iLife '04. When you choose this option, your DVD player skips around through the DVD and plays back those portions of the DVD that relate to new iLife '04 features.

Extras for your Mac. If your Mac has a DVD drive, check out the Extras folder. It contains a collection of software, GarageBand loops, sample files, and other goodies that you can use with the iLife '04 programs.

The Book, the DVD, the Web Site

There's just one thing this book and DVD don't cover: tomorrow. The iLife scene is always evolving as new programs and new developments change the way we work with digital media.

That's why this book and DVD also have a companion Web site: www.macilife.com. At this site, you'll find links to the products discussed in the book and on the DVD as well as tips and news items, updates, and reviews of iLife-related products.

Introducing
iLife

The Macintosh
iLife '04

Personal Computers Get Personal

Music, photographs, and movies can inspire, amuse, persuade, and entertain. They're time machines that recall people and places. They're vehicles that carry messages into the future. They're ingrained in infancy and become intensely personal parts of our lives. And they've all gone digital.

It's now possible to carry a music library in your pocket, to take photos without film, and to edit video in your den—or on a cross-country flight. It's easier than ever to combine music, images, and video. And it's easy to share your finished product, whether with loved ones in the living room, clients in a conference room, or a global audience on the Internet.

Behind this digital age are breakthroughs in storage technologies, processor speed, chip design, and even in the types of connectors and interfaces used to attach external gear. In the past, personal computers weren't powerful enough to manage the billions of bits that make up digital media. Today, they are.

You might say that personal computers have finally become powerful enough to become truly personal.

Audio

1962
Bell System begins first digital phone transmissions.

1972
Nippon Columbia Company begins digitally recording master tapes.

1979
Sony's Walkman is the first portable music player.

1982
Billy Joel's 52nd Street is the first album released on CD.

1988
CDs outsell vinyl albums for the first time.

Imaging

1969
Bell Labs researchers invent the charge-coupled device (CCD).

1991
Kodak adapts Nikon F-3 camera with 1.3-megapixel CCD.

1992
Kodak's Photo-CD system puts scanned images on CDs.

1994
Apple's QuickTake 100 camera debuts at $699.

1997
The Associated Press switches to digital photography.

Video

1956
First videotaped TV program is broadcast.

1967
Sony delivers first portable videotape recorder.

1975
Bell Labs demonstrates CCD TV camera. Sony Betamax debuts.

1983
Sony's Betamovie is the first one-piece camcorder.

1985
Small, 8 mm tape cassettes allow for compact camcorders.

Storage

1956
IBM disk system holds 5 megabytes and uses disks two feet wide.

1973
First hard disk: 30MB on an 8-inch disk platter.

1980
Philips and Sony develop the compact disc standard.

1984
First Mac hard disks store 5MB and cost over $2500.

1992
Apple includes CD-ROM drives with Macs.

1989
MP3 audio
compression
scheme is
patented.

1990
Digital audio
tape (DAT)
recorders debut.

1996
Fraunhofer
releases MP3
encoder and
player for
Windows PCs.

1999
Napster and
other Internet
services enable
swapping of
MP3 files.

2001
Apple introduces
iPod. First
copy-protected
audio CDs
appear amid
controversy.

2003
iTunes Music
Store debuts
for Macs and
Windows.

2004
iPod mini and
GarageBand
debut.

Truly
Personal
Computing

1998
1-megapixel
cameras
proliferate.
Online photo
sites offer
prints and other
services.

1999
2-megapixel
cameras, led by
Nikon's $999
Coolpix 950,
are the rage.

2000
3-megapixel
cameras add
movie modes.
Digital cameras
represent
18 percent of
camera sales.

2001
Consumer
cameras hit
4 megapixels.
Digital cameras
comprise
21 percent of
camera market.

2002
Apple introduces
iPhoto. Consumer
cameras reach
5 megapixels.

2003
Sony introduces
first 8-megapixel
consumer digital
camera.

2004
Digital camera
sales projected
to exceed
film camera
sales.

1989
Hi-8 format
brings improved
image and
sound quality.

1991
Apple's
QuickTime 1.0
brings digital
video to the
Macintosh.

1994
miniDV format
debuts: digital
audio and video
on 6.3 mm
wide tape.

1995
FireWire,
invented by
Apple in the
early 90s,
is adopted
as industry
standard.

1999
Apple builds
FireWire into
Macs and
releases
iMovie 1.0.

2001
Apple wins
Primetime Emmy
Engineering
Award for
FireWire.

2004
Apple releases
iLife '04,
incorporating
iMovie 4.

1993
A 1.4GB hard
drive costs
$4559.

1995
DVD standard
is announced.

1999
IBM MicroDrive
puts 340MB
on a coin-sized
platter.

2001
5GB Toshiba
hard drive uses
1.8-inch platter;
Apple builds
it into the
new iPod.

2001
Apple begins
building
SuperDrive
DVD burners
into Macs.

2002
Apple delivers
PowerBooks
with DVD
burners.

2004
Apple updates
iDVD.

A Sampling of the Possibilities

This technological march of progress is exciting because it enables us to do new things with age-old media. I've already hinted at some of them: carrying a music library with you on a portable player, shooting photographs with a digital camera, and editing digital movies.

But the digital age isn't about simply replacing vinyl records, Instamatic cameras, and Super 8 movies. What makes digital technology significant is that it lets you combine various media into messages that are uniquely yours. You can tell stories, sell products, educate, or entertain.

And when you combine these various elements, the whole becomes greater than the sum of its parts.

Go Digital

Pictures That Move

The miniDV format has transformed video for amateurs and professionals alike. Shoot sparkling video with stereo sound using a camcorder that fits in the palm of your hand. Transfer your footage to the Mac, then edit to tell your story.

Forget Film

Use a digital camera just once, and you'll never want to go back to film. Review your shots instantly. Delete the ones you don't want. Transfer the keepers to your Mac, and then share them—through the Internet, through CDs and DVDs, and much more.

Bring It All Together

Preserve the past.
Relive a vacation
with pictures, video,
and sound.

Create for the future.
Produce a book that
commemorates a baby's
first year.

Become a digital DJ.
Assemble a music library and
create music mixes that play
back your favorites. Then take
it all on the road.

Tell a story.
Interview relatives and
create a multimedia
family history.

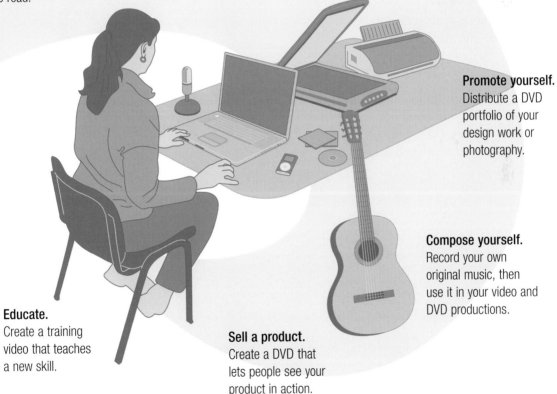

Promote yourself.
Distribute a DVD
portfolio of your
design work or
photography.

Compose yourself.
Record your own
original music, then
use it in your video and
DVD productions.

Educate.
Create a training
video that teaches
a new skill.

Sell a product.
Create a DVD that
lets people see your
product in action.

Where the Mac Fits In

All of today's personal computers have fast processors, fat hard drives, and the other trappings of power. But powerful hardware is only a foundation. Software is what turns that box of chips into a jukebox, a digital darkroom, a movie studio, and a recording studio.

Software is what really makes the Macintosh digital hub go around. Each of Apple's iLife programs—iTunes for music, iPhoto for photography, iMovie for video editing, iDVD for creating DVDs, and GarageBand for recording music—greatly simplifies working with, creating, and combining digital media.

Similar programs are available for PCs running Microsoft Windows. But they aren't included with every PC, and they lack the design elegance and simplicity of Apple's offerings. It's simple: Apple's iLife has made the Mac the best personal computer for digital media.

iMovie

· Capture video from camcorders
· Edit video and create titles and effects
· Add music soundtracks from iTunes
· Add photographs from iPhoto
· Save finished video to tape or disk

iDVD

· Create slide shows from iPhoto images
· Add music soundtracks from iTunes
· Present video created in iMovie
· Distribute files in DVD-ROM format

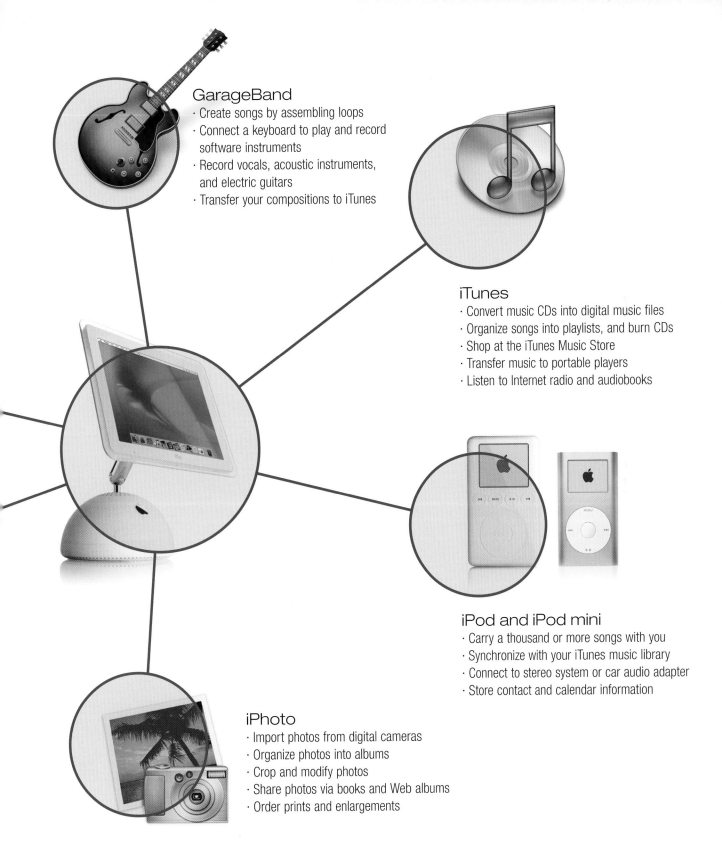

GarageBand
· Create songs by assembling loops
· Connect a keyboard to play and record software instruments
· Record vocals, acoustic instruments, and electric guitars
· Transfer your compositions to iTunes

iTunes
· Convert music CDs into digital music files
· Organize songs into playlists, and burn CDs
· Shop at the iTunes Music Store
· Transfer music to portable players
· Listen to Internet radio and audiobooks

iPod and iPod mini
· Carry a thousand or more songs with you
· Synchronize with your iTunes music library
· Connect to stereo system or car audio adapter
· Store contact and calendar information

iPhoto
· Import photos from digital cameras
· Organize photos into albums
· Crop and modify photos
· Share photos via books and Web albums
· Order prints and enlargements

No Medium is an Island

Combining multiple media is a key part of audio-visual storytelling—even silent films had soundtracks played on mighty Wurlitzer theater organs.

Combining media is easy with the iLife programs. There's no need to plod through export and import chores to move, say, a photograph from iPhoto into iMovie. iPhoto, iMovie, and iDVD each have media browsers that put all your media just a few mouse clicks away, no matter which program you're using. Most of the media browsers also have Search boxes to help you find the music track, photo, or movie you want.

You can also move items between programs by simply dragging them. Drag a photo from iPhoto into iMovie or iDVD. Drag a music track from iTunes into iPhoto, iMovie, or iDVD. And when you've finished a hot tune in GarageBand, add it to your iTunes music library with a click of the mouse.

The iLife programs work together in other ways, which I'll describe as we go. In the meantime, think about ways to marry your media and tell a stronger story.

iMovie

If you edit a movie after adding it to iDVD, your edits are reflected in iDVD.

iMovie iPhoto browser

When making movies, you can add photos from your iPhoto library. Use the Ken Burns pan-and-zoom feature to add dynamism to static photos.

iMovie iTunes browser

You can give your movies music soundtracks from your iTunes library.

GarageBand

Export your finished songs to your iTunes music library.

iTunes

If you modify your iTunes library or playlists, the changes immediately appear in the other programs' media browsers.

iDVD

In iDVD, your music, photos, and movies are a button away. Add movies to a DVD, create DVD slide shows, and add music from iTunes.

iPhoto iTunes browser

When creating an iPhoto slideshow, you can add a music soundtrack from iTunes.

iPhoto

If you edit a photo after adding it to iDVD, your modifications are reflected in iDVD.

Putting the Pieces Together

Software is important, but so is hardware. Several aspects of the Mac's hardware make it ideally suited to digital media work. One is the speed of the PowerPC, the central processor at the heart of each Mac.

Converting audio CD tracks into digital music files, generating special video effects, playing back multiple tracks of music and sound, preparing video for burning onto a DVD—these are demanding tasks, far more demanding than moving words around, calculating budget spreadsheets, or displaying Web pages. But the PowerPC chip contains special circuitry—Apple calls it the Velocity Engine—which specializes in performing complex calculations.

Another factor in the hardware equation is ports: the connection schemes used to attach external devices, such as portable music players, digital cameras, camcorders, printers, and speakers. Every Mac contains all the ports necessary for connecting these and other add-ons.

And finally, the Mac's hardware and software work together smoothly and reliably. This lets you concentrate on your creations, not on your connections.

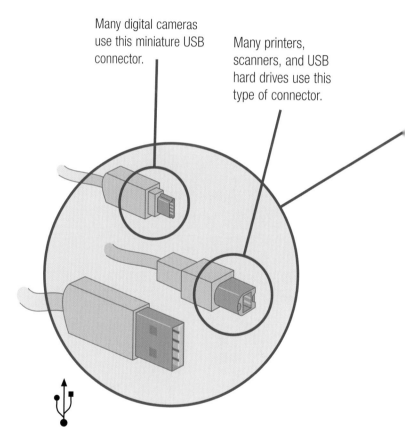

Many digital cameras use this miniature USB connector.

Many printers, scanners, and USB hard drives use this type of connector.

Universal Serial Bus (USB)

Connects to digital cameras, scanners, some speaker systems, microphones, printers, some music keyboards and interfaces, and other add-ons.

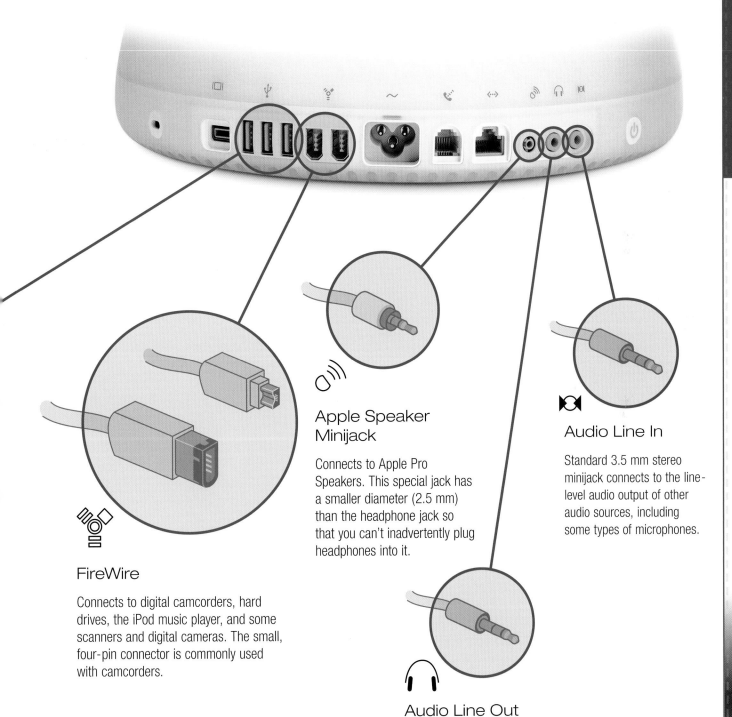

Apple Speaker Minijack

Connects to Apple Pro Speakers. This special jack has a smaller diameter (2.5 mm) than the headphone jack so that you can't inadvertently plug headphones into it.

FireWire

Connects to digital camcorders, hard drives, the iPod music player, and some scanners and digital cameras. The small, four-pin connector is commonly used with camcorders.

Audio Line In

Standard 3.5 mm stereo minijack connects to the line-level audio output of other audio sources, including some types of microphones.

Audio Line Out

Standard 3.5 mm stereo minijack connects to head-phones, amplifiers, and other audio equipment.

11

Essential Add-Ons: Outfitting Your Mac for Digital Media

With their built-in USB and FireWire ports, today's Macs are well equipped to connect to cameras, portable music players, camcorders, and other digital devices.

But there's always room for improvement. To get the most out of iLife, consider upgrading several key components of your Mac. Here's a shopping list.

Memory

Adding memory is a great way to boost any Mac's overall performance. And with most Macs, you can install a memory upgrade yourself. (With older iMac models that have tray-loading CD-ROM drives, it's a good idea to have memory installed by a qualified technician.)

Add as much memory as you can afford. I consider 384 megabytes (MB) to be a bare minimum for the iLife programs; 512MB or more are better.

Hard Drive

All digital media eat up a lot of disk space—except for video, which utterly devours it. If you're serious about digital media, you'll want to expand your Mac's storage.

It's easy to do. If you have a tower-style Mac, you can install a second hard drive inside the Mac's case. For iMacs and PowerBooks, you can connect an external FireWire hard drive—or several of them, if you like.

External FireWire hard drives are available in a wide range of capacities and case sizes. Portable drives are particularly convenient: they fit in a shirt pocket and can draw power from a Mac's FireWire jack—no separate power supply needed. On the downside, though, portable drives cost more than conventional external drives.

Speakers

Some Mac models include the Apple Pro Speakers, lovely transparent orbs that sound surprisingly rich for their small size.

You can also buy the Apple Pro Speakers separately, but note that they require a Mac containing a special jack. They work with flat-panel iMacs and newer Power Mac models, but not with Power Macs introduced prior to 2001.

The small size of the Apple Pro Speakers makes their bass response a bit anemic. If you crave that deep, gut-punching bass, get a speaker system that includes a *subwoofer.*

This is a large speaker that you stash under your desk or in a similarly unobtrusive place; because our ears aren't very sensitive to where low-pitched sounds are coming from, it doesn't much matter where you put a subwoofer.

If you don't yet have a speaker system, Harmon Kardon's SoundSticks system is a great choice. It includes an exotic-looking subwoofer and two see-through acrylic satellite speakers that sit on either side of the Mac.

The original SoundSticks system connects to the Mac's USB jack, but the newer SoundSticks II system is more versatile: it connects to the Mac's headphone jack—or to an iPod or other sound source that uses a standard stereo miniplug.

JBL's Creature system costs less and also connects to any audio source, but its subwoofer is smaller and its amplifier doesn't put out quite as much sound.

FireWire and USB Hubs

The Mac's FireWire connectors are durable, but they aren't indestructible. All that plugging and unplugging of camcorders, hard drives, iPods, and other doodads can take its toll. What's more, many Macs have just one FireWire connector, limiting the number of devices you can connect directly to the Mac.

A FireWire hub is an inexpensive add-on that addresses both issues. A hub is to FireWire what a power strip is to a wall outlet: it provides more jacks for your devices. After connecting the hub to your Mac, you can connect several devices to the hub.

You can also buy USB hubs that provide the same expansion benefits for USB devices.

A .Mac Account

Okay, so this isn't an add-on per se, but it is something you may want. If you sign up for a subscription to Apple's .Mac service, you can create your own Web page and Web photo albums using iPhoto. You'll also be able to access Apple's iDisk remote storage service, where you'll find lots of software downloads as well as a library of royalty-free music that you can use in your digital hub endeavors.

To sign up for .Mac, go to www.mac.com. If you aren't sure whether .Mac is for you, sign up for a free trial membership.

More Accessories You Might Want

While you're filling your shopping cart, you might also want to consider some accessories that will help you get more out of your digital devices.

Memory Cards

Many digital cameras come with "starter" memory cards that will fill up after half a dozen shots. Don't run out of digital film—buy a couple of extra memory cards. They're available in many capacities: 128 megabytes (MB), 512MB, even a gigabyte or more.

How big a card should you buy? That depends on your camera's resolution. For a two-megapixel camera, consider a 128MB card. It will store 100 or more photos (the exact number depends on your camera's settings). For a camera whose resolution is four megapixels or higher, consider a 256MB or 512MB card. I tend to avoid cards larger than this—I just don't feel comfortable storing many hundreds of photos on one card.

Memory Media Reader

Speaking of memory, another accessory you might consider is a memory reader. Insert your memory card into the reader, then use iPhoto or the Mac's Finder to import your photos. Because you aren't using your camera to transfer photos, its batteries will last longer. And if you get a reader that supports the Mac's FireWire interface, you can transfer images much faster than when using a USB connection.

FM Transmitter

With an FM transmitter, you can broadcast the audio from your iPod or your Mac throughout your house—or your car. In my house, we use an FM transmitter to broadcast streaming Internet audio throughout the house.

A number of FM transmitters are available, and in my experience, most of them work poorly. I have found one exception, though—C. Crane Company makes an FM transmitter that delivers excellent sound quality and very good range. Check it out at www.ccradio.com.

And from the "something completely different" category, there's Griffin Technology's iTrip, an FM transmitter that plugs into the top of an iPod music player. The iTrip gets power from the iPod itself, so it doesn't require its own batteries.

Cassette Adapter

Here's another alternative for listening to your iPod in the car. Plug the cassette adapter into the iPod, and insert its cassette assembly into your car's tape deck. The sound quality won't do justice to the iPod's capabilities, but it's an inexpensive and easy way to hear your tunes in the car.

iPod Accessories Galore

If you're listening to the iPod in the car, why not charge it at the same time? XtremeMac and Belkin are just two companies that sell cables for charging an iPod on the road. One end of the cable plugs into the car's cigarette lighter, while the other end plugs into the iPod's FireWire jack or dock connector.

And the accessory shopping doesn't stop there. With Belkin's Media Reader for iPod, you can use your iPod to store digital camera photos. And with the Belkin Voice Recorder or Griffin Technology's iTalk, you can turn your iPod into a voice recorder. Note that these accessories do not work with the iPod mini.

iTunes and iPod:
Listening to Music

iTunes at a Glance

Music, photographs, and movies may have gone digital, but music was there first. In the 1980s, the compact disc format turned the clicks and pops of vinyl into relics of the past—at least until hip-hop DJs brought them back.

In the late 1990s, the grassroots groundswell behind Napster and the MP3 format led to a frenzy of illegal music swapping over the Internet. Indications are that music theft has begun a slow decline, but still keeps recording industry executives awake at night and puts food on the table for more than a few lawyers.

The fact is, the digital audio revolution has created a new era of musical freedom. This freedom is not license to steal—copying an artist's efforts without paying for them is just plain wrong—but freedom to arrange songs in whatever order you like and to play those songs on a variety of devices.

iTunes is the program that brings this freedom of music to the Mac. With iTunes, you can create digital music files from your favorite audio CDs. You can buy and *legally* download music from the iTunes Music Store. You can create your own music mixes by creating playlists. And you can listen to your playlists on a Mac, burn them onto CDs, or transfer them to an iPod portable music player.

Let's put a quarter in the Mac's digital jukebox.

The arrow buttons skip to the previous or next song in a playlist. To skip forward and backward within a playing song, click on an arrow and hold down the mouse button.

Play/Pause (keyboard shortcut: spacebar).

Adjusts the volume (keyboard shortcut: ⌘-up arrow and ⌘-down arrow).

Click to display the iTunes Library, which lists all of your songs.

Use the Party Shuffle playlist to have iTunes quickly create a mix for you (page 64).

Click to switch to iTunes' Internet radio mode (page 56).

Click to shop at the iTunes Music Store (page 30).

Add songs to playlists to control their playback order and create your own music mixes. Use smart playlists (⚙) to have iTunes create playlists for you.

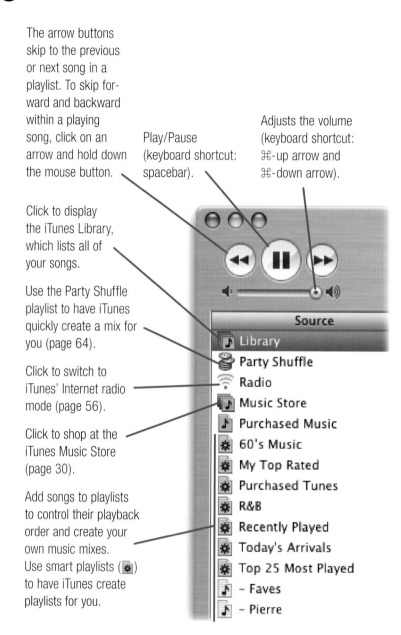

See iTunes and the iPod in action.
⊚ iTunes and iPod: Making Music

Click this tiny button to switch between song information and iTunes' spectrum animation.

Share your playlists with iMix playlist publishing (page 39).

Click the time display and artist name to view other time options and album information.

Drag the diamond left or right to scan through a song.

Display related songs in the iTunes Music Store (page 32) or your library (page 45).

To quickly locate the currently playing song, click the SnapBack button (page 63).

Use the Browse button to view your music by artist and album (page 44).

Use the Search box to quickly locate songs (page 44).

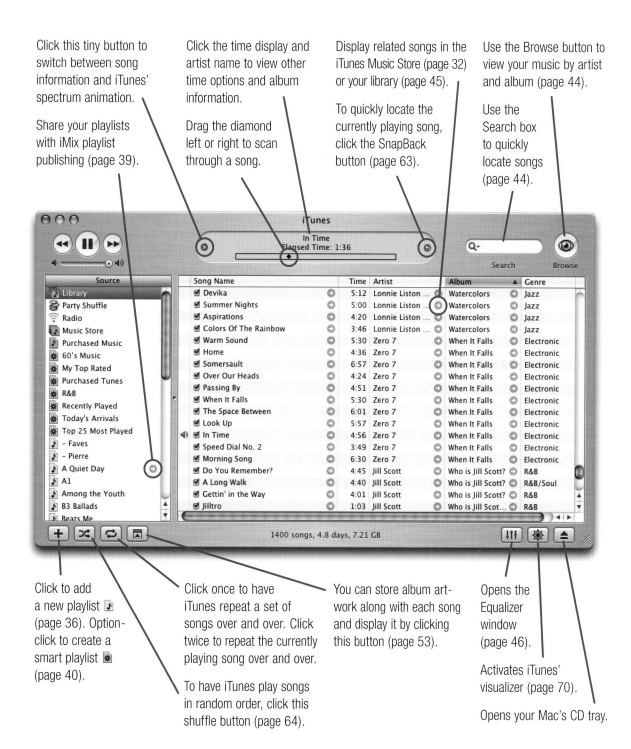

Click to add a new playlist 🎵 (page 36). Option-click to create a smart playlist ⚙ (page 40).

Click once to have iTunes repeat a set of songs over and over. Click twice to repeat the currently playing song over and over.

To have iTunes play songs in random order, click this shuffle button (page 64).

You can store album artwork along with each song and display it by clicking this button (page 53).

Opens the Equalizer window (page 46).

Activates iTunes' visualizer (page 70).

Opens your Mac's CD tray.

19

Importing Music from CDs

The first step in stocking your digital juke-box will probably involve bringing in music from your audio CDs. Apple calls this process *importing*, but most digital music fans refer to it as *ripping* (from the Latin, meaning "to rip off").

Whatever you call this process, iTunes is good at it. Insert a compact disc into your Mac's CD drive, and iTunes launches, connects to the Internet, and retrieves the name of the CD and its tracks. Click iTunes' Import button, and the program converts the CD's contents into digital music files that are stored on your Mac's hard drive.

That's the big picture. You can create a vast digital music library with iTunes without having to know any more than that. But iTunes has several features that give you more control over the ripping process. You can, for example, specify that iTunes import only certain songs—no need to waste disk space by storing songs you don't like.

And as I describe on the following pages, you can choose to store your digital music library in a variety of formats, each with its own advantages and drawbacks.

Just want to play a CD instead of ripping it? Click the play button or double-click on any track.

Indicates which songs to rip. Don't like some songs? Uncheck their boxes, and iTunes will not import them.

Tip: To uncheck all tracks, press ⌘ while clicking on a track's check box (☑).

Rips all tracks with check marks before their names.

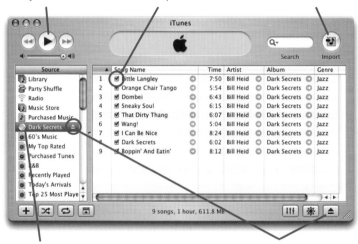

Shows the currently inserted CD.

Ejects the CD.

Joining Tracks to Eliminate Gaps

In some cases, you might not want a gap of silence between songs. For example, the songs on a CD might be composed so that one flows seamlessly into the next.

iTunes indicates joined tracks with a bracket.

You can prevent a gap between two or more songs by importing them as joined tracks. Select the tracks, then choose Join CD Tracks from the Advanced menu. iTunes will import the tracks as one file. If you decide to not

join the tracks after all, choose Unjoin CD Tracks from the Advanced menu.

Note that you can't join tracks that you've already imported.

See an iTunes importing session.
◉ **Importing a CD**

How iTunes Retrieves Track Names

Back in the late 1970s, when the compact disc standard was being developed, no one foresaw the iLife era. As a result, the developers of the CD standard didn't create a way for CDs to store artist, album, and track names.

So how can iTunes retrieve this information? The answer lies in the fact that no two audio CDs are the exact same length. A CD is comprised of a specific number of blocks, each of which is one seventy-fifth of a second long. You might say that every CD has its own unique digital fingerprint.

In 1996, some clever programmers in Berkeley, California, realized they could create a database that would link these fingerprints to specific information. The compact disc database, or CDDB, was born. Soon, CDDB spawned a company, Gracenote, which provides disc-lookup features to Apple and other companies that have digital music products.

When you insert a CD, iTunes calculates its digital fingerprint and then sends it over the Internet to Gracenote's server. If Gracenote finds a match, it transmits the corresponding information back to iTunes, which displays it.

Just how big is Gracenote's database? As of 2004, it contained more than 2.5 million CDs, representing over 33 million songs. That's even bigger than my iTunes library.

Incidentally, the audio CD specification now contains provisions for storing track information on a CD. It's called "CD-Text," but its support in the music industry is spotty. Sony has been including CD-Text information on its releases for several years, but many record labels don't support it.

Power Ripping: Changing CD Insert Preferences

Doing some binge ripping? Save yourself time and set up iTunes to automatically begin importing as soon as you insert a CD. Choose Preferences from the iTunes menu, then check the setting of the On CD Insert pop-up menu. Choose Import Songs or, better yet, Import Songs and Eject.

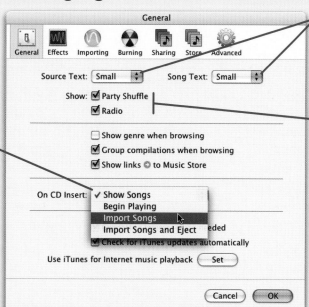

Aging eyes? Use these pop-up menus to have iTunes display large text.

You can control which items iTunes displays in its Source list.

Choosing an Audio Format

The factory settings that iTunes uses for importing music are perfectly fine for most music lovers and listening scenarios. So if you'd rather explore some of the more musical and less technical aspects of iTunes, feel free to skip on to page 30. But if you're an audiophile or are just curious, read on for a look at how audio compression works—and at how you can adjust the way iTunes applies it.

CD-quality stereo sound requires about 10MB of disk space per minute. By using *compression*, iTunes can lower audio's appetite for storage by a factor of 10 or more. Audio-compression schemes use something called *perceptual encoding*, which eliminates those portions of an audio signal that our ears don't hear well anyway. Because some information is lost in the process, this form of compression is called *lossy*.

iTunes supports two lossy compression schemes: MP3, the format that helped fuel the Internet music revolution; and a newer method called AAC (short for *Advanced Audio Coding*). Each scheme has advantages and drawbacks.

Beginning with version 4.5, iTunes also offers a lossless compression scheme called *Apple Lossless* encoding. It doesn't provide nearly as much compression as MP3 or AAC—files are only about half the size of the original. But true to its name, Apple Lossless imposes no quality loss. If you're a golden-eared audiophile with plenty of hard drive space, you might prefer to rip your CDs using the Apple Lossless encoder.

Changing Importing Settings

From the factory, iTunes is set up to encode in AAC format. By adjusting the Importing options in the Preferences dialog box, you can change the encoding settings to arrive at your own ideal balance between sound quality, storage requirements, and listening plans.

Step 1.

Choose Preferences from the iTunes menu.

Step 2.

Click the Importing button.

Encoder Options at a Glance

Encoder	Comments
AAC	Best balance between sound quality and small file size.
MP3	Not as efficient as AAC, but broadly compatible with non-Apple portable players and computer systems.
Apple Lossless	Creates much larger files than the MP3 or AAC encoders, but with no audio quality loss. Files won't play on older iPods; see page 76.
WAV and AIFF	Create uncompressed files that use 10MB of disk space per minute. (AIFF, which stands for Audio Interchange File Format, is a standard audio format on the Mac; WAV is its equivalent on Windows. Both formats are broadly supported on Macs and Windows.)

Step 3.

Adjust importing settings as shown below.

Fine-tune compression settings (page 24).

If you plan to burn MP3-format CDs, consider checking this box (page 50).

If a song that you've imported has audible pops or clicks, consider checking this box and then importing the song again.

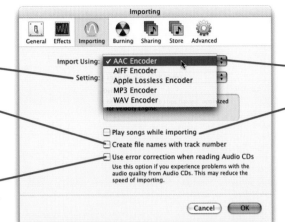

Specify how you'd like iTunes to rip your CDs.

Want to listen while you rip? Check this box.

AAC: More Bang for the Byte

You want the storage efficiency that a lossy encoder provides. Should you rip your CDs using the AAC encoder or the MP3 encoder? If you'll always use iTunes, an iPod, and the other iLife programs to play music, by all means use AAC—I do. But if you anticipate transferring tunes between computers or non-Apple portable players, use MP3.

Here's why. Audio compression is measured in terms of *bit rate*, the average number of bits required for one second of sound. To obtain near CD-quality audio, MP3 requires a bit rate in the range of 128 to 192 kilobits

per second (kbps). Higher bit rates mean less compression and better sound quality.

AAC is more efficient than MP3—it does a smarter job of encoding music, which means you can use lower bit rates and still get great sound quality. Audiophiles love to argue the fine points, but to most ears, a 128 kbps AAC file sounds at least as good as an MP3 file encoded at 160 kbps.

What does this mean to you? If you use AAC when importing CDs, you'll use disk space more efficiently. This can help you

shoehorn a mammoth music library onto an iPod.

The downside to AAC? Your music files will be less compatible with other music software and hardware. MP3 is supported by every music program, personal computer, and portable music player; AAC isn't.

There's one more reason you might consider using MP3 instead of AAC. If you plan to burn CDs in MP3 format as described on page 50, you should rip your music in MP3 format.

Any Mac with version 6.4 or later of QuickTime can play AAC

audio. For best compatibility with all of the iLife '04 programs, use QuickTime 6.5.1 or a later version, if available. You can also play AAC audio on a Windows computer after installing QuickTime for Windows (which is included with iTunes for Windows).

One more thing. As page 30 describes, the iTunes Music Store delivers its tracks in AAC format. The AAC music you buy contains some copying restrictions. But AAC files that you rip from your own CDs contain no such restrictions.

Fine-Tuning Compression Settings

Adjusting MP3 Settings

iTunes is set up to encode MP3 at a bit rate of 160kbps. To change the bit rate and other MP3 settings, choose Custom from the Setting pop-up menu.

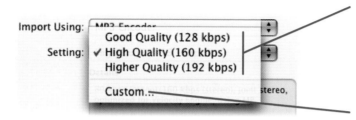

128 kbps is closer to FM-radio quality than to CD quality—you may notice a swirling quality to instruments that produce high frequencies, such as strings and cymbals. 192 kbps delivers better quality than 160 kbps, though my ears have trouble detecting it.

To explore the kinds of adjustments MP3 allows for, choose Custom to display the dialog box shown below. See below for custom setting choices.

Variable bit rate (VBR) encoding varies a song's bit rate according to the complexity of the sound. For example, a quiet passage with a narrow range of frequencies is less "demanding" than a loud passage with a broad range of frequencies. VBR uses disk space more efficiently and, according to many MP3 fans, sounds better, too. Many MP3 users turn on VBR and then lower the bit rate—for example, encoding at 128 kbps with VBR instead of at 160 kbps without VBR.

Restores iTunes' original settings.

iTunes will filter out inaudible, low frequencies. Leave this one checked.

Specify the bit rate here.

Tweaks your encoding settings for the best quality given the bit rate settings you've specified. You can usually leave this box checked, but if you're a control freak who doesn't want iTunes making adjustments for you, uncheck it.

For most uses, leave this menu set to Auto. If you're encoding a voice recording, however, you can save disk space by lowering the sample rate to 22.050 KHz or even 11.025 KHz.

In the Auto setting, iTunes detects whether the original recording is in stereo or mono. To force iTunes to encode in mono—for example, to save disk space—choose Mono.

Our ears have trouble discerning where high frequencies are coming from. Joint Stereo encoding exploits this phenomenon by combining high frequencies into a single channel, saving disk space. Careful listeners say they can sometimes hear a difference in the spatial qualities of a recording.

Adjusting AAC Settings

iTunes is set up to encode AAC at a bit rate of 128 kbps. To change the bit rate, choose Custom from the Setting pop-up menu, then choose the desired bit rate.

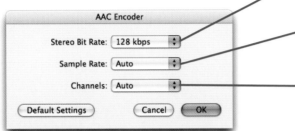

Choose the desired bit rate. Lower bit rates yield smaller files and poorer sound quality.

You can choose a 44.1 KHz or 48 KHz sample rate. Use the Auto setting: iTunes encodes to match the original recording.

You can choose to encode in mono or stereo. Use the Auto setting: iTunes detects whether the original recording is monophonic or stereophonic, and encodes to match.

Converting from MP3 to AAC and Apple Lossless

iTunes can convert existing MP3s to AAC, but you'll lose quality in the process. That's because both AAC and MP3 are lossy formats: each discards audio information in order to save disk space. Thus, when an MP3 file is compressed with AAC, the lossiness is compounded.

Bottom line: To take advantage of AAC's space savings, re-rip your original CDs instead of recompressing existing MP3s.

This re-ripping requirement also applies if you want to take advantage of the Apple Lossless encoder introduced in iTunes 4.5.

You can't convert an MP3 (or an AAC) file into Apple Lossless and gain the quality benefits of the latter—the sonic damage has already been done.

iTunes has some smarts that make re-ripping less laborious: If you re-rip a CD that iTunes already has in its library, iTunes tells you that the songs have already been imported and asks if you want to import them again. Thus, you're spared from having to rebuild your playlists, retype any song information, or manually delete your old MP3s.

Note: If you've edited a song's information—changed its name or that of the artist or album as described on pages 28 and 29—iTunes won't recognize that you're importing it again, and you'll end up with two copies of the same song.

To avoid this, make the same edits before you import the CD, or edit the song information of the existing MP3s to match that of the audio CD. Or just make a mental note to delete the old MP3 files after re-ripping.

To replace the existing MP3 version, click Replace Existing.

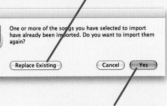

To import the CD without replacing the MP3 versions, click Yes. You'll end up with two versions of each song.

How Audio Compression Works

You don't have to understand how audio compression works in order to use iTunes, but you might wonder how an MP3 or AAC file can be roughly one-tenth the size of an uncompressed audio file and still sound nearly the same.

MP3's origins go back to the 1980s, when researchers began exploring ways to reduce the storage requirements of digital audio. One of the standards that came from these efforts was MPEG (Moving Picture Experts Group) Audio Layer III—MP3 for short.

AAC is a newer kid on the block. Conceptually, AAC and MP3 are very similar: both reduce the storage requirements of sound by "shaving off" audio information that our ears have trouble hearing. But scientists have learned a lot about audio compression and human hearing in the decades since MP3 was created, and AAC takes advantage of these breakthroughs to provide better sound quality at smaller file sizes.

As for the Apple Lossless encoder that debuted in iTunes 4.5, it doesn't "shave off" any audio information. Instead, it uses compression techniques that are similar to those of a file archiving program such as StuffIt. You don't save nearly as much space, but there's no loss in sound quality either.

Will your ears be able to tell the difference? Do some tests and find out. One thing is for certain: your hard drive and your iPod will know the difference. Apple Lossless files require dramatically more storage space than AAC or MP3 files.

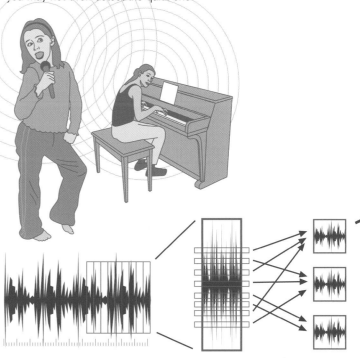

The uncompressed audio on a CD contains more information than our ears can detect. For example, if a loud sound and a quiet one reach your ears simultaneously, you may not even detect the quiet one.

An encoder's first step is to break the original audio into a series of *frames*, each a fraction of a second in length.

The encoder further breaks down each frame into *sub-bands* in order to determine how bits will need to be allocated to best represent the audio signal.

The encoder compares the sub-bands to *psychoacoustics tables*, which mathematically describe the characteristics of human hearing. This comparison process, along with the bit rate that you've chosen for encoding, determines what portion of the original audio signal will be cut and what portion will survive.

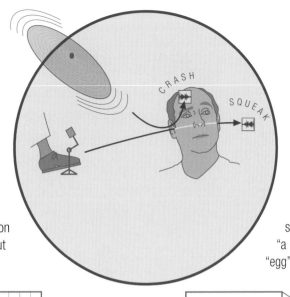

Finally, the encoded data is further compressed by about 20 percent using *Huffman* compression, which replaces redundant pieces of data with shorter codes. You do the same thing every time you say "a dozen eggs" instead of saying "egg" twelve times.

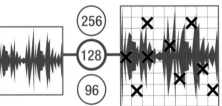

6 of ◣   2 of ◢
4 of ◥   6 of ◤

Where iTunes Stores Your Tunes

iTunes stores your music library in your Music folder. The fastest way to locate the Music folder is to choose Home from the Finder's Go menu.

You don't have to venture inside the Music folder—indeed, you should always add and remove songs to and from your music library by using iTunes itself, not by dragging files into and out of the Music folder.

iTunes 4 Music Library

If you're curious, here's how the Music folder is organized. The Music folder contains another folder named iTunes, and inside *this* folder is a file named iTunes 4 Music Library. This file contains a database of all the songs you've added to iTunes, as well as all the playlists you've created. But it doesn't contain the song files themselves. Those files live in the folder named iTunes Music.

Note that you don't have to store your music in the Music folder. You might want to store it elsewhere—on a portable FireWire hard drive, for example. To specify a different location for your music library, choose Preferences from the iTunes menu, click the Advanced button, and then specify the desired location.

To tell iTunes where to store your music, click Change.

To restore the default location, click Reset.

Note: If you've been using iTunes for a while, you may find older music library files in your iTunes folder. For example, if you upgraded from iTunes 4.2 to iTunes 4.5, you'll have an icon named iTunes 4 Music Library (Old). It's safe to delete these older library files.

Editing Song Information

A digital music file holds more than just music. It also holds information about the music: the song's name, the name of the artist who recorded it, the year it was recorded, and more.

There may be times when you'll want to edit this information. Maybe the song is from an obscure CD that isn't in Gracenote's CDDB, and iTunes has given its tracks generic names like *Track 5*. (This will also happen if you rip a CD when not connected to the Internet.) Or maybe CDDB stored the song names in all-lowercase or all-capital letters, and you'd like to correct that.

Or maybe you've encountered a problem similar to the one illustrated at right. I ripped two CDs from jazz piano giant, Bill Evans. For one of the CDs, CDDB retrieved the artist name as *Bill Evans*, but for the other CD, it retrieved the name as *Bill Evans Trio*. When I transfer those songs to my iPod, I have two separate listings in the Artist view—even though both listings refer to the same artist.

For situations like these, you can use iTunes' Get Info command to edit the information of one or more songs. First, select the song whose attributes you want to edit, and then choose Get Info from the File menu, or press ⌘-I.

You can also edit song information directly within the iTunes window: simply select the song and then click on the item you want to edit.

To edit a song's information, click Info (see opposite page).

Change equalization, volume, and other playback settings here (see page 62).

Add and remove album artwork here (see page 53).

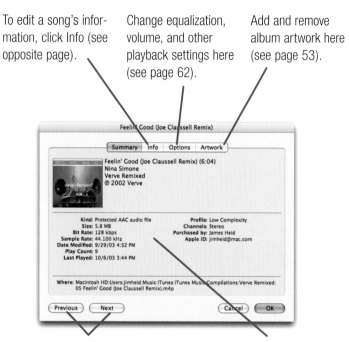

Need to edit information for multiple songs? Rather than repeatedly choosing Get Info, just click Previous to display information for the previous song (the one above the current song in iTunes' window) or Next to get info for the next song.

Information about how the song is encoded appears here.

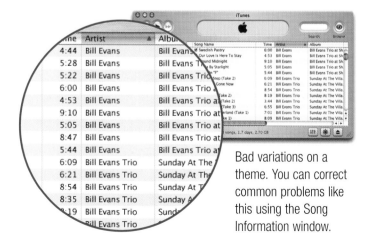

Bad variations on a theme. You can correct common problems like this using the Song Information window.

See links to useful iTunes utilities.
www.macilife.com/itunes

Tips for Editing Song Information

To edit information for a song, click the Info button in the song information dialog box. While many of the items in the Info area are self-explanatory, some aren't. Let's take a look.

As you delve into this dialog box, keep in mind that you don't have to play by the rules. For example, you can store *any* piece of text in the Composer field—iTunes won't complain. Feel free to use the more obscure items in this dialog box to describe and categorize your music library as you see fit. Your efforts will pay off when you start creating smart playlists (described on page 40).

Correct common problems (like the one described on the opposite page) here.

On many CDs, some tracks may be related to each other. For example, a classical CD may contain two Mozart symphonies, with tracks 1 through 4 representing one work and tracks 5 through 8 representing the second work. You can use the Grouping box to store this kind of information: in the Mozart example, you might select tracks 1 through 4, choose Get Info, and then type the name of the work here. But the fact is, you can store whatever information you like here—the names of soloists who play on a given track, or even a sub-genre, such as *smooth jazz* or *Euro techno*.

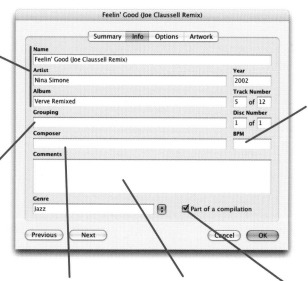

With some genres—particularly classical—a work's composer is at least as important as the name of the artist who performed it. You can use the Composer field to hold any information, but it's intended for storing the name of the person who composed a given piece. On the iPod, you can browse by composer.

Use the Comments box to hold anything you like: a list of musicians, the record label's name, the city where it was recorded, the name of its recording engineer—or just comments such as *This song rocks!* When creating smart playlists, you can search for part or all of a comment.

BPM stands for *beats per minute*—this field is designed to hold a numeric value that corresponds to how many beats per minute are in a song. DJs can use this information when compiling smart playlists. Don't know the exact tempo of a song? Some iTunes users create codes that represent a song's tempo: 1 for a ballad, 2 for a medium-tempo song, 3 for an up-tempo song, and so on. If you use a scheme like this, you can use smart playlists to gather and play songs in a similar tempo range.

Indicates that the song is part of a compilation; when browsing, you can have iTunes display a Compilations category to make it easy to find albums featuring multiple artists (see page 45).

Shopping at the iTunes Music Store

At the iTunes Music Store, you can search for, browse, audition, and buy music. Wander the store's virtual aisles or search for specific songs or artists. Listen to 30-second clips of your finds. Buy just the songs you want, or buy entire albums. iTunes downloads your purchases into your music library, from which you can add them to playlists, burn them to CDs, and transfer them to an iPod.

If you've experimented with music-swapping services, you'll find the iTunes Music Store easier to use and much more reliable. And you'll be able to take off that eye patch, since you won't be pirating from your favorite artists.

You can use the music store with any kind of Internet connection, but a high-speed connection—for example, a cable modem or DSL line—works best. Music takes a long time to download over a slow modem connection.

Before you can buy music, you must set up an account by providing billing information and creating a password. Once that's done, you can buy songs and albums with a couple of mouse clicks.

The music you buy is stored in AAC format and is tied to your account in ways that guard against the piracy that pervades the MP3 scene. And yet you still have plenty of freedom to burn CDs and move your music between computers.

Let's go shopping.

Getting Set Up: Signing In

Step 1:
Step into the Store

Be sure you're connected to the Internet, then click the Music Store item in the iTunes Source list. iTunes connects to the music store. You can browse and search at this point, but you can't buy music until you sign in.

Step 2: Sign In

To sign in, click the Sign In button in the upper-right corner of the store, then complete the dialog box below.

If you don't have an Apple account, click Create New Account and then supply your billing information.

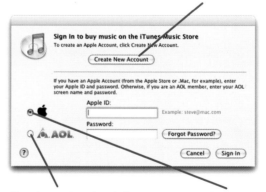

If you're an America Online subscriber, you can charge your purchases to your AOL account. Click AOL, specify your screen name and password, then click Sign In.

If you're a .Mac member, have purchased from the Apple online store in the past, or have ordered prints or books through iPhoto, you already have an Apple account. Specify your ID and password here, then click Sign In.

See how to go shopping.
◉ Shopping at the iTunes Music Store

The Music Store at a Glance

Navigate within the store (see below).

Each genre has its own area of the store; choose a genre to display its area.

Publish your favorite playlists for others to see and rate (page 39).

Featured items appear in these virtual aisles. To move within an aisle, click the blue arrows at the edges of the aisle.

Browse by genre, artist, and album (page 33).

Search the store. To search only by artist, album, song name, or composer, click the magnifying glass and choose a category. After typing search criteria, press the Return key to do the search.

What's everyone else buying? Top song and album downloads appear here.

Getting Around in the Store

The navigation bar changes as you move within the store; click the buttons to jump to areas that relate to what's on your screen.

Go back or forward one screen.

Go to the front of the music store.

The current genre appears here; click it to go to that genre's main screen.

To go to the current artist's discography, click the artist's name. Some discographies have photos, videos, and links to artist Web sites.

The album you're currently viewing.

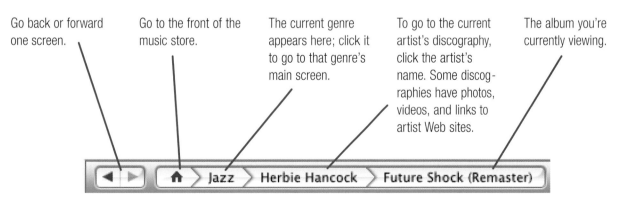

From Browsing to Buying

Once you've created an account and signed in, you're ready shop at the iTunes Music Store. You might start by browsing the store's virtual aisles, clicking on the little album thumbnail images or the text links around them. (The links are underlined when you point to them.)

You might jump to a genre by using the Choose Genre pop-up menu. You might use the Browse button to quickly navigate genres, artists, and albums. Or you might use the Power Search option to home in on exactly what you're looking for.

The end result of any searching or browsing session is a list of songs. Here's where you can play 30-second song previews, locate additional songs from an artist or album, and most important, buy songs and albums. You can also burn your purchases to audio CDs and transfer them to an iPod.

Working with a Song List

You've searched or browsed your way to a list of songs. What happens next is up to you.

Go elsewhere: Click an album name or photo to display its songs. Click an artist name for a discography. Click the genre name to go to that genre.

Follow the pack: The most popular songs and artists that complement your search appear here, each as a clickable link.

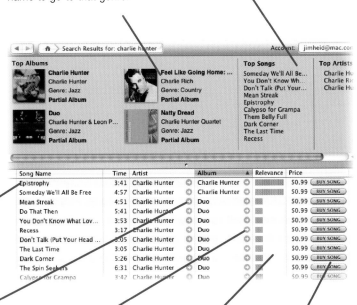

Play a preview: Double-click a song to hear a sample.

See more: In the Artist column, click the arrow for the artist's discography.

Drill down: In the Album column, click the arrow to show the entire album.

Who cares? The Relevance column isn't very useful. To hide it, Control-click on its heading and uncheck Relevance. (You can show and hide other columns, too.)

Buy: To buy a song, click its Buy Song button.

Learn how to shop faster.
⊙ **Tips for the iTunes Music Store**

To Shop Faster, Browse

If you're the type who heads for a mall directory instead of wandering around, try the music store's browse mode, where you can quickly home in on genres, artists, and albums. Browsing is efficient, and because it discards graphics in favor of all-text displays, it's fast, even over slow Internet connections.

Step 1. With the music store displayed, click the Browse button in the upper-right corner of the iTunes window.

Step 2. Choose a genre, then an artist.

Tip: You can navigate the browse boxes with the keyboard. Use the arrow keys to move up and down, or type the first few letters of a word to jump to it. To jump between boxes, press Tab or Shift-Tab.

Power Searching

With the music store's Power Search feature, you can specify multiple search criteria at once—for example, to search for only those versions of *Giant Steps* performed by John Coltrane.

Step 1. Click the music store's Power Search option, or choose Power Search from the search box's pop-up menu.

Step 2. Specify your search criteria and click Search.

Tips for the Music Store

Stopping Stutters

Saddled with a slow connection? Improve song previewing by tweaking iTunes' preferences.

Choose Preferences from the iTunes menu, click the Store button, and then check the box labeled Load Complete Preview Before Playing. From now on, iTunes will load the entire preview before playing it. You'll wait longer to hear the preview, but at least it won't be interrupted.

Authorizing and Deauthorizing

Unlike the music files that iTunes creates when you rip a CD, the music tracks you buy contain some playback and copying restrictions designed to prevent music thieves from sharing the songs through Internet file-swapping services.

When you buy a song, the iTunes Music Store embeds your Apple ID in the music file that downloads to your hard drive. To play the song, you must authorize your Mac, a one-time process that simply involves typing your Apple ID and password. You can authorize up to five Macs (or Windows PCs) per Apple ID.

If you've already authorized five computers to play your purchases and you want to play them on a sixth computer, you'll have to deauthorize one of the other five. Choose Deauthorize Computer from the

Advanced menu, choose Apple Account in the subsequent dialog box, and then type your Apple ID and password. You must be connected to the Internet to deauthorize a computer.

Burning What You Buy

You can burn purchased songs to audio CDs, but iTunes imposes a minor restriction on your burning endeavors. If a playlist contains purchased music, you can burn a maximum of seven CDs containing that playlist.

Binge Buying? Get a Cart

When you go into a store, chances are you don't just buy one thing. Most of the time, you grab a shopping cart so you can haul all of your purchases to the cashier at once.

iTunes provides a shopping cart, and using it is a better way to shop when you're picking up several songs.

When the shopping cart is active, iTunes doesn't download each purchased song immediately. Instead, it slings them into a shopping cart. When you're ready to check out, a couple of clicks buys the songs and begins their download.

Shopping for multiple tunes is more convenient in shopping-cart mode. Navigating the music store is faster, too, since iTunes isn't downloading a song in the background while you shop.

To use the shopping-cart mode, choose Preferences from the iTunes menu, click Store, and then click the option labeled Buy Using a Shopping Cart. The Buy Song button that appears next to each song now reads Add Song: click it to add a song to your cart.

ADD SONG

To buy the songs in your cart, click the Shopping Cart item in the Source list, then click the Buy Now button near the lower-right corner of the iTunes window.

Keep Informed

If you use iCal (page 86), you can subscribe to daily calendar updates of top songs, albums, and new releases by going to Apple's iCal site (www.apple.com/ical).

And if you use a newsreader program such as NetNewsWire, you can create RSS newsfeeds containing this information by going to www.applemusic.com.

When Downloads Go Awry

If your Internet connection is interrupted during a download, you haven't lost your money. Simply reconnect and choose Check for Purchased Music from the Advanced menu. iTunes will resume any incomplete downloads.

The "Purchased Music" Playlist

Once you start buying tunes, iTunes creates a playlist for you named Purchased Music. iTunes adds songs you buy to this playlist; it's a handy way to get an at-a-glance look at the music you've bought—and to preview your next credit card bill.

Because the Purchased Music playlist is something new, iTunes displays a small information window each time you select the playlist. To bypass this message, check the box labeled Do not show this message again.

You can delete songs from the Purchased Music playlist; doing so does not delete them from your music library. And though I'm not sure why you'd want to, you can also add songs you've ripped to the Purchased Music playlist.

You can even delete the Purchased Music playlist entirely, although I don't recommend it—this playlist pairs up nicely with iTunes' backup features (described on page 50).

Get that Song's Address

Every song and album in the music store has its own Internet address. You can copy this address and include it in an email, or link to it from your personal Web site. Using this address is a fun way to let other people know about the music you've found.

To copy an item's Web address, point to the item, press the Control key (that's Control, not ⌘), and choose Copy iTunes Music Store URL from the shortcut menu that appears.

Next, switch to your email program, create a blank email, then paste the address into the body of the email.

You can also drag a song to the desktop; this creates an icon that, when double-clicked, takes iTunes to the appropriate song or album. If you've stumbled on an interesting-sounding album but you want to wait and explore it later, use this technique to put a temporary bookmark on your desktop.

Hiding the Link Buttons

The music store has always had link arrows (⬤) that let you jump to a page for an artist, album, or song. Starting with iTunes 4.5, these buttons also appear when you're viewing your music library or a playlist. The buttons are Apple's way of letting you search for (and buy) songs relating to ones you already have.

If you'd rather not see these buttons—maybe so you don't accidentally click one and beam yourself into the music store—you can turn them off. Choose Preferences, click the General button, then uncheck the box labeled Show Links to Music Store.

What Are They Playing in Peoria?

With the Radio Charts category, you can get a list of top songs from more than 1000 radio stations in over 100 cities.

First, click Radio Charts in the Choose Genre area (or in Browse mode). A list of cities appears. Click a city name, and an often-diverse list of stations appears. Click a station to see its top tunes. It's a fun way to see what people are listening to in your home town, in a popular college town, and yes, in Peoria.

Sequencing Songs with Playlists

Once you've created a digital music library, you'll want to create playlists: collections of songs sequenced in whatever order you like.

You might create playlists whose songs set a mood: Workout Tunes, Road Trip Songs, Romantic Getaway Music.

You might create playlists that play all your favorite tunes from specific artists: The Best of U2, John Coltrane Favorites, The Artistry of Britney Spears. (That last one is pretty small.)

With playlists, you can mix and match songs in any way you see fit. You can add a song to as many playlists as you like, or even create a playlist that plays one song five times in a row.

Once you've created playlists, you can, of course, play them. But you can also transfer them to an iPod portable player (page 74) and burn them to create your own compilation CDs (page 48).

This section describes how to create playlists "by hand." You can also use iTunes' smart playlists feature to have the program create playlists for you. For details on smart playlists, see page 40.

Once you've created some playlists, share them with the rest of us. As page 39 describes, you can publish your playlists on the iTunes Music Store for everyone to see—and rate.

Step 1.
Create a New Playlist

To create a new playlist, click the plus sign or choose New Playlist from the File menu.

Step 2.
Rename the
New Playlist

Type a name for the new playlist.

Step 3.
Drag Songs to the Playlist

You can drag songs into the playlist one at a time or select a series of songs and drag them all at once. To select a range of songs that are adjacent to each other, use the Shift key: click on the first song, then Shift-click on the last one. To select songs that aren't adjacent to one another, press ⌘ while clicking on each song.

Viewing and Fine-Tuning a Playlist

To view a playlist's contents, simply click on its name. To change the playlist's name, click again and then edit the name. To delete a playlist, select it and press Delete. (Deleting a playlist *doesn't* delete its songs from your Library.)

To change the playback order of the songs in the playlist, drag songs up or down. Here, the last song in the playlist is being moved to between songs 1 and 2.

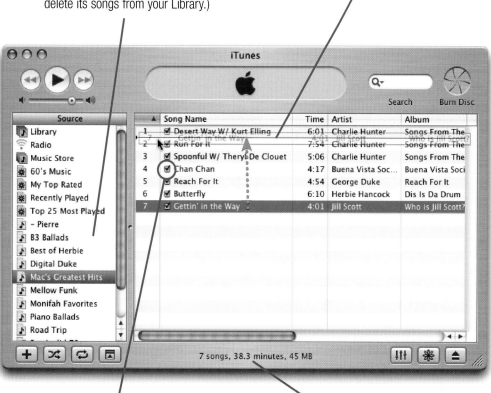

To omit a song from a playlist, select the song and press the Delete key. To omit the song without deleting it—for example, if you want to keep it in the playlist but not burn it or play it back this time—uncheck the box next to the song's name.

iTunes displays the playlist's statistics, including its duration, here.

Important: If you're burning an audio CD, keep the playlist's duration under 74 minutes.

iMix and More: Playlist Tips

Opening a Playlist in a Separate Window

To open a playlist in its own window, double-click the playlist's name. iTunes opens the playlist in a new window, and switches its main window to the Library view.

You can open as many playlist windows as you like, and drag songs between them, as shown here. As I demonstrate on the DVD, it's a handy way to work, since it lets you see the contents of your Library and your playlist at the same time.

Previews in Playlists

Beginning with iTunes 4.5, you can drag a song preview from the music store into a playlist. This can be a handy way to put together a temporary shopping list—drag previews into a playlist, then go back and review them again before deciding what to buy.

You can also publish a wish list of tunes: Drag previews into a playlist, then publish the playlist as described on the next page. Your friends won't be able to buy the tunes for you—the music store's copy-protection system prohibits that—but they could buy you gift certificates. Hint, hint.

To help you tell a preview from a full-length song, iTunes displays a little badge (⑨) adjacent to a preview song's name.

Creating a Playlist From a Selection

Here's a shortcut for creating a playlist: in the Library view, select the songs you want to include in a playlist, and then choose New Playlist From Selection from the File menu. iTunes will add the songs to a new playlist, which you can then rename.

Naming Playlists with iPod in Mind

If you plan to transfer your playlists to an iPod, there's a trick you can use to ensure that a given playlist will appear at the top of the iPod's Playlists menu. This cuts down on the time and scrolling required to find a specific playlist.

To have a playlist appear at the top of the iPod's Playlists menu, precede the playlist's name with a hyphen (-) character, as in - *Mac's Greatest Hits*.

A few other punctuation characters, including period (.), will also send a playlist to the top of the heap.

Adding One Playlist to Another

You can add the entire contents of one playlist to other playlists. In the Source area of the iTunes window, simply drag one playlist to another.

Where Have I Used that Song?

Curious about which playlists contain a particular song? Hold down the Control key and click on the song. A shortcut menu appears containing a Playlists submenu. Open the submenu to see a list of playlists containing the song. To jump to a specific playlist, choose its name from the Playlists submenu.

From CD to Playlist in One Drag

You're about to rip an audio CD and you're planning to add some of its tracks to a playlist. Here's a shortcut: simply drag the tracks from the CD list to the playlist. iTunes will import the tracks and add them to the playlist for you.

See tips for working with playlists.
◉ Playlist Tips
◉ Naming with iPod in Mind

iMix: Publishing Your Playlists

You've crafted the perfect playlist? Share it with the rest of us. Beginning with iTunes 4.5, you can publish a playlist on the iTunes Music Store. (You must have an account at the music store or with America Online before you can publish a playlist.)

A published playlist is called an *iMix*, and it appears in its own screen, much like an artist or album page. Each iMix is available for one year. After you create one, you can tell your friends by sending them e-cards or by publishing your iMix's address on a Web site.

Creating an iMix

Step 1. Select the playlist you want to publish, and click the arrow next to its name.

If iTunes displays its sign-in screen, supply your account name and password.

Step 2. Describe your iMix.

iTunes creates a collage based on the artwork for the songs in the playlist.

Type a description of your iMix and change its name, if you like.

To publish the iMix, click Publish.

Step 3 (optional). Tell the world, or at least a friend.

To let someone know about your iMix, click the Tell a Friend button that appears after you publish the iMix.

After your iMix is published, you'll receive an email containing a summary of its tunes as well as a link that you can include in an email or on a Web page.

If your playlist includes songs that are *not* available at iTunes Music Store, those songs don't appear in your iMix.

---

iMix Tips

Exploring iMixes. To explore the iMixes that other people have created, click the iMix item in the Genre area of the music store's home screen.

You can view mixes chronologically or in order of their rating. Highly rated iMixes also appear in relevant artist and album pages.

What else? If you like someone's iMix, you might want to explore other iMixes that he or she has created. In an iMix window, click the link that reads *See more iMixes by this user.*

Linking to an iMix. Want to grab the Internet address for an iMix? Control-click on the iMix's name or artwork, and choose Copy iTunes Music Store URL from the shortcut menu. Paste the resulting link into an email or the Web tool of your choice.

As with individual songs, you can also create a desktop icon for an iMix—just drag its title or artwork icon to the desktop.

Updating an iMix. To make changes to an iMix, edit the original playlist, then publish it again. When you've published a playlist, a link arrow appears next to it, even when the playlist isn't selected.

Smart Playlists: iTunes as DJ

iTunes can create playlists for you based on criteria that you specify. When you're in a hurry—or if you're just curious to see what iTunes comes up with—use iTunes' *smart playlists* feature to quickly assemble playlists. Smart playlists take advantage of all that information that's stored along with your music—its genre, artist, year, and more—to enable you to enjoy and present your music library in some fun ways.

Creating a smart playlist involves specifying the criteria for the songs you want included in the playlist—for example, songs whose genre is jazz and whose year is in the range of 1960 to 1969. You can choose to limit the size of the playlist using various criteria, including playing time (don't create a playlist longer than 74 minutes); disk space (don't create a playlist larger than 2 GB); number of songs (limit this playlist to 20 songs); and much more. You'll find some smart playlist ideas on page 42.

The smart playlists feature is really just a sophisticated search command. But a good playlist is more than just a series of songs that meet certain rules—it also presents those songs in a musically and emotionally pleasing way. A ballad may segue into an up-tempo tune, for example, or a laid-back instrumental may follow a dramatic vocal.

So go ahead and use iTunes' smart playlist feature to quickly throw together playlists. But to really do justice to your music, fine-tune the order of the songs in the smart playlists that iTunes creates. Or build your playlists by hand.

Creating a Smart Playlist

To create a smart playlist, choose New Smart Playlist from the File menu or press the Option key while clicking the playlist button (⚙) in the lower-left corner of the iTunes window.

What are you interested in? Choose options from the pop-up menus and type text in the box. Here, I'm building a smart playlist of all my Herbie Hancock tunes.

iTunes normally organizes the songs in a smart playlist in random order, but you can choose to organize them by artist name, song name, and other criteria.

Want to be more specific? Click ⊕ to add another criterion (see opposite page).

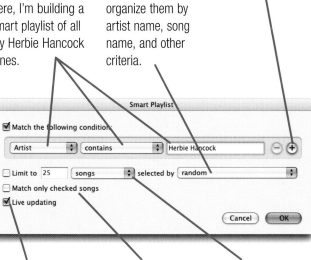

iTunes updates a smart playlist's contents as you add songs to (or remove them from) your music library.

To turn a smart playlist into a static one, uncheck Live Updating.

To have iTunes search only those songs that have a checkmark next to them in your library, click this box.

You can limit the size of the smart playlist to a maximum number of songs, minutes, hours, megabytes (MB), or gigabytes (GB).

See how to create and modify smart playlists.
◉ **Creating Smart Playlists**
◉ **Refining a Smart Playlist**

Changing a Smart Playlist

To modify a smart playlist's criteria or update settings, select the smart playlist and choose Edit Smart Playlist from the File menu (or press ⌘-I).

Be More Specific:
Adding Criteria

When you want to be more specific, use more than one criterion in your smart playlists. In this example, my smart playlist will contain all George Duke songs from the 70s that are under five minutes long.

To have iTunes apply all of your criteria as it searches and compiles the playlist, choose All. If you choose Any, iTunes adds a song if it matches any of your criteria.

You can choose from and combine criteria in more than twenty categories. For some inspiration, see the following pages.

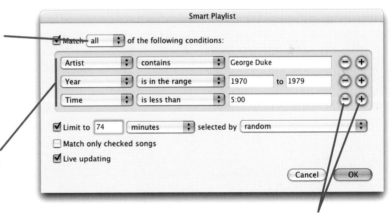

To add another criterion, click the plus button (⊕). To remove a criterion, click the minus button (⊖) .

Built-in Smart Playlists

iTunes includes several simple smart playlists, including "60's Music" and "My Top Rated." Feel free to delete or modify them.

A Cookbook of Smart Playlists

Some smart playlist ideas are obvious: a playlist containing songs from your favorite artist, a playlist of dance tunes, and so on.

But smart playlists aren't just a quick way to create playlists; they're also a great way to rediscover your music and explore your library in ways you might not think of otherwise. In short, don't restrict yourself to the obvious.

Here are some smart playlist ideas to get your creative juices flowing.

Smart Playlist Suggestions

For a Compilation of	Specify These Criteria
Short dance tunes	Genre is *Dance* and Time is less than 5:00 minutes
The same song performed by various artists	Song Name is equal to *name*
Songs added to your library recently	Date Added is in the last 1 week (adjust date value as desired)
Songs from a particular artist and era	Artist is *name* and Year is in the range *years here*.
Songs you haven't listened to recently	Last Played is not in the last *x* days (adjust date value as desired)
Songs by any of a few favorite artists	Artist is *name* or Artist is *name* (add a criterion for each artist and choose Any from the Match pop-up menu)
Audio files that are not in MP3 format	Kind is not "MPEG audio file" (don't type the quotes)
Songs you've added but never listened to	Play Count is 0 (zero)
Songs you've created in GarageBand and exported to iTunes	Kind contains "AIFF audio file" (don't type the quotes)
Audiobooks downloaded from Audible.com	Kind contains "audible" (don't type the quotes)
Songs from your high-school days (assuming that you've reached them)	Year is in the range 1975 to 1978 (for example)
Songs you've purchased from the iTunes Music Store	Kind contains "protected AAC" (don't type the quotes)

Smart Playlist Tips

Smart Playlists and Purchased Music

On page 35, I mentioned that iTunes creates a Purchased Music playlist when you begin buying songs at the iTunes Music Store. However, the Purchased Music playlist lists only songs you've purchased using that particular computer. If you move those purchased songs to a different computer, they won't show up in its Purchased Music playlist. And that can complicate backup sessions.

The solution? You could use the iTunes Export Song List command to export the Purchased Music playlist and then move it over to the other computer. But there's an easier way: Create a smart playlist containing only music you've purchased. Set up the Smart Playlist window to read *Kind contains "protected AAC"* (don't type the quotes). Keep the Live Updating box checked, and you'll always have a full list of your purchases, no matter which Mac you use to do your buying.

Including or Excluding Existing Playlists

Beginning with iTunes version 4.5, you can have iTunes include or exclude specific playlists when putting together a smart playlist. Choose the Playlist item from the leftmost pop-up menu, choose "is" or "is not" from the middle pop-up menu, then choose a playlist name from the rightmost pop-up menu.

This gives you more control over which songs iTunes selects. For example, to put together a playlist of all the jazz you've bought from the iTunes Music Store, create two criteria: Genre is jazz, and Playlist is Purchased Music.

Or, assemble a playlist of the highest rated songs in a favorite playlist: My Rating is greater than three stars, and Playlist is My Favorites (for example).

You can also use this feature to create more sophisticated search rules. For example, say you want to assemble a smart playlist of your R&B and jazz tunes from the 60s. First, create a smart playlist that locates all your R&B and jazz. Create two criteria: Genre is R&B *and* Genre is Jazz, then choose Any from the Match pop-up menu. Name this playlist something like "R&B and Jazz."

Next, create another smart playlist with the following two criteria: Playlist is "R&B and Jazz" and Year is in the range 1960 to 1969.

Don't Forget Comments

As described on page 29, you can assign comments and other tidbits of information to your songs. These tidbits pair up beautifully with smart playlists. For example, if you're a jazz buff, you might use the Comments field to store the sidemen who appear on a given song—Ron Carter on bass, Freddie Hubbard on trumpet. You could then create a smart playlist containing songs in which Freddie Hubbard appears: Comment contains *Freddie Hubbard.*

Something Completely Different

Want to explore your music library in a completely different way? Try making a smart playlist built around the Track Number field. For example, to create a smart playlist containing the first song in all of your albums, specify Track Number is 1. If one of your favorite artists always starts his or albums with a particularly cool track, add the artist's name: Artist is George Duke and Track Number is 1.

Want More?

Looking for even more smart playlists? Believe it or not, there's a Web site devoted to them: www.smartplaylists.com. Check it out for smart playlist ideas and iTunes tips of all kinds.

Find that Tune: Searching and Browsing

As your music library grows, you'll want to take advantage of the features iTunes provides for locating songs, artists, and albums.

With the iTunes Search box, you can quickly narrow down the list of songs displayed to only those songs that match the criterion you typed.

With the Browse button, you can quickly scan your music library by artist, album name, or genre.

And with the Show Song File command in the File menu, you can quickly display the actual disk file that corresponds to a given song in your library or in a playlist.

Searching

As you type in the Search box, iTunes narrows down the list of songs displayed. iTunes searches the album title, artist, genre, and song title items. To see all the songs in your library or playlist, select the text in the Search box and press Delete, or simply click the ⊗ in the Search box.

Narrow Your Searches

Want to search with more precision? Click on the magnifying glass, then choose an option from the pop-up menu. For example, to find songs by Jennifer Love Hewitt without also retrieving songs with "love" in their names, choose Artists.

Finding a Song's Disk File

There may be times when you want to locate a song's disk file on your hard drive—to back it up, for example, to move it to another drive, or to simply determine where it's stored.

To locate a song's disk file, select the song and choose Show Song File from the File menu (or press ⌘-R). iTunes switches you to the Finder, opens the folder containing the song, and highlights the song file.

See iTunes' searching and browsing features in action.
◉ **Searching for Songs**
◉ **Browsing Your Song Library**

Browsing

The Artist pane lists all the artists in your library. Select an artist name, and iTunes displays that artist's albums in the Album pane.

Use the link arrows to quickly browse your library: press the Option key while clicking on the link arrow for an artist, song, or album. (To customize this feature, see page 67.)

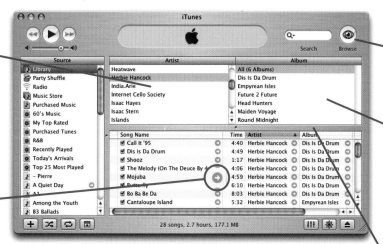

To browse your music library by artist and album name, click the Browse button.

The Album pane lists all the albums in your library or those from a selected artist. Select an album name, and iTunes displays the songs from that album.

Drag the separator up or down to resize the window panes.

Browsing by Genre

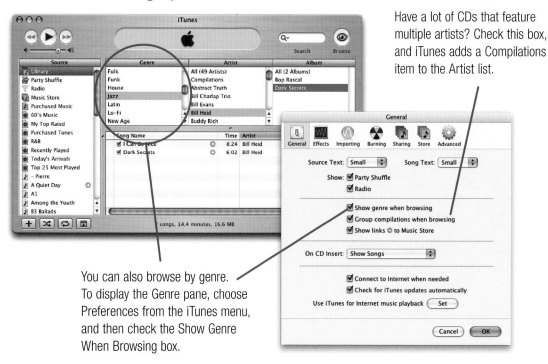

Have a lot of CDs that feature multiple artists? Check this box, and iTunes adds a Compilations item to the Artist list.

You can also browse by genre. To display the Genre pane, choose Preferences from the iTunes menu, and then check the Show Genre When Browsing box.

Improving Sound Quality with the Equalizer

The iTunes *equalizer* lets you boost and attenuate various frequency ranges; think of it as a very sophisticated set of bass and treble controls. You might pump up the bass to make up for small speakers. You might boost the high frequencies to make up for aging ears. Or you might increase the mid-range frequencies to improve the clarity of a spoken recording.

The iTunes equalizer (EQ) divides the audio spectrum into ten *bands*, and provides a slider that lets you boost or attenuate frequencies in each band. The bands start at 32 hertz (Hz), a deeper bass than most of us can hear, and go all the way up to 16 kilohertz (KHz), which, while short of dog-whistle territory, approaches the upper limits of human hearing. (If you've been around for more than several decades or have listened to a lot of loud music, 16 KHz is probably out of your hearing range.)

iTunes provides more than 20 equalization presets from which to choose. You can listen to all your music with one setting applied, or you can assign separate settings to individual songs. You can also adjust EQ settings by hand and create your own presets.

To display the equalizer, click the Equalizer button (▥) near the lower-right corner of the iTunes window, or choose Equalizer from the Window menu (⌘-2).

Finding Your Way Around the Equalizer

Click to turn on the equalizer.

Drag a slider up to boost the frequencies in that range; drag it down to attenuate them.

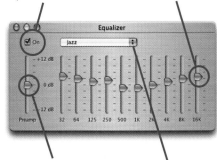

The preamp boosts or attenuates the volume for all frequencies equally.

Choose a preset, create a new preset, or manage your list of presets.

Creating Your Own Preset

1. To save a customized preset, choose Make Preset from the preset pop-up menu.

2. Type a name for the preset and click OK.

The new preset appears in the pop-up menu.

Assigning Presets to Individual Songs

If you've turned on the equalizer, iTunes applies the current EQ setting to any song you play back. However, you can also assign EQ settings on a song-by-song basis.

First, choose View Options from the Edit menu and verify that the Equalizer box is checked.

Next, choose the desired preset from the pop-up menu in the Equalizer column.

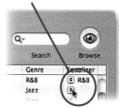

To change the EQ settings for several songs at once, select the songs and choose Get Info from the File menu. Then choose the desired EQ setting.

Presets that Make You Smile

You may have noticed that many of iTunes' presets have a smile-like appearance: the low- and high-frequency ranges are boosted to a greater degree than the mid-range frequencies.

Audio gurus call this shape the *Fletcher-Munson curve*. It reflects the fact that, at most listening levels, our ears are less sensitive to low and high frequencies than they are to mid-range frequencies.

Chances are your stereo system has a Loudness button. When you turn it on, the stereo applies a similar curve to make the music sound more natural at lower volume levels.

Classical

Jazz

Rock

Latin

"That Song Needs a Bit More 250"

Being able to control the volume of 10 different frequency ranges is great, but how do you know which ranges to adjust? Here's a guide to how frequency ranges correlate with those of some common musical instruments and the human voice. Note that these ranges don't take into account harmonics, which are the tonal complexities that help us discern between instruments. Harmonics can easily exceed 20 KHz.

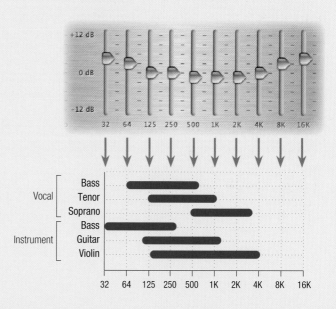

47

Burning Audio CDs

It may be on life support, but the compact disc player isn't dead yet. If your Mac contains a CD burner (all current models do), you can create your own audio CDs—to play in the car, in the living room, on a boombox, or at a friend's house.

To burn some songs onto a CD, you must first add them to a playlist. Once you've done that, burning a CD is a two-click proposition.

iTunes also has some advanced burning features that enable you to burn other types of discs; for details on them and for tips for all your burning endeavors, see page 50.

And by the way, if you have an older Mac that lacks a built-in CD burner, consider buying an external burner that connects to the USB or FireWire jack. iTunes supports many third-party external burners. For a list of supported burners, see www.apple.com/macosx/upgrade/storage.html.

Step 1.
Select the Playlist You Want to Burn

If the playlist contains a song that you don't want to burn, uncheck the box next to the song's name.

iTunes displays the playlist's total duration here.

Important: If you're burning an audio CD, keep the playlist's duration under 74 minutes. If your entire playlist won't fit on one audio CD, iTunes will offer to burn additional discs.

Watch the CD-burning process.
◉ **Burning an Audio CD**

Step 2.
Click the Burn Disc button

When you click Burn Disc, iTunes opens your Mac's CD tray and instructs you to insert a blank CD.

Note: As an alternative to clicking the Burn Disc button, you can choose Burn Playlist to Disc from the File menu.

To cancel the burn, click here.

Step 3.
Begin the Burn

iTunes displays the number of songs it will burn and their total duration.

To begin burning, click Burn Disc again.

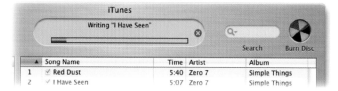

As the CD burns, iTunes displays a status message. You can cancel a burn in progress by clicking the ⊗ button, but you'll end up with a *coaster*— a damaged CD blank whose only useful purpose is to sit beneath a cold drink.

Tips for Your Burning Endeavors

By adjusting burning preferences, you can control the pause between songs, volume levels, and even the format of your final CD. Choose Preferences from the iTunes menu, click the Burning button, and then read on.

Gap Control

When iTunes burns an audio CD, it uses a two-second gap to separate songs. Depending on what you're burning, you may want to omit, or at least change, that gap. On many so-called concept albums, one song flows seamlessly into the next. When burning these kinds of tracks, close the gap: choose None from the Gap Between Songs pop-up menu. Unfortunately, because of the nature of audio compression, you may still hear a tiny gap between songs. If you can't bear even the smallest pause, rip the songs from an audio CD using the Join Tracks option (page 20).

Volume Control

Not all albums are mastered at the same volume level, and if you mix and match tracks from a few CDs, some songs may sound much quieter than others. Don't reach for the volume knob—click the Sound Check box before burning, and iTunes adjusts each track to make the final CD's levels consistent.

You can also apply Sound Check when playing music in iTunes; see page 62 for details.

Burning MP3 CDs

Normally, iTunes burns CDs in standard audio CD format. But you can also burn tracks as MP3 files; this lets you take advantage of MP3's compression so you can squeeze more music onto a CD— roughly ten times the number of songs that an audio CD will hold.

But there are a couple of catches. Catch Number One: Most audio CD players can't play MP3-format CDs. If you're shopping for a CD or DVD player, you may want to look for one that supports MP3 playback.

Catch Number Two: When you burn a playlist in MP3 format, iTunes skips over any songs that are stored in AAC format. If you're taking advantage of AAC's superior efficiency—or if you've built a library of purchases from the iTunes Music Store—the MP3 CD format won't be of much use to you.

To have iTunes burn in MP3 format, click the Burning button in the iTunes Preferences dialog box. Click the MP3 CD button, and then click OK.

When ripping CDs that you'll subsequently be burning in MP3 format, you might find it useful to activate the iTunes track numbering option: in the Preferences dialog box, click Importing and then check the box labeled Create file names with track number.

Track numbering is useful because many players play the songs on MP3 CDs in alphabetical order—activating track numbering will enable the tracks to play back in the correct order.

Back Up Your Tunes

You've bought some music—and then your Mac's hard drive dies. The songs you bought are gone, and the only way to download them again is to buy them again.

Clearly, backing up is good to do. iTunes can help.

Choose Preferences from the iTunes menu, click Burning, then choose the Data CD option. Next, create a playlist of the songs you want to back up. (If you want to back up only the songs you've purchased, just click the Purchased Music playlist or the smart playlist I described on page 43.) Finally, burn that playlist to a CD or DVD.

If you have more music than will fit on a single CD or DVD, iTunes displays a message letting you know. Verify that you have a few blank discs available, then click the Data Discs button.

Another way to back up a huge music library is to drag it to a second hard drive. An external FireWire hard drive is inexpensive and makes great backup media for music and photos alike. Go to your Home directory (choose Home from the Finder's Go menu), then locate and double-click your Music folder. Locate the folder named iTunes and drag it to the other hard drive. Unlike the burning approach, this technique also backs up all of your playlists.

Blank Advice

Many brands of CD-R media are available, and some people swear by a given brand. Some users even claim that certain colors of CD-R blanks are better than others.

My advice: Don't sweat it—just buy name-brand CD-R blanks. And don't fret about their colors. Color varies depending on the organic dyes used by the CD-R's manufacturer, and different manufacturers use different dye formulations. Color isn't a useful indicator of CD-R quality anyway.

How long will your burned CDs last? Manufacturers toss out figures ranging from 75 to 200 years, but these are only estimates based on accelerated aging tests that attempt to simulate the effects of time.

One thing is certain: a CD-R will last longer when kept away from heat and bright light. Avoid scratching either side of a CD-R—use a felt-tipped pen to label it, and don't write any more than you need to. (The solvents in the ink can damage the CD over time.)

Also, think twice about applying a peel-and-stick label to the CD. The label's adhesive can damage the CD over time, and if you don't center the label perfectly, the CD will be out of balance as it spins, which could cause playback problems.

To learn more about CD-R media, visit the CD-Recordable FAQ at www.cdrfaq.org.

Burning to CD-RW Media

For broadest compatibility with CD players, you'll want to burn using CD-R blanks, which can't be erased and reused. But the CD burners in all current Macs can also use CD-RW media—rewritable media, which costs more but can be erased and reused again and again.

A growing number of CD players can play back rewritable media, and if yours is among them, you might consider using rewritable media for some burning jobs. It's also ideal for backing up your iTunes music library.

Note that iTunes can't erase a CD-RW disc. To do that, use Mac OS X's Disk Utility program; it's located in the Utilities folder, inside the Applications folder.

Finishing Touches:
Printing Case Inserts and More

After you've burned a CD, you might want to print an insert that you can slide into the disc's jewel case. Apple added printing features to iTunes 4.5 that let you do this and more.

When printing a case insert, you can choose from a variety of insert designs, called *themes*. Some themes take advantage of the album artwork feature described on the opposite page. If your playlist's songs have corresponding album art, iTunes uses the art for the front and back of the case insert. With a few mouse clicks, you can even put your own artwork on a jewel case insert.

You can also print several types of song and album lists. They're a great way to produce a hard-copy reference of your music library and favorite playlists.

If your playlist contains songs from multiple albums, you can use the Mosaic themes to produce a collage of album art.

Want to use just one album's art for the cover? Before you choose Print, select the song containing that art.

To Print a Jewel Case Insert

Step 1. In the Source area, select the playlist for which you want a case insert.

Step 2. Choose Print from the File menu and choose a theme.

Step 3. Adjust Page Setup options as needed, then click Print or press Return.

Step 4. Trim the case insert, using the crop marks as a guide.

India.Arie and Zero 7
ACOUSTIC SOUL

1. Intro / India.Arie — 0:50
2. Vidéo / India.Arie — 4:10
3. Promises / India.Arie — 4:37
4. Brown Skin / India.Arie — 4:56
5. Strength, Courage, & Wisdom / India.Arie — 4:57
6. Nature / India.Arie — 4:24
7. Back To The Middle / India.Arie — 5:11
8. Ready For Love / India.Arie — 4:28
9. Interlude / India.Arie — 1:24
10. Always In My Head / India.Arie — 4:40
11. I See God In You / India.Arie — 3:17
12. Simple / India.Arie — 3:26
13. Part Of My Life / India.Arie — 4:03
14. Beautiful / India.Arie — 4:05
15. In Time / Zero 7 — 4:56
16. Speed Dial No. 2 / Zero 7 — 3:49
17. Over Our Heads / Zero 7 — 4:24
18. Morning Song / Zero 7 — 6:30
19. Look Up / Zero 7 — 5:57
20. Passing By / Zero 7 — 4:51
21. Warm Sound / Zero 7 — 5:30

Printed with iTunes

ZERO7
WHEN IT FALLS

More About Artwork

iTunes can store album artwork—for example, an image of a CD cover—along with your music. The artwork is embedded into a music file itself, so if you move the file to another Mac, the art moves along with it.

Music that you buy from the iTunes Music Store usually has artwork. To display it, click the Show/Hide Artwork button.

To switch between the currently playing song and the currently selected song, click here. A song can contain multiple images; click the little arrows to display other images.

To hide (or show) the artwork, click this button.

To display the artwork in a larger window, click here. To add an image to the currently selected song, drag an image here. To copy the art into another program, drag it from here to the program.

Adding Artwork to Songs

What about all the songs in your library that don't have artwork? If you'd like to add art to them, you have several options. Some free utilities will search for, and retrieve, artwork over the Internet; I use a program called Fetch Art, by Yoel Inbar. Like other artwork utilities, it looks up the name of an album on Amazon.com, then retrieves the artwork from Amazon's site.

For more artwork-related utilities, see macilife.com/itunes.

To rearrange the images, drag them left and right. To use a specific image in a jewel case insert, drag it so that it's the first image in the list.

To add another image, click Add. To delete an image, select it and then click Delete.

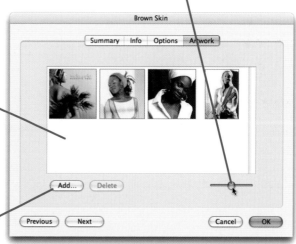

More Artwork Tips

You can also view and modify a song's artwork by using the Song Information dialog box. Select a song, choose Get Info from File menu, and click the Artwork option. In the example below, the song contains four images. You can store even more, but keep in mind that each image increases the size of your music file, thus leaving less free space on your hard drive and iPod.

To make the thumbnail images smaller or larger, drag the slider.

Tip: You can print your own artwork—including a photo from your iPhoto library—on a jewel case insert. First, add the image to a song. (For a photo, simply drag it from the iPhoto window to the artwork area.) Drag the image so it's the first image in the list, then print. To reduce the size of the song file, delete the image after printing.

Sharing Music on a Network

If you have multiple Macs or Windows PCs on a network, you can use iTunes' sharing feature to turn them into jukeboxes whose music other computers can play. (You'll need to install iTunes for Windows on the PCs).

Sharing enables all manner of music networking options. You might keep all of your music on one Mac—no wasting disk space by storing a music library on each Mac or PC in your network. Conversely, you might prefer to segregate your music—put your kids' music on their iMac and your music on yours—while still giving each Mac access to every song. You might want to set up a jukebox Mac to dish out tunes to the office. Or use AirPort wireless networking to listen at poolside using your PowerBook.

The sharing feature relies on streaming: when you listen to another Mac's music, the song files are streamed across your network. The files are never actually copied from one Mac to another. It's the same concept I discuss on page 57, except it happens on your local network, not the Internet.

Note: Be sure you're using the same version of iTunes on each computer in the network. Apple has changed the iTunes sharing feature a couple of times, and as a result, different versions of iTunes aren't always able to share libraries. If a shared library appears grey and an error message appears when you select it, it's probably because the shared library is coming from an older version of iTunes.

Activating Sharing

To share your music library with other Macs on your network, choose Preferences from the iTunes menu, then click the Sharing button.

To have your Mac automatically connect to shared libraries on your network, check this box.

To share your music, check this box.

You can share your entire library or only selected playlists. To share a specific playlist, click its check box.

When other users connect to your shared music, this name will appear in their copies of iTunes.

Don't want your kids (or parents) to access your shared library? Check this box, then specify a password.

When sharing is on, the Status area also shows how many users are connected.

See music sharing in action.
⊚ **Sharing Music on a Network**

Accessing Shared Music

If you've checked the Look for Shared Music box in the Sharing portion of the Preferences dialog box, iTunes automatically scans your network and finds shared libraries.

To view a shared library, click its name in the Source list. If the library requires a password, a dialog box appears.

To view playlists in a shared library, click the little triangle next to the library's name.

Tips for Sharing

Shared Songs Are Play-Only

Because shared songs don't reside on your hard drive, you can't add them to playlists, delete them, burn them to a CD, or modify their information.

Up to Five

Up to five computers can connect to a shared library. If a sixth user tries to connect, he or she sees an error message.

To free up a connection, you'll need to disconnect one of the currently connected computers, as described in the following tip.

Disconnecting

To disconnect from a shared library—for example, to free up a connection for someone else—click the Disconnect button (⏏) in the lower-right corner of the iTunes window, or Control-click on the library in the Source list and choose Disconnect from the pop-up shortcut menu.

Authorization

If you want to play a purchased song from a shared library, you'll have to authorize your Mac by supplying your account name and password. As noted on page 34, you can authorize up to five computers per account.

Tuning In to Internet Radio

The Internet is transforming a lot of things, and broadcasting is one of them. You can tune into thousands of streaming Internet radio stations using iTunes and other programs.

Many of these stations are commercial or public broadcasters that are also making their audio available on the 'net. But most stations are Internet-only affairs, often set up by music lovers who simply want to share their tastes with the rest of us. You can join them—create your own radio station using a service such as Live365 (www.live365.com) or a streaming server program such as Rogue Amoeba's NiceCast, a trial version of which is included in the DVD's Extras folder.

If part of streaming audio's appeal is its diversity, the other part is its immediacy. Streaming playback begins just a few seconds after you click on a link—there's no waiting for huge sound files to download before you hear a single note.

Several formats for streaming audio exist, and MP3 is one of them. Using the iTunes Radio tuner, you can listen to Internet radio stations that stream in MP3 format.

You can't use iTunes to listen to Internet radio stations that use formats other than MP3. To tune in the full range of Internet streaming media, use Apple's QuickTime Player (www.apple.com/quicktime), Microsoft's Windows Media Player (www.windowsmedia.com), and Real-Networks' RealOne (www.real.com).

Turn on the Tuner

The first step in using iTunes to listen to Internet radio is to activate the iTunes radio tuner.

Click Radio to switch the iTunes view to the radio tuner. To display the tuner in its own window, double-click.

Note: If you don't see the Radio item, choose Preferences from the iTunes menu, click General, and be sure the Radio check box is selected.

iTunes retrieves its list of Internet radio categories and stations from the Internet. Click Refresh to have iTunes contact the tuning service and update its list of categories and stations.

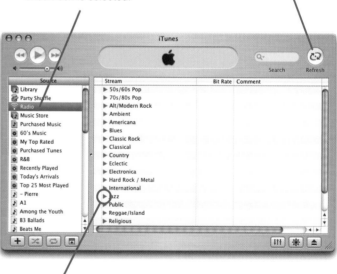

iTunes groups Internet radio stations by genre; to display the stations in a genre, double-click the genre name or click on the triangle to its left.

Bandwidth:
Internet Radio's Antenna

The quality of your Internet radio "reception" depends in part on the speed of your Internet connection.

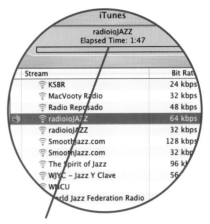

With Internet radio, information listed in the Bit Rate column is particularly important. It reflects not only how much the audio has been compressed, but also how fast a connection you'll need in order to listen without interruption. For example, if you have a 56 kbps modem connection, you won't be able to listen to a stream whose bit rate is higher than 56 kbps. (Indeed, even a 56 kbps stream may hiccup occasionally.)

iTunes shows how long you've been listening to a stream. Notice that when you're listening to a live stream, there is no control for skipping forward and backward within a song.

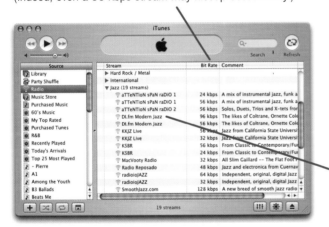

To listen to a station, double-click the station's name.

How Streaming Works

When you begin playing back an Internet radio stream, iTunes connects to a streaming server, which downloads several seconds' worth of audio into an area of memory called a *buffer.* When the buffer is full, playback begins. The player then continues downloading audio into the buffer while simultaneously playing back the audio that it has already buffered. It's this just-in-time downloading that gives streaming its near-immediate gratification— most of the time, anyway.

If Internet congestion or connection problems interrupt the incoming stream, the buffer may empty completely, stalling playback while the buffer refills.

Recording Internet Radio and More

Internet radio is a fleeting affair—just as your radio doesn't store programs, iTunes and other streaming players don't store Internet audio on your hard drive. That means you can't add your favorite Internet radio programming to your iTunes library or listen to it on your iPod.

At least not without a little help. Several free or inexpensive programs can record streaming audio on your hard drive. In fact, they can record any sound your Mac can play. Thus, you can also record audio from DVDs: record some tunes from a favorite concert movie—or some dialog from your favorite Cheech and Chong romp—and burn an audio CD to play in the car.

If you use Apple's iChat AV to conduct audio chats, you can use one of these programs to record your conversations. You can also record real-time performance effects in GarageBand (page 255). You can even record the soundtrack and explosions of a favorite video game, if that's your idea of easy listening.

Let's look at the tools and techniques behind recording the unrecordable.

Hijacking in Three Easy Steps

The top tool for recording the unrecordable is Rogue Amoeba Software's Audio Hijack (see opposite page for a look at other tools). Here's how to use it.

Step 1. Hijack

Create a preset for the program whose audio you want to record. If you like, set a timer to start or stop recording at specific times. You can also specify that Audio Hijack run an AppleScript after recording (see page 70 for an introduction to AppleScripts). Audio Hijack includes scripts that use iTunes to encode a recording into AAC or MP3 format.

Step 2. Click the Record button and start playback.

Click Audio Hijack's Record button and then begin playing back the audio. Audio Hijack starts recording when playback begins.

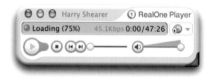

Step 3. Add to iTunes and tweak track info.

Add the recording to iTunes if necessary (if you run either of the encoding scripts after recording, this happens automatically). Locate the track in your iTunes library, choose Get Info from the File menu, and edit the song information.

For more information about adding audio files to iTunes "by hand," see page 68.

Getting the Best Sound

When recording Internet audio, you'll often have to make audio-quality decisions.

The right rate. Internet audio is often heavily compressed to allow streaming over slow modem connections. To avoid degrading the sound quality even more, encode at a relatively high bit rate, such as 96kbps for spoken-word programming, and 128 or 160kbps for music.

If you're recording talk radio, record in mono rather than stereo.

As for format decisions, as I've mentioned elsewhere, AAC provides better sound quality at a given bit rate than does MP3.

Before or after? With some programs, including Audio Hijack Pro, you can choose these settings before you record. With most of the other tools, you must use iTunes to encode after you record.

Being able to encode as you record is a timesaving convenience that uses disk space more efficiently. On the downside, you don't have the opportunity to experiment with different encoding settings. If you're recording music and want to get the best sound quality, record in uncompressed AIFF format first, then use iTunes to encode, experimenting with different bit rates and formats until you arrive at the combination that sounds best to your ears.

Which Program to Use?

Several stream recorders are available, and each fills a useful niche.

The casual recorder. You want to record the unrecordable only occasionally. You don't want or need complicated features, and heaven forbid that you should have to pay a dime.

For you, there's Ambrosia Software's free WireTap. WireTap couldn't be simpler: start the audio playing and click WireTap's Record button. The only other control WireTap provides is a button for pausing and resuming recording—great for cutting out talk radio commercials.

When you click WireTap's Stop button, you have an audio file

that you can immediately play back in Apple's QuickTime Player or in iTunes.

One downside to WireTap's simplicity is that it records *every* sound your Mac produces. If your email program chimes while you're recording some talk radio, the chime will be in your final recording. When you want to be more selective about your sound, you need a more sophisticated tool.

Serious sound. The premiere programs for recording the unrecordable are Rogue Amoeba Software's Audio Hijack and Audio Hijack Pro; both can snag the sound from specific programs. And if you don't want to hear the audio as you're record-

ing it, one click of the Mute button silences the stream even at it's being recorded.

Both Audio Hijack programs have VCR-like timers that let you start and stop recording at specific times. Both programs also allow you to make bass and treble adjustments as you record, and both provide a feature that removes some of the muddiness associated with Internet audio. Audio Hijack Pro goes much further, providing a broad selection of audio-processing effects: apply the reverberation effect, and you can make Howard Stern sound like he's in a cathedral— at least from an acoustical standpoint.

For the radio lover. Bitcartel's RadioLover specializes in record-

ing MP3 stations, such as those that iTunes can tune in. Many MP3-based stations send artist and song information along with their streams, and RadioLover can use this information to create separate song files as it records. Set up RadioLover to record for a few hours, and you'll return to find dozens of separate MP3 tracks, already named and ready to add to your iTunes library. It's the kind of feature that makes recording executives reach for antacid, but it's a fabulous way to discover new music. It's also imperfect: the beginning or end of a song is almost always cut off. (You can sometimes fix the problem by adjusting the program's recording preferences.)

Converting Old Tapes and Albums

If you're like me, you're desperate to recapture the past: you want to create digital audio files from audio cassettes and vinyl albums.

Bridging the gap between the analog and digital worlds requires some software and hardware. The process involves connecting your Mac to an audio source, such as a cassette deck or stereo system, and then using recording software to save the audio on your hard drive as it plays back. You can encode the resulting files into AAC or MP3 format and add them to your iTunes music library.

Most current Mac models contain audio-input jacks to that you can connect to a sound source, such as a cassette deck or stereo system. If your Mac doesn't have an audio-input jack, you'll need an adapter such as Griffin Technology's iMic (below), which is inexpensive and does a fine job. Griffin, M-Audio, and other companies also sell more sophisticated (and better-sounding) audio hardware that you might prefer if you're an audiophile or you plan to record acoustic instruments using GarageBand.

Step 1.
Make the Connections

Recording analog sources is easiest when you connect the Mac to the audio output of a stereo system. This will enable you to record anything your stereo can play, from vinyl albums to cassettes to FM radio.

Most stereo receivers have auxiliary output jacks on their back panels. To make the connection, use a cable with two RCA phono plugs on one end and a ⅛-inch stereo miniplug on the other. Connect the phono plugs to the receiver's output jacks, and the miniplug to the input jack on your Mac or audio adapter.

Step 2.
Prepare to Record

Before you record, set your audio levels properly: you want the audio signal to be as loud as possible without distorting the sound.

Fire up your audio recording software (Roxio's CD Spin Doctor is shown here), and adjust its recording levels so that the loudest passages of music fully illuminate the volume meters.

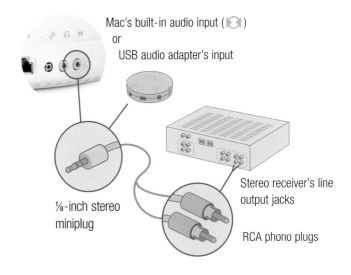

Mac's built-in audio input ( ) or USB audio adapter's input

⅛-inch stereo miniplug

Stereo receiver's line output jacks

RCA phono plugs

Step 3. Record

First, do a test recording. Activate your software's Record mode and begin playing back the original audio, preferably a loud passage. After a minute or two, stop and play back the recorded audio to verify that the recording levels you set are correct. Listen for distortion in loud passages; if you hear any, decrease the levels slightly.

Once you've arrived at the correct setting for recording levels, record the original audio in its entirety.

Step 4. Encode and Edit Song Information

Your completed recording will almost certainly be stored in uncompressed AIFF format—the format used by Mac recording programs.

To save disk space, you'll probably want to encode the recording into AAC or MP3 format. Naturally, you can use iTunes to do this.

Before encoding your recordings, use the Preferences command to choose your preferred encoding settings as described on page 22. Next, hold down the Option key and check out the Advanced menu— you'll see a command that reads Convert to AAC. (If you specified the MP3 encoder in the Preferences dialog box, the command reads Convert to MP3.)

Choose the Convert to AAC (or Convert to MP3) command, and then locate and double-click on the recording you just made. iTunes will encode the track and store the resulting digital audio file in your iTunes library.

iTunes can also encode multiple recordings in one operation. After choosing Convert to AAC (or Convert to MP3), simply ⌘-click on each file you want to import.

After you've encoded your recordings, edit their song information as described on pages 28 and 29. By adding song, artist, album, and genre information, you'll be able to conveniently browse your converted recordings on an iPod and include them in smart playlists.

Choosing a Recording Program

Plenty of audio-recording programs are available, ranging from free programs such as TC Works' SparkME to shareware programs such as Amadeus II to commercial programs such as Bias' Peak and TC Works' SparkXL.

One of my favorite programs for recording analog audio is CD Spin Doctor, included with Roxio's Toast Titanium CD burning software. CD Spin Doctor creates AIFF files, which you can encode into AAC or MP3 format using iTunes, as described above.

A few features make CD Spin Doctor particularly ideal for converting analog recordings into digital form. One is the Auto-Define Tracks command: choose it, and CD Spin Doctor scans a recording, detects the silence between each song, and then divides the recording into multiple tracks. This makes it easy to record one side of an album and then divvy it up into separate tracks.

CD Spin Doctor also has noise and pop filters that can clean up abused records, as well as an "exciter" filter that enhances old recordings by beefing up bass and improving the sense of stereo separation.

Another recording program is Griffin Technology's Final Vinyl, which works only with Griffin recording hardware. For links to these and other audio programs, visit the iTunes page on macilife.com.

Tips for Playing Music

iTunes and Your Stereo

Once you've assembled a music library on your Mac, you'll probably want to listen to it on your stereo system. If your Mac and your stereo are in the same room, you can unite the two using a cable. Simply get a cable with a ⅛-inch stereo miniplug on one end and two RCA phono plugs on the other. Connect the miniplug to the Mac's headphone jack and the phono plugs to an auxiliary input on your stereo.

What if your Mac and stereo aren't close together? Several companies sell receiver/transmitter products that let a computer pipe its audio into a stereo system. Some products use wireless technology, while others use long cables. My advice: don't bother with any of them. Spend your money on an iPod, and simply connect the iPod to your stereo as described on page 81.

If you own a digital video recorder from TiVo (www.tivo.com), you have another option. TiVo's Home Media Option enables the latest TiVo players to access music on a Mac or PC via a home network. You summon playlists and individual tracks using the TiVo's remote control and on-screen menus, and the TiVo retrieves the tunes from your Mac and plays them through your stereo.

But there's a big downside: Home Media Option does not support the AAC music format—it's limited to MP3 only. Home Media Option also lets you view an iPhoto library on your TV set. But for music, it's a second-best option— an iPod remains the best way to conveniently play your music anywhere.

Crossfading Songs

You hear it on the radio all the time: as one song nears its end, it begins to fade as the next song starts to play. You can recreate this effect in iTunes. First, choose Preferences from the iTunes menu, click the Effects button, and then check the Crossfade Playback box.

With crossfading, one song fades out...

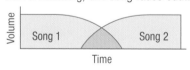

...as the next song fades in.

Dock Control

When iTunes is running, you can start and stop playback and perform other tasks using the iTunes icon in your dock. Point to the icon and hold down the mouse button (or simply Control-click on the icon), then choose the desired command from the shortcut menu. For even more control over iTunes, check out Synergy, described on page 71.

Adjusting a Song's Volume

When you create a playlist containing songs from numerous albums, you may notice that some songs are louder than others. One way to compensate for this is by adjusting the playback volume for specific songs. First, Control-click on a song and then choose Get Info from the contextual pop-up menu.

In the Options tab of the Song Information dialog box, drag the Volume Adjustment slider to decrease or increase the song's playback volume.

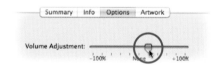

Optimizing Levels with Sound Check

A faster alternative to adjusting playback levels for individual songs is to use the Sound Check option, which optimizes playback volumes so that all songs play back with similar volume levels. To turn Sound Check on, choose Preferences from the iTunes menu, click the Effects button, then check the Sound Check box.

The Sound Enhancer

You can add aural punch by improving what audio gurus call *presence*, the perception that the instruments are right in the room with you. To do this, use the Sound Enhancer option in the Effects tab of the Preferences dialog box. Drag the slider toward the High setting, and you may notice brighter-sounding high frequencies and an enhanced sense of stereo separation. Experiment with the setting that sounds best for your ears—and your audio equipment.

Skipping to the Next or Previous Album

As I noted on page 18, you can skip to the next song by clicking ⏭ and to the previous song by clicking ⏮. To skip to the next or previous album, press the Option key while clicking these buttons.

You can also skip to the next and previous album using the keyboard: press Option along with the right-arrow or left-arrow key.

Adjusting Volume with a Scroll Wheel Mouse

Many third-party mice have a scroll wheel. If your rodent is so equipped, you can use the scroll wheel to adjust the volume when iTunes is in its tiny-window mode—that is, when you've clicked the rightmost gumdrop in the upper-left corner of the iTunes window.

Snapping Back: Showing the Current Song

Here's a common scenario: As you listen to a tune, you begin browsing your music library or maybe even shopping at the iTunes Music Store. Then you decide to add the currently playing song to a playlist.

How can you quickly find it? Easy: choose Show Current Song from the File menu (⌘-L). Choose this command, and iTunes displays and highlights the song that's currently playing.

Beginning with iTunes 4.5, there's also a button you can click. It's called the SnapBack button, and it appears near the right-hand side of the iTunes LCD—that wide area at the top of the iTunes window.

How to "Crop" Songs

Scenario #1: You have an album that was recorded live, and each song starts with a long, rambling introduction by the recording artist. You'd like to cut out that intro and just start with the music.

Scenario #2: There's a song you really want to like, but two thirds of the way through, it degenerates into an ear-bleeding cacophony of noise.

iTunes has a little-used feature that beautifully addresses both of these scenarios: You can "crop" a song—lop off part of the beginning, part of the end, or both—to hear only the part you want to hear. This cropping is even retained when you transfer the song to an iPod. And best of all, it's easy.

First, listen to the song you want to crop, and use the iTunes time display to note where the offensive portion ends or begins. Now select the song, choose Get Info from the File menu, and click the Options button.

Next, configure the Start Time and/or End Time boxes as needed. In the example below, I'm skipping over the first 34 seconds of the song.

Click OK when you've finished, and you're done. And if you ever do want to hear that cropped-out portion, you can do so by simply dragging the little playback diamond that appears near the top of the iTunes window.

Surprise Me: Shuffle Playback Options

When long-playing albums appeared in the 1940s, recording artists gained the ability to present more than one song at a time. LPs enabled artists to present songs in a sequence of their choosing. And for the next forty years or so, music lovers would be locked into their choices.

Then compact discs appeared. Unlike phonographs, CD players could instantly access any part of an album. To take advantage of this, player manufacturers added *shuffle* features: press a button, and the player skipped around within a CD, playing tracks at random. One comedian even worked the concept into his routine: "I ran into a famous musician on the street and I told him, 'I'm familiar with your latest CD—but not in the order you want me to be.'"

iTunes takes the shuffle concept to the next level. Sure, you can play tracks or albums at random, but with the Party Shuffle playlist that debuted in iTunes 4.5, you can combine the serendipity of shuffle mode with the forethought of a well-crafted playlist.

Some music lovers want full control over playback; others love the game of chance that shuffle modes provide. One thing is certain: random-playback features are a great way to rediscover songs you haven't listened to in a while.

Here's how turn your music jukebox into a slot machine.

Pick a Song, Any Song: Shuffle Mode

The simplest form of random playback is shuffle mode. To play random songs from your library, select the Library item, then click the Shuffle button (⤨).

Shuffling a playlist. You can apply shuffle mode to a playlist in a couple of ways. To simply hear a playlist in random order, select the playlist, then click the shuffle button.

If you'd like to see what kind of random order iTunes comes up with, click the playlist's leftmost column heading to sort it in numeric order, *then* click the shuffle button.

Keeping a shuffle. Sometimes a random pick is perfect—just ask any lottery winner. If you like the way iTunes has shuffled a playlist, you can tell iTunes to reorder the songs so that they always play back in that order. Simply Control-click on any song in the shuffled playlist and then choose Copy to Play Order from the shortcut menu.

Album shuffle. Normally, shuffle mode plays back songs in random order. You can, however, also choose to shuffle by album. In album-shuffle mode, iTunes plays back an entire album in its original song order, then randomly chooses another album and plays all of it.

To use album shuffle, choose Preferences from the iTunes menu, click the Advanced button, and in the Shuffle By area, click the Album button.

Are random-playback modes evil?
Read some differing opinions.
www.macilife.com/itunes

Mix it Up: Party Shuffle

iTunes 4.5 introduced the Party Shuffle playlist, a hybrid of random shuffle mode, smart playlists, and conventional playlists.

To use Party Shuffle, click it in the Source list of the iTunes window ( ). iTunes instantly assembles a list of songs.

The blue bar separates songs that have been played from upcoming songs (see related tip, right).

Another good reason to rate your music (page 66): you can have iTunes weight its selection toward higher-rated songs.

Don't like what iTunes has come up with? Click Refresh, and iTunes rolls the dice and chooses another batch of songs.

You can tell iTunes to narrow its pool of eligible songs to specific playlists. **Tip:** To create a party shuffle mix based on a specific genre, create a smart playlist for that genre (for example, genre is rock), then specify that smart playlist here (see related tip, below).

You can have iTunes display the last songs it played from the shuffle, and up to 100 upcoming songs.

Party Shuffle Tips

Customizing the mix. As with other types of playlists, you can change the Party Shuffle playlist on a song-by-song basis: drag songs up or down to change their playback order, delete songs you don't want to hear, and manually add songs from your iTunes library by dragging them into the playlist.

Adding a song. You can add a song to the Party Shuffle playlist by simply dragging it, but there's a shortcut. Control-click on a song, then, from the shortcut menu, choose either Play Next in

Party Shuffle (to hear the song next) or Add to Party Shuffle (to add the song to the end of the Party Shuffle playlist).

Selecting from multiple playlists. To base a party shuffle mix on more than one playlist, create a smart playlist that selects those playlists (for example, Playlist is *My Favorites* and Playlist is *Jazz Hits*), then specify that smart playlist.

Freeze the mix. If you like what Party Shuffle comes up with, you can save the mix as a conven-

tional playlist: choose Select All (⌘-A), then choose New Playlist from Selection (Option-⌘-N).

Drag the blue bar. As described above, the blue bar separates songs that have played from upcoming songs—when a song finishes playing, it moves above the bar.

You can also use the blue bar in another way. If you like some, but not all, of the songs that iTunes has chosen, you can retain the songs you like, then have iTunes choose more at random.

First, choose 0 (zero) from the Recently Played Songs pop-up menu. Now drag the songs you want to keep in the playlist to the top of the list. Next, tell iTunes to display some recently played songs—choose 5 or 10 or any other value from the pop-up menu. Finally, drag the blue bar so that it's just below the last song you want to keep.

Now click Refresh. iTunes whips up a fresh batch of random selections, but retains the songs that appear above the blue bar.

Tips for Customizing and More

Customizing Columns

You can specify which columns of information iTunes displays in its windows—to remove columns you never use, or to add ones that iTunes normally doesn't display.

One way to customize columns is to use the Edit menu's View Options command. Here's an easier way: Control-click on any column heading, and uncheck or check columns in the shortcut menu.

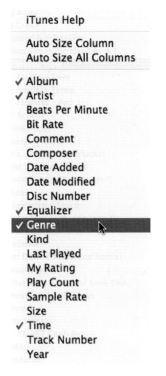

You can also use the shortcut menu to automatically resize columns to fit the

longest item in each one. You can also change the order of the columns themselves, moving them left and right to suit your tastes. To move a column, click on its heading and then drag left or right.

Some Program to Watch Over Me

While you're listening, iTunes is watching: the program keeps track of how many times you listen to a song and when you last listened to it.

iTunes displays this audio odometer in its Play Count and Last Played columns. This means you can sort your music library or a playlist according to how many times you listened to a song (click the Play Count column heading) or when you last listened to it (click the Last Played column heading). Note that you'll probably have to scroll the iTunes window to the right to see these columns.

You can also use these data as criteria when creating a smart playlist (see page 40)—have iTunes create a playlist of your favorite songs or of those you haven't listened to lately.

Everyone's a Critic: Rating Your Songs

iTunes lets you express your inner music critic by assigning a rating of between one and five stars to songs. You don't have to assign ratings, but if you do, you

can use the Ratings category as a criterion when creating smart playlists. You can also have iTunes take ratings into account when compiling Party Shuffle playlists (page 65).

You can also sort your music library or playlists in order of your favorites: simply click on the My Rating column heading.

The fastest way to rate a song is to Control-click on it and then choose the desired rating from the My Rating popup menu.

You can also rate songs by clicking within the My Ratings column in the iTunes window or by opening the Options portion of the Song Info dialog box. In both cases, simply click the tiny dots that represent placeholders for each star. Drag to the right to add stars, or to the left to remove them.

And finally, you can rate the song that is currently playing by using the iTunes icon in your dock. Control-click on the iTunes icon, and a pop-up menu appears. Use the My Ratings submenu to assign a rating.

Exporting and Importing Playlists

You've crafted the perfect playlist and now want to move it over to a different Mac or email it to a friend. Here's how: select the playlist, then choose Export Song List from the File menu. In the Save dialog box, choose XML from the Format pop-up menu, then click Save.

Next, move the playlist over to a different computer. On that computer, choose Import from the File menu. Locate the playlist and double-click its name. You're done.

Note that iTunes exports and imports only *information* about the songs in a playlist—it doesn't copy the songs' music files themselves. If any of the songs are missing on the importing computer, iTunes displays a warning and removes those songs from the imported playlist.

To export all of your playlists (an ideal prelude to backing them up), choose Export Library from the File menu.

Export Playlists as Plain Text

By choosing the Plain Text format in the Export Playlist dialog box, you can export a playlist in text format—perhaps to bring it into a database manager or spreadsheet program. (Hey, some iTunes users are very obsessive audio librarians.)

When you export a playlist in this way, iTunes creates a text file containing all the information about each song, from its name to its bit rate. You can open this text file using a word processor, or you can import it into a spreadsheet or database program. The items—artist, song name, album name, and so on—in an exported playlist are separated by tab characters. (In geek speak, this command creates a *tab-delimited* text file.) Most spreadsheet and database programs can read these tabs and use them to put each piece of information in its own spreadsheet cell or database field.

AppleScript Export Options

Some programmers have created free AppleScripts that provide more control over playlist exporting. (To learn about expanding iTunes with AppleScript, see page 70.) The Doug's AppleScripts for iTunes Web site (www.malcolmadams.com/itunes/) contains a great selection, including an AppleScript that will create a Web page showing a playlist's contents.

Printing to PDF

Another way to publish a song list is to use the Print command introduced in iTunes 4.5. With Mac OS X's ability to "print" to a PDF file, you can create a PDF listing of songs, then email it or post it on a Web site.

In the Print dialog box, click the Song Listing or Album Listing option, pick a theme, then click Print. Click Save As PDF in the next dialog box, and give the PDF name. Now share the PDF as you see fit.

Tip: Looking for yet another way to get information from iTunes into another program? Print to a PDF, then open the PDF, copy its text, and paste it elsewhere.

Customizing the Link Arrows

As described on page 35, beginning with iTunes 4.5, link arrows appear next to all the songs in your library. Click a link arrow, and iTunes beams you to the music store and displays relevant songs. Option-click an arrow, and iTunes switches into browse mode and displays relevant songs in your library.

By using an AppleScript that's included on your DVD, you can reverse this behavior so that a simple click switches you to browse mode and an Option-click takes you to the music store.

Open the Extras folder of the DVD, then open the For iTunes folder. Inside you'll find a folder named Arrow Scripts. This folder contains two scripts: Set iTunes Arrows to Local and Set iTunes Arrows to Music Store. You can run these scripts right from the Finder—just double-click whichever one you want. Or, install them in the iTunes Scripts menu to be able to toggle iTunes' behavior from within the program itself. To do the latter, follow the directions on page 70.

Tips for the iTunes Library

Adding Music from Other Sources

You've built a digital music library by importing audio CDs and buying music from the iTunes Music Store. That's great—but don't stop there. Thousands of songs are available for free (and legal) downloading from the Internet. Some of these freebies are encoded in Windows Media format, and thus won't work with the Mac version of iTunes. But many free songs are available in MP3 format and are iTunes-ready.

A great place to locate free MP3 downloads is David Lawrence's Legal MP3 Downloads site (www.onlinetonight.net/mp3). And, although record industry executives wouldn't want me to say so, you can also download MP3s using utilities such as LimeWire (www.limewire.com) to access file-sharing networks such as Gnutella. Note that downloading via Gnutella may make you a thief—most of the songs available through file-swapping networks have been shared without the permission of their copyright holders.

Regardless of where your other songs come from, you can add them to your iTunes music library by simply dragging them into the iTunes window or by using the File menu's Add to Library command.

Keeping Your Music Library Organized

iTunes normally stores your music in the Music folder, as described on page 27. If you download an MP3 file from the Internet and drag it into the iTunes window, you'll actually have two copies of the MP3 file on your hard drive.

If you don't want this—if you'd prefer to have your music files scattered throughout your hard drive—choose Preferences from the iTunes menu, click the Advanced button, and then uncheck the box labeled Copy Files to iTunes Music Folder When Adding to Library. You can also temporarily override the copying feature: press Option while dragging a file into the iTunes window. Note, though, that having music scattered across your hard drive makes backing up your music library much more cumbersome. I don't recommend it.

Tip: If you already have files scattered across your hard drive and you want to move them all to the Music folder, choose Consolidate Library from the Advanced menu.

The How and Why Behind Specifying Compilations

Chances are you have some compilation CDs in your music collection: *Solid Gold 70s, The Best of Bartok, Tuvanese Throat Singing Mania*, and so on. You can have iTunes store the music files for compilations in a separate folder within your iTunes Music folder. This helps reduce folder clutter and makes it easier to locate and manage your music files.

For example, say you have a compilation CD that contains tracks from a dozen different artists. Normally, iTunes creates a separate folder for each artist—even though that folder might contain just one music file. But if you designate those songs as being part of a compilation, iTunes will store all of those tracks together in their own folder.

To tell iTunes that a song is part of a compilation, select the song and choose Get Info from the File menu or press ⌘-I. In the Info area of the Song Information window, check the Part of a Compilation box. As with other tag-editing tasks, you can do this for multiple songs at once by selecting them all before choosing Get Info.

iTunes stores compilations within a folder whose name is, you guessed it, Compilations. Within this folder, iTunes creates a separate folder for each compilation you've specified.

Fixing "Anonymous" Music Tracks

You've ripped a few audio CDs while on a cross-country flight. Since you didn't have Internet access, iTunes wasn't able to retrieve album and song information, and now you have songs named Track 01, Track 02, and so on.

Must you venture into the Song Information dialog box to manually enter album, song, and artist information? Of course not. Simply connect to the Internet, select those "anonymous" tracks, and then choose Get CD Track Names from the Advanced menu. iTunes connects to CDDB and retrieves the information you crave.

Keep Your Music Library Healthy

I've already mentioned the importance of backing up your iTunes playlists and your music (page 50). This message bears repeating. Make a habit of backing up your playlists by using the Export Library command in the File menu, and of backing up your music files by burning them to CDs or DVDs. Or simply drag your entire iTunes Music folder to an external hard drive every now and then.

Recreating a Damaged Music Library

Sometimes the worst happens—a power failure or other glitch may damage your iTunes 4 Music Library file, that all-important music database that I described on page 27. If this file becomes corrupted, you may see an error message when you start iTunes—something along the lines of "The iTunes Music Library file cannot be read because it does not appear to be a valid library file."

Don't despair. Okay, go ahead and despair, but don't lose hope. Your entire music library is almost certainly still intact; it's just that the librarian has lost its mind. Here's how to restore some sanity to the situation.

Got backup? If you have a current backup of the files named iTunes 4 Music Library and iTunes Music Library.xml, you'll be up and running again in seconds. Quit iTunes, then open your iTunes folder (unless you've moved it elsewhere, it's inside the Music folder of your home directory). Next, locate the files named "iTunes 4 Music Library" and "iTunes Music Library.xml" and drag them to the trash. Finally, copy the back-ups of these files to your iTunes folder. You're done.

No backup? If you don't have current backups of your iTunes 4 Music Library and iTunes Music Library.xml files, you have more work to do. First, locate the corrupted versions of these files and drag them to the Trash. If you also find older Music Library files there (for example, one named iTunes 3 Music Library), drag them to the Trash—these files are left over from older versions of iTunes that you had installed on your computer, and you don't need them anymore. Do not delete anything inside the iTunes Music folder—as you'll recall from page 27, this folder contains your digital music files.

Next, start up iTunes. When you do, you'll notice its library window is completely empty. Let's fix that. Choose Add to Library from the File menu, navigate to your iTunes Music folder, and click Open. iTunes will read all your music files and recreate your library.

Alas, performing these steps will cause you to lose the playlists you've created. To avoid this heartache, back up your iTunes Music Library.xml file now and then—by dragging it to another drive, by burning it to a CD, or by using the File menu's Export Library command.

Adding On: Scripts and Beyond

I've already mentioned that you can enhance the capabilities of iTunes through AppleScripts that automate iTunes in various ways.

You can also enhance the iTunes visualizer—the feature that displays those psychedelic patterns as your music plays back—by adding plug-ins. Visualizer plug-ins may not be as practical as AppleScripts, but on-screen psychedelics can often be more fun than practicalities.

Here's how to download and install iTunes AppleScripts and visualizer plug-ins, as well as information on some other programs that can round out the audio spoke of your digital hub.

Visualize Cool Graphics

If you're a fan of the iTunes visualizer, try out some of the free visualizer plug-ins available on the Web. My favorite is Andy O'Meara's free G-Force, which goes well beyond the built-in iTunes visualizer. For example, you can "play" G-Force—controlling its patterns and colors—by pressing keys on your keyboard as a song plays back.

You can find G-Force and other visualizer plug-ins by going to www.macilife.com/itunes.

Most visualizers include installation programs that tuck the plug-ins into the appropriate spot. But, just for the record, iTunes visualizer plug-ins are generally located within the iTunes folder of your Library folder.

Automating with AppleScript

AppleScript is a powerful automation technology that is part of the Mac OS and many Mac programs, including iTunes. AppleScript puts your Mac on autopilot: when you run a script, its commands can control one or more programs and make them perform a series of steps.

Dozens of useful scripts are available for iTunes. You might start by downloading the set of scripts created by Apple (www.apple.com/applescript/itunes). After you've experimented with them, sprint to Doug's AppleScripts for iTunes (www.malcolmadams.com/itunes), where you'll find the best collection of iTunes AppleScripts, some of which are included in the Extras folder of your DVD.

Installing scripts. After you've acquired an iTunes AppleScript, you need to move it to a specific place in order for iTunes to recognize it. First, quit iTunes. Then, click the Home button or choose Home from the Finder's Go menu. Next, locate and open the Library folder, and then locate and open the iTunes folder within that Library folder. Create a folder named Scripts inside this iTunes folder and stash your scripts here.

Find iTunes add-ons aplenty.
www.macilife.com/itunes

Completing Your Audio Arsenal

Dozens of programs are available that enhance or complement iTunes. You can find links to them at the Web address above. In the meantime, here's a quick look at a few of my favorite audio things.

Synergy

This inexpensive program lets you control iTunes without having to switch into iTunes. Synergy provides keyboard shortcuts that let you play, pause, change volume, and even assign ratings to songs—no matter which program you're using at the moment. Synergy also adds a menu to your Mac's menu bar that lets you start and stop playback, skip to a particular playlist, and much more. When a song begins playing, Synergy displays a cool-looking "floater" containing the song and artist name, album cover art, and other information. If you frequently listen to iTunes while you work, you'll want Synergy.

Toast Titanium

Roxio's Toast Titanium is a burning program for serious CD arsonists. This application can burn DVDs as well as audio and data CDs, and provides more control over the burning process. Just one example: while iTunes puts the same amount of time between each song on a CD, Toast Titanium lets you specify a different interval for each song. Toast Titanium also includes the CD Spin Doctor audio-recording program discussed on page 61.

Toast also works together with iTunes. As shown above, you can drag and drop songs from iTunes directly into Toast.

Salling Clicker

If you have a Bluetooth-equipped Mac and a Bluetooth-equipped Palm handheld, you can turn the handheld into a powerful remote control for iTunes (and many other Mac programs, including iPhoto and OS X's DVD Player). A version of Salling Clicker is also available for Bluetooth-equipped cell phones, including the popular Sony Ericsson T618, T616, Z600, and Z608.

Clutter

The freeware Clutter puts the iTunes album-artwork feature to work in a genuinely useful way. Clutter displays a CD's artwork in a Now Playing window and in the Mac OS X dock. But here's the slick part: drag the artwork from the Now Playing window to your desktop, and Clutter creates a small button containing the artwork image. Double-click that button, and the CD begins playing back.

Having a party? Create a few on-screen stacks of your favorite CDs and let folks riffle through them. Have a few favorite discs? Stack them on your desktop, where they're just a couple of clicks away.

You can resize Clutter's buttons, stack them atop one another, or arrange them in any way you like. And when you're tired of the clutter, just quit the program, and the buttons disappear. (They reappear the next time you run Clutter.)

Books on Bytes: Listening to Audiobooks

iTunes isn't just about tunes. You can also use it to listen to recorded *audiobooks* that you can buy and download from the iTunes Music Store or from Audible.com (www.audible.com). Listen to a novel on your next flight, burn it to a CD so you can listen to it in the car, or transfer it to your iPod and listen while you jog. You can buy audio versions of novels, magazines, newspapers, comedy shows, and much more.

The easiest way to shop for audiobooks is to use the iTunes Music Store. Simply go to the Music Store's main screen and choose the Audiobooks option from the Choose Genre pop-up menu.

If you want a larger selection, shop at Audible.com's Web site. Buying audiobooks through Audible.com is a bit trickier than buying them through the iTunes Music Store. You'll also have to perform an extra couple of steps to add your purchased audiobooks to your iTunes library. These steps are outlined at right.

And to ensure that your Mac handles audiobooks correctly, be sure iTunes is set up to handle Internet playback. Quit your Web browser and email program, then choose Preferences from the iTunes menu. Click the General button at the top of the Preferences window, and click the Set button that appears next to the label Use iTunes for Internet Music Playback.

Now your Mac is ready to read aloud.

Working with Audiobooks

If you already have an Apple account, you're ready to buy audiobooks from the iTunes Music Store. If you're interested in the broader selection available from Audible.com's site, visit www.audible.com and create an account. Then read on for details on working with Audible.com files.

Step 1. Purchase and Download

When buying an audiobook from Audible.com's Web site, you typically have a choice of formats, which are numbered 1 through 4. The iPod supports formats 2, 3, and 4. Which should you use? If you're using a modem connection, you might choose format 2—its files are smaller and thus download faster. If you have a fast connection, you might lean toward formats 3 or 4. They sound better, but they'll take longer to download and use more disk space on your Mac and iPod. (Audiobooks that you buy from the iTunes Music Store are available in AAC format only.)

Step 2. Add the Audiobook to Your iTunes Library

When you download an audiobook from Audible.com's site, its icon appears on your Mac's desktop. Audiobooks end with the file extension .aa. Drag this icon into the iTunes window. (This step isn't necessary if you buy from the iTunes Music Store, which downloads audiobooks directly into your iTunes library.)

Step 3.
Specify Account Information

The first time you add an audiobook to iTunes, you must specify the user name and password you created when signing up at Audible.com. iTunes contacts Audible.com to verify your account information.

Step 4.
Listen

An audiobook appears in your iTunes library, just like any other song. You can listen to it, apply equalization to it, and burn it to a CD.

Audiobooks Tips

One Account

As with the iTunes Music Store, you can use one Audible.com account with up to three computers. If you try to add an account to a fourth computer, an error message appears. If you want to add the account to that computer, you must deauthorize one of the other three. Choose Deauthorize Computer from the Advanced menu, choose the Audible account button, and click OK.

To remove an account, choose Remove Audible Account from the Advanced menu.

Audiobookmarks

The audiobook format provides bookmarks: when you pause or stop an audiobook, iTunes creates a bookmark at the point where you stopped. When you resume playing the audiobook, playback resumes at the bookmark's position.

It gets better. The iPod also supports audiobookmarks, and it synchronizes them with iTunes when you synchronize your music library. This synchronization process works in both directions: if you pause an audiobook on your iPod, the bookmark is transferred to your Mac when

you sync. Thus, you can use your iPod to start listening to an audiobook on your evening commute, then use your iMac to pick up where you left off when you get home.

Chapter Markers

On the latest iPods and the iPod mini family, audiobooks can have chapter markers that allow for convenient navigation between chapters or other sections. To jump from one chapter to the next, press the iPod's Select button while the audiobook is playing. If the audiobook has section markers, they appear as vertical bars in the iPod's

on-screen navigation bar. Use the Rewind and Fast Forward buttons to jump between chapters.

Burning a Book

To burn an audiobook to a CD, create a playlist and drag the audiobook to the playlist. Next, select the playlist and click the Disc Burn button.

If your audiobook is longer than roughly one hour, it won't fit on a standard audio CD. No problem. iTunes will burn as much as will fit on one CD, and then prompt you to insert additional blank discs until you've burned the entire book.

iPod: Music to Go

It's hard to appreciate the significance of the iPod until you load it up with hundreds of songs and begin carrying it around with you.

Then it hits you: all of your favorite songs are right there with you, ready to play—in the car, on a walk, in the living room, on a plane. There's no finding and fumbling with CDs, and every song is only a couple of button presses away.

Several factors work together to make the iPod the best portable music player, starting with its capacity: no other portable player of its size can store as many tunes.

Another factor is the iPod's integration with iTunes: connect the iPod to your Mac, and iTunes automatically synchronizes your music library and playlists. And, the synchronization occurs over FireWire, which is many times faster than the USB connections used by other portable players.

And finally, there's the iPod's versatility. Its ability to store contact information, your calendar, appointment schedule, and other files make the iPod more than a portable music player.

Life with an iPod

Step 1.
Build a Music Library

Use the techniques described earlier in this section to import songs from audio CDs, buy music from the iTunes Music Store, assign equalization settings (optional), edit song information (if necessary), and create playlists.

Step 2.
Transfer to the iPod

Connect the iPod to your Mac using the included FireWire cable. Some iPod models include a dock that makes connecting to the Mac even faster and more convenient (see page 77). Whether you use the dock or just a cable, when you connect the iPod to a Mac, iTunes copies your music library and playlists to the iPod.

While the iPod is connected, its battery charges. The battery charges to 80 percent of its capacity in an hour, and charges fully in about three to four hours.

The iPod's battery gauge is located in the top left corner of its screen.

You can adjust settings for updating the music on your iPod by using the iPod Preferences dialog box, described on the following pages.

Watch an iPod synchronization session.
⊙ **Synchronizing with an iPod**

Step 3. Listen and Repeat

Disconnect the iPod and start listening. When you modify your iTunes music library or playlists, you can update the iPod's contents to match by simply connecting the iPod again.

If you don't have a dock, you can use the headphones jack to connect the iPod to a stereo system or other audio hardware, such as an FM transmitter. To connect to a stereo system, use a cable with a ⅛-inch miniplug on one end and two RCA phono plugs on the other. Connect the cable as described on page 81.

To the right of the iPod's audio-output jack is the Hold button. Slide it to the left to disable the iPod's buttons. This is useful when you're transporting the iPod in a briefcase or purse, where its buttons could get pressed, causing the battery to drain.

To pause and resume playback, press the Play/Pause button. To turn off the iPod, press and hold this button for a few seconds.

The battery gauge shows how much power remains.

To back up to the previous list of choices, press the Menu button.

The iPod's menu system uses a "drill-down" scheme: select an option and press the Select button, and you drill down one level to another menu or list of choices.

To skip to the previous or next song, press the Previous or Next button.

To choose an item in a menu, press the Select button.

Use the scroll wheel to move the menu highlight up and down, and to adjust the playback volume.

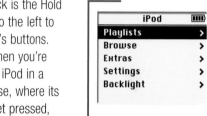

The iPod Family Tree

The iPod has changed since its debut in 2001, and it continues to evolve. Sometimes the changes are simple: bigger hard drives to store even more songs. Sometimes the changes are significant: a new hardware design, such as that of the iPod mini.

Each new generation brings improvements and enhancements to the software inside the iPod. Apple usually makes these enhancements available as software updates for older iPods, although the oldest models have been left behind by some upgrades. For example, older iPods (specifically, ones that do not have dock connectors) can't play back songs compressed using the Apple Lossless encoder, nor do they provide as many menu-customizing options.

But every iPod, from the latest mini to the original 5GB granddaddy, can play back songs purchased at the iTunes Music Store. (With the oldest iPods, you must download and install a software update that teaches them about the AAC format.)

The features change, but the iPod's name remains the same. Because of this, the iPod family is often categorized according to "generations." Here's a look at each generation.

First and Second Generation

The first two iPod generations shared the same overall appearance.

First generation (1G). Introduced in October 2001, the original iPod had a 5GB hard drive and had a mechanical *scroll wheel* that rode on ball bearings. A 10GB model shipped in March 2002.

Second generation (2G). Introduced July 2002, the 2G iPod came in 10GB and 20GB models, some of which included a wired remote control. A non-moving *touch wheel* replaced the mechanical scroll wheel.

Third Generation (3G)

Introduced in April 2003, the third-generation iPod is smaller than its predecessors and supports a convenient dock. The dock connector also supports accessories, such as voice recorders and camera media readers (page 83). The 30GB and 40GB models are slightly thicker and heavier than the 10GB and 15GB models.

Earbuds and, in some models, a small remote control, connect to ports on the top.

With the On-The-Go playlist, you can build a playlist on the road (see page 82). But please wait until you're stopped at a red light.

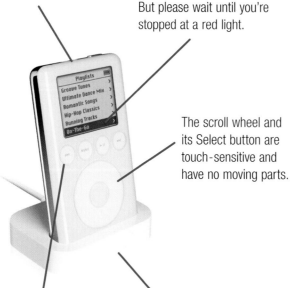

The scroll wheel and its Select button are touch-sensitive and have no moving parts.

Backlit buttons, from left to right: Previous/Rewind, Menu, Play/Pause, Next/Fast Forward.

Note: You can customize the main menu (page 82).

Plant it here: the dock connects to an AC adapter or a FireWire port and has a jack for stereo connections. Most 3G models include a dock; you can also buy one separately.

iPod mini

Introduced in January 2004, the iPod mini provides the same basic capabilities as the larger iPods, but sacrifices capacity for size and cost. About the height and width of a business card, the iPod mini debuted with a 4GB capacity.

On top are a hold switch and jacks for earphones and an optional remote control.

The 1.6-inch display is bright and crisp but smaller than that of other iPods.

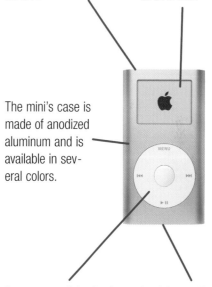

The mini's case is made of anodized aluminum and is available in several colors.

A compact *click wheel* combines touch wheel and navigation buttons into one control. Spin your thumb around the wheel to scroll; press one of the button labels to navigate.

A mini-specific dock is optional. The iPod mini's dock connector works with most iPod 3G accessories, but not Belkin's Media Reader or Voice Recorder.

Setting iPod Preferences

Normally, iTunes will synchronize all your playlists and your entire music library, or at least as much of it as will fit on the iPod.

But there may be times when you want to manually control which playlists and songs iTunes copies to the iPod. Maybe your iTunes music library is larger than will fit on the iPod, and you'd like to specify what you want to copy. Or maybe you listen to some songs on your Mac but not on your iPod, and you don't want to waste iPod disk space by copying those songs.

Whatever the reason, you can use the iPod Preferences dialog box to specify updating preferences.

You can also use this dialog box to activate *disk mode*, in which the iPod appears on your desktop just like a hard drive (which, of course, it is). In disk mode, you can use the Mac's Finder to copy files to and from the iPod's hard drive. This is a handy way to shuttle documents to and from work, or to carry backups of important programs or files with you on the road.

Opening iPod Preferences

When you connect the iPod to the Mac and start iTunes, the iPod appears in the Source pane of the iTunes window, and an iPod preferences icon appears next to the Equalizer button.

The graph shows how much iPod disk space you've used and how much remains.

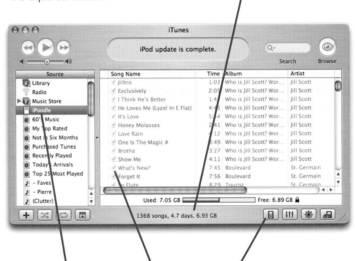

iPoodle

To rename the iPod, click its name and then type a new name. The name appears in iTunes, as shown above, and in the Finder (left) when the iPod is in disk mode. It also appears in the iPod's Info screen.

To display the iPod Preferences dialog box, click the Options button (▣).

If iTunes is configured to update automatically (below), the iPod's contents appear dimmed (above) and you can't manually change them.

iPod Preferences

◉ Automatically update all songs and playlists
○ Automatically update selected playlists only:

iPod Preferences Settings

To control which playlists are copied, click this option and check the box next to each playlist you want to copy.

Normally, iTunes copies everything when you connect the iPod.

To update songs and playlists by hand, click this option. After you click OK, the iPod's contents in the iTunes window are no longer dimmed, and you can drag songs and play-lists from iTunes to the iPod. See "Manual Management" on page 80.

To have your Mac automati-cally start iTunes when you connect the iPod, choose this option. Use this option along with automatic updating when you want convenient, no-fuss updating.

To use the iPod as a hard drive, choose this option. (You must do so to add con-tacts and notes to the iPod; see page 84.)

If you've chosen automatic updating but don't want to copy all new songs to the iPod, check this box and then, in the Library, uncheck any new songs that you do not want copied. When you next update the iPod, only the new songs that are checked will be copied to it.

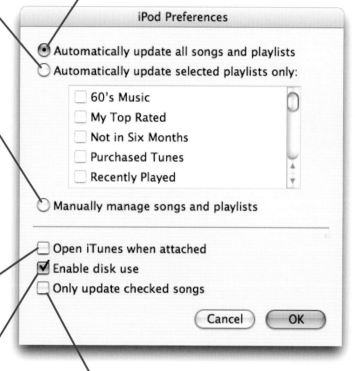

iPod Preferences

- ◉ Automatically update all songs and playlists
- ○ Automatically update selected playlists only:
  - ☐ 60's Music
  - ☐ My Top Rated
  - ☐ Not in Six Months
  - ☐ Purchased Tunes
  - ☐ Recently Played
- ○ Manually manage songs and playlists

- ☐ Open iTunes when attached
- ☑ Enable disk use
- ☐ Only update checked songs

Cancel   OK

iPod Tips

Here are some tips for getting more out of your iPod and appreciating its finer points.

Not So Loud!

Do you love music? Then turn it down. At the risk of sounding like a nagging parent, I'm telling you that you shouldn't listen to music at high volume levels, especially when you're wearing headphones or earbuds. Your brain can acclimate to loud volume levels, but your ears can't—they'll be damaged.

When you're wearing headphones or earbuds, set the iPod's volume so that it's *just* loud enough. When you start playing back a tune, you should be thinking to yourself, "I wish that was a just a little bit louder."

Pay attention, kids. In a couple of decades, a lot of iPod users are going to be cupping their ears and saying, "Pardon me?" Don't be one of them. Just remember: your hearing is the only sense you can damage with too much of a good thing.

Scrubbing within a Song

You can quickly move around, or scrub, within a song while it plays. Press the Select button, and the elapsed-time gauge on the iPod's screen is replaced with a little diamond—just like the one iTunes displays during playback. Using the scroll wheel, move the diamond left and right to scrub within the song.

Extending Battery Life

To get the longest playing times, turn off the screen's backlighting, avoid jumping between songs frequently (the hard drive is one of the iPod's biggest power consumers), and use the Settings menu to turn off the iPod's equalizer. And remember, you can play songs when the iPod is plugged in to its power adapter. If you put the iPod in manual-updating mode or use one of the iPod utilities discussed here, you can even play songs while the iPod is connected to (and charging from) the Mac.

When the Music Dies

The iPod's battery doesn't last forever, and many iPod users were incensed when their batteries began dying and Apple seemed to turn a deaf ear.

The good news is, Apple has launched a $99 iPod battery-replacement program. Some companies also sell replacement batteries that you can install yourself—if you dare to crack open the iPod's case and venture inside. One source is www.ipodbattery.com.

For details on replacement batteries and on iPod batteries in general, see www.ipodbatteryfaq.com.

iPod Utilities

Apple built a simple anti-piracy system into the iPod: its music files are stored in an invisible folder on the iPod's hard drive. Thus, you can't use the Finder to copy music files from the iPod to your hard drive. Music transfer is a one-way street: from the Mac to the iPod.

However, several free or inexpensive utilities let you directly access the music files on an iPod. I'm fond of Findley Designs' iPod Access, which lets you access and play music on an iPod as well as copy it to your Mac's hard drive. Another popular iPod utility is CrispSofties' iPod.iTunes. You can find these and other iPod utilities at software download sites.

Manual Management

When you have the iPod set up for manual updating, you can use iTunes to create playlists that exist only on the iPod. In the Source area of the iTunes window, select the iPod and then create the new playlist.

When manual updating is active, you must manually unmount the iPod when you're done with it. You can do this in iTunes (select the iPod in the Source list and then click the Eject button) or by using the Finder (drag the iPod's icon to the Trash or select it and press ⌘-E).

If you ever decide to switch back to iTunes' automatic updating mode, iTunes will replace the iPod's contents with the current music library and playlists.

Playing While Charging

When the iPod is connected to the Mac, its menus aren't available, preventing you from playing music located on the iPod. One way to work around this is to put the iPod in manual-updating mode, as described previously. You can then play tunes on the iPod by using the iTunes window. The other technique is to use a direct-access utility such as iPod Access.

Library Too Big?

The time may come when your music library is larger than will fit on your iPod. One solution is to use the iPod Preferences dialog box to switch into manual-management mode. In this mode, you can drag songs from the iTunes library into the iPod. You can also delete songs from the iPod by selecting them and pressing the Delete key.

There's also an automatic alternative. Beginning with version 4.2, iTunes can create a playlist containing only songs that will fit on your iPod. This playlist is called the iPod Selection playlist, and iTunes will offer to create it for you if it determines that your library won't fit on your iPod.

The iPod Selection playlist uses a five-step process to determine which songs will be copied to your iPod.

1. iTunes groups all tracks into albums.

2. iTunes calculates an average play count and average user rating for each album.

3. iTunes begins filling the iPod with albums that have non-zero average play counts and non-zero ratings, in descending order. In other words, albums with higher play counts and higher ratings get higher priority.

4. If Step 3 completes and there's still some free space, iTunes starts copying albums that were recently played or recently added to your library.

5. If there's *still* some free space after Step 4 completes, iTunes adds random albums until the iPod is filled to the gills and loosening its belt.

If there's a lesson here, it's this: rate your music. Ratings clearly play an important role in the iPod Selection play-list, so if you rate your songs, you'll stand a better chance of shoehorning your favorites into your iPod.

Of course, in the end, there's no substitute for your own smarts: you can probably do a better job of budgeting iPod disk space by manually managing your iPod's library.

The Stereo Connection

Don't just listen to your iPod through headphones—connect it to your home or car stereo system, too. To connect the iPod to a stereo system, use a cable with a ⅛-inch stereo miniplug on one end and two RCA phono plugs on the other. Plug the miniplug into the iPod (or its dock, if you have one), and connect the phono plugs into a spare set of inputs on the back of your stereo—they're usually labeled AUX or something similar.

The Car Connection

One way to listen to an iPod in the car is by using a cassette adapter, available at Radio Shack and other electronics stores. Plug the adapter's cable into the iPod, and insert the adapter into your car's cassette deck.

You can also use an FM transmitter, which plugs into the iPod and then transmits its signal so that you can tune it in on your radio. Most FM transmitters don't work all that well, though I've found one that does. It's available from C. Crane Company (www.ccradio.com).

(Incidentally, an FM transmitter is also a great way to beam your Mac's audio signal throughout the house—tune in streaming Internet radio on your kitchen-table radio.)

A better way to listen to the iPod in your car is to use a cabling system that enables the iPod's audio output to go directly into your car stereo's amplifier. Several companies sell cabling kits that let an iPod tap into the audio inputs that would otherwise be used for a trunk-mounted CD changer. Check out the Ice-Link from Dension (www.densionusa.com), as well as the offerings from rcainput.com, logjamelectronics.com, and soundgate.com.

And if you're shopping for a new car stereo system, you might consider one of the iPod-ready systems from Alpine (www.alpine-usa.com). Connect your iPod to a compatible system, and you can stash the iPod in the glove compartment and control it using the knobs on the stereo system. The systems even display the name of the currently playing song. Now *that's* traveling in style.

More iPod Tips

Customizing the iPod's Main Menu

You can add and remove items from the iPod's main menu. For example, if you frequently browse your library by artist, add an Artist menu to the main menu. Go to Settings > Main Menu, then scroll to Artists and press Select. While you're there, check out the other customizing options and tweak your iPod's main menu to contain the commands you use most.

Menu customizing is not available on 1G and 2G iPod models.

The On-The-Go Playlist

You have a sudden hankering to hear some songs from six different albums, but you're on the road and thus can't build a new playlist using iTunes. Solution: the On-The-Go playlist, a special, temporary playlist that lives within the iPod.

To add a song to this playlist, scroll to the song and then press and hold the Select button until the song flashes a few times. Repeat for the next song.

You can even add entire albums, artists, genres, and playlists to the On-The-Go playlist. Simply scroll to the item you want and hold down Select.

To clear the On-The-Go playlist, navigate to it, scroll to the bottom of the song list,

and choose Clear Playlist. The playlist is also cleared when you connect the iPod to your Mac, but if you've set up iTunes to automatically update the iPod when you connect it, the On-The-Go playlist will be copied to iTunes so you can use it again.

The On-The-Go playlist is not available on the 1G and 2G iPod models.

Time for the iPod

The iPod's alarm clock feature lets you wake up to music (or to a beep). You can also have the iPod always display the current time in the title bar area at the top of its screen. Choose Extras > Clock > Date & Time > Time in Title. Now you'll always know what time it is.

The iPod syncs its clock with your Mac's, and if you use the Network Time option in Mac OS X's Date & Time system preference, your iPod's clock will always be accurate.

Add Bookmarking to an AAC Song

On page 73, I mentioned that audiobooks provide a bookmarking feature that lets you pick up where you left off after listening to part of an audiobook.

You can add bookmark support to any AAC-format file. Listen to part of a long symphony, and then later on pick up where you left off.

The easiest way to make an AAC file bookmarkable is by using a free AppleScript called Make Bookmarkable, from Doug Adams; it's included in the Extras folder of your DVD.

You can also add bookmarking to a file "by hand." To do so, you'll need a program that lets you edit the song's file type. (This is an "invisible" code that's embedded in a file and identifies it.) FileMatch X is one popular file-type editor; it's free and available for downloading from sites such as VersionTracker.

Once you've downloaded a file-type editor, use it to change an AAC's file's type to "M4B "—that's a capital M, numeral 4, capital B, and a space.

Charging a mini via USB

To update an iPod mini's music library, you need to connect it via FireWire—you can't use USB to copy songs to the iPod mini unless you're using a Windows computer.

You can, however, *charge* an iPod mini by connecting it to the USB 2.0 jack that many newer Mac models provide. If you're on the road with a PowerBook and its FireWire jack is otherwise occupied, you can still top off your mini's charge—just connect it to the PowerBook's USB 2.0 jack.

iPod AppleScripts

Apple has created some free AppleScripts that exploit the note-storage feature that the 3G and iPod mini models provide. For example, one script lets you create a note from any text that you've copied to the Clipboard. Get the scripts at www.apple.com/applescript/ipod.

Updating Older iPods

If you have an older iPod and you want to play purchased music on it, you'll need to install a free software update available at Apple's Web site. The update also improves battery life. But it doesn't add goodies such as Apple Lossless encoding playback, a customizable main menu, text notes, On-The-Go playlist, or enhanced clock features. For those, you'll need a new iPod. And that was enough of an excuse for me.

iPod Accessories

Shopping for iPod accessories? Here are a few ideas and sources for iPod add-ons.

Dock. A dock makes it easy and convenient to update your iPod, charge its battery, and connect the iPod to a stereo system. If your iPod didn't include a dock, consider springing for one. If your iPod included a dock, consider a second one—connect one to your Mac for quick updating, and another to your stereo for convenient listening.

Voice recorders. Belkin and Griffin Technology each offer add-ons that enable a 3G iPod to record voice memos.

iPod Key Sequences	
To Do This	**Do This**
Turn off the iPod	Hold down Play
Restart the iPod	**Large iPods:** Hold down Menu and Play/Pause until the Apple logo appears on the screen (five to 10 seconds).
	iPod mini: Toggle the Hold switch, then hold down Menu and Select until the Apple logo appears (about six seconds).
Force the iPod into disk mode (useful if you're using an old Mac or Windows PC containing a non-powered FireWire add-on card)	**Large iPods:** Restart (see above), then immediately hold down Previous and Next.
	iPod mini: Restart (see above), then immediately hold down Select and Play/Pause.
Have the iPod scan its hard drive for problems	Restart, then immediately hold down Previous, Next, Menu, and Select.
	Note: Don't jostle the iPod during disk scanning.
Have the iPod perform self-diagnostic tests	Restart, then immediately hold down Previous, Next, and Select.
Play the built-in games	Go to Extras > Games.

Media reader. With the Belkin Media Reader and Digital Camera Link add-ons, your 3G iPod can store photos from your digital camera.

Case. Many companies sell iPod cases in all styles. My 3G iPod wears the Showcase, a rugged plastic case from Contour Designs (www.contourdesign.com).

Battery and car chargers. Griffin Technology, Belkin, and XtremeMac are among the companies selling car chargers and other power-related add-ons. With Belkin's Backup Battery Pack, you can power your 3G iPod using standard AA batteries.

iPod as Address Book and More

You can store more than just music on your iPod. You can also store names and addresses and short text notes.

The iPod's address book feature is made possible by an Internet standard called vCard. All current email programs support vCard, as does the Mac OS X Address Book program. You'll also find support for vCard in Palm- and PocketPC-based hand-held computers and even some cell phones.

Mac programmers, intrepid folks that they are, have taken the vCard ball and run with it. Numerous utilities are available that let you peck out notes and store them in vCard format, or that let you convert notes and calendar entries from Microsoft Entourage into vCard format. So your iPod's Contacts menu isn't just an address book—it can store any text tidbits you want.

Before you can add vCards to your iPod, you must activate the iPod's disk mode. With the iPod connected, open iTunes and click the iPod Preferences button. In the iPod Preferences dialog box, check the Enable Disk Use box. Remember to remove the iPod's icon from your desktop before disconnecting the iPod from your Mac.

You can also store text notes that are accessible through the iPod's Notes menu item: simply peck your notes into a text-only file and then copy the file to the iPod's Notes folder.

Adding Contacts from Microsoft Entourage X

In order for the iPod to recognize vCards, you must store them in the iPod's Contacts folder. To copy contacts from Microsoft Entourage to the iPod, open Entourage X's address book and select the contacts you want to copy to the iPod. Next, drag those contacts to the iPod's Contacts folder.

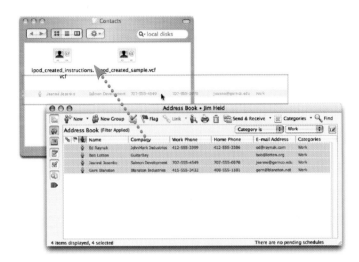

Deleting Contacts

To remove contacts from the iPod, open the Contacts folder, select the contacts you don't want, and drag them to the Trash.

Find these and other iPod utilities.
www.macilife.com/itunes

iPod Scripts

Numerous programmers have created useful AppleScripts for the iPod that enable you to manage playlists, copy songs, and more. The best source for these scripts is Doug Adams' excellent Doug's AppleScripts for iTunes site, mentioned earlier.

Synchronizing with iSync

With Apple's iSync utility, you can automatically update the contacts and calendars on your iPod. Simply run iSync, choose the desired options, and click Sync Now. iSync will copy your contacts from Mac OS X's Address Book program as well as any iCal calendars you've created or subscribed to. (See the following page for more details on iCal.)

Beyond Music: A Sampling of iPod Utilities

Dozens of free or inexpensive utilities are available that enable you to store all manner of information on an iPod. Here's a sampling of a few noteworthy offerings.

iSpeakIt. With Michael Zapp's iSpeakIt (www.zapptek.com), you can create your own audiobooks—kind of. iSpeakIt turns any text file or Microsoft Word document into an MP3 or AAC audio file. Add the resulting file to your iTunes music library, and listen.

iSpeakIt uses the Mac's text-to-speech technology to create its files, so your homemade audiobooks will have a decidedly robotic quality to them. But you can get used to the sound. One of my business partners uses iSpeakIt to "read" an assortment of daily newspapers and magazines during long commutes: he copies and pastes text from Web sites into iSpeakIt, and then generates audio files that help while away the miles.

iPod It. Also from Michael Zapp, iPod It can export calendar events, email, notes, and contacts from Microsoft Entourage X, iCal, and the Mac OS X Mail program. It can also download news headlines and weather forecasts.

Text2iPod. This freeware utility by Benoît Terradillos will convert any text-only file into a note file that you can read on the iPod.

PodQuest. This slick little utility from Mibasoft (www.mibasoft.dk) downloads driving directions from MapQuest and stores them

in the iPod's Notes folder. Just remember to pull over to the side of the road before trying to read them.

The Rise of the Lost. A full-fledged adventure game on the iPod? You bet. In "The Rise of the Lost," you're a knight who battles an evil wizard to determine the fate of the Kingdom of Valance. Make the right decisions, and you'll save the kingdom. Make the wrong ones, and, well, it's curtains for Valance.

iPod as Calendar: Using iCal

With Apple's iCal software, you can keep track of appointments, schedules, and events of all kinds. You can create multiple calendars—for example, one for personal events such as birthdays and another for work appointments.

Use iCal to display multiple calendars at once to quickly identify schedule conflicts. You can also share calendars—with friends, coworkers, or complete strangers—by *publishing* them through your .Mac account.

You can even download and use calendars that other people have created. Hundreds of free calendars are available in categories ranging from TV schedules to holidays to the phases of the moon. To learn more about iCal and get your own copy, visit www.apple.com/ical.

What does all this have to do with the iPod? Simply this: You can copy your calendars to the iPod and view them on the road. You can also set up alarms in iCal and have your iPod beep to notify you of important appointments. Or TV shows.

Your iPod isn't just a pocket-sized jukebox and address book—it's a calendar, too.

Copying Calendars to the iPod

To copy a calendar to the iPod, export it, saving the exported calendar in the iPod's Calendars folder.

Step 1.
Get Connected

Connect the iPod to your Mac and activate the iPod's disk mode (described on page 78).

Step 2.
Export or Copy the Calendar

In iCal's Calendars list, select the calendar you want to export and then choose Export from the File menu. In the Export dialog box, navigate to your iPod's Calendars folder. Type a name and click the Export button. Unmount your iPod by dragging its icon to the Trash. You can now access the calendar using the iPod's menus, as described to the right.

You may also have calendar files that originated somewhere other than in your copy of iCal—perhaps you downloaded a calendar from a Web site, or someone emailed it to you as an attachment, or you simply copied it from a different Mac. To add a calendar file to the iPod, drag its icon into the Calendars folder.

You can also use Apple's iSync program to automatically synchronize calendars between your Mac and your iPod. To learn more about iSync, visit www.apple.com/isync.

Navigating Calendars and Events

As with music and addresses, the iPod uses a drill-down menu scheme for calendars and events: the deeper you go, the more detail you get.

To display calendars, go to Extras > Calendar.

Each calendar appears as a separate menu item. To display a specific calendar, use the scroll wheel to highlight it, then press the iPod's Select button.

Days that have events associated with them are indicated with a small dot. To see a day's events, highlight the day, then press the iPod's Select button.

The iPod displays a summary of the event. To see event details, select the event and press the Select button again.

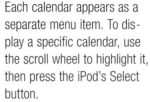

Calendar Tips

iCal Calling iTunes

Doug Adams' iCal Calling iTunes is a slick AppleScript that turns iCal and iTunes into a musical alarm clock: it enables iTunes to play a specific playlist at a time you specify.

iCal Calling iTunes is a cinch to use. Simply create an iCal event whose name is the same as one of your iTunes playlists. When the event time arrives, iTunes begins playing the playlist.

Silencing Alarms

If you've used iCal to specify that some events have alarms, your iPod will beep at the specified times. But there may be times when you don't want the iPod to beep.

To silence the iPod's alarms, go to Calendar > Alarms where you'll find three options: On (the iPod beeps and the alarm text appears on the iPod's screen); Silent (no beep but the alarm text still appears); and Off (no beep or alarm text).

Dates of All Kinds

You don't use iCal to manage your schedule? Don't let that stop you from sampling the world of calendars that other people have published on the Web. You can download hundreds of calendars in dozens of categories: sports schedules, TV schedules, lunar phases, celebrity personal appearances, holidays of all kinds, and more.

One place to find calendars is Apple's iCal Web site, but the ultimate collection of calendars lives at an independent site called iCalShare (www.icalshare.com). I downloaded the Moon Phases calendar, and now my iPod knows the phases of the moon through the year 2015.

So even if you don't use iCal to manage your appointments, you might find it a useful tool for keeping track of events that take place elsewhere in the solar system.

iPhoto:
Organizing and
Sharing Images

iPhoto at a Glance

Millions of photographs lead lives of loneliness, trapped in unorganized boxes where they're never seen. Their digital brethren often share the same fate, exiled to cluttered folders on a hard drive and rarely opened.

With iPhoto, you can free your photos—and organize, print, and share them, too. iPhoto simplifies the entire process. You begin by *importing* images from a digital camera, your hard drive, a CD from a photofinisher, or other source. Then you can create *albums*, organizing the images in whatever order you want. You can even have iPhoto create the albums for you.

Along the way, you might also use iPhoto's editing features to retouch flaws, improve brightness and contrast, remove red-eye, and crop out unwanted portions of images. And you might use iPhoto's keyword features to help you file and locate images.

When you've finished organizing and editing images, you can share them in several ways, from printing them to publishing them to creating on-screen slide shows, complete with music from your iTunes library.

Welcome to the Photo Liberation Society.

Add an album.　　Play a slide show.　　View information.　　Rotate images.

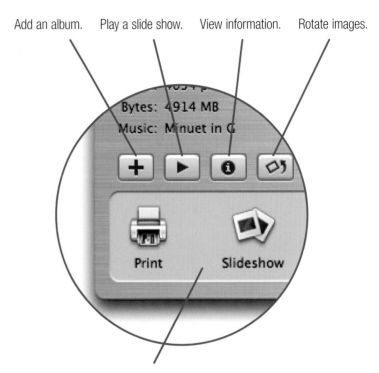

This window pane changes depending on which mode button you've selected. The Organize pane, shown here, contains the iPhoto functions you're likely to use often.

To quickly access photos from a specific recent year, click the triangle (page 98).

To quickly see the last set of images you imported, click Last Roll (page 98).

The Photo Library contains all the images you import into iPhoto, whether from a digital camera or a disk file (page 94). Each set of images you import is called a *roll*.

To resize the album area, drag this vertical bar left or right.

You can name each roll of images. To show a roll's images, click on the triangle next to the roll's name. Click the triangle again to hide the images.

Note: If your photos aren't being displayed by roll, choose Film Rolls from the View menu.

Use smart albums to have iPhoto create albums for you (page 104).

You can assemble photos into albums, and then share the albums (pages 120–125).

The Trash holds photos you delete; photos aren't removed from your hard drive until you empty the Trash by choosing Empty Trash from the File menu.

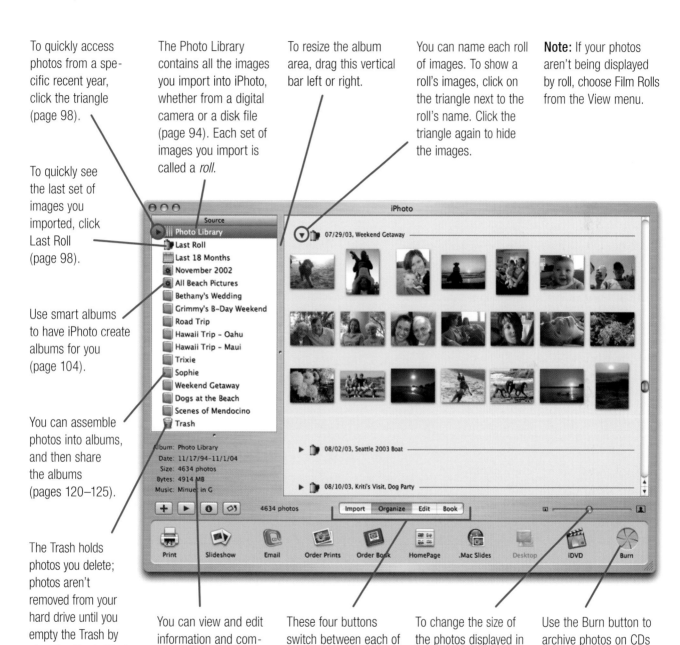

You can view and edit information and comments for images or entire rolls (page 96).

These four buttons switch between each of iPhoto's primary modes.

To change the size of the photos displayed in iPhoto's window, drag the size slider.

Use the Burn button to archive photos on CDs or DVDs (page 136).

The Essentials of Digital Imaging

Like the digital audio world and other specialized fields, digital imaging has its own jargon and technical concepts to understand. You can accomplish a lot in iPhoto without having to know these things, but a solid foundation in imaging essentials will help you get more out of iPhoto, your digital camera, and other imaging hardware.

There are a few key points to take away from this little lesson. First, although iPhoto works beautifully with digital cameras, it can also accept images that you've scanned or received from a photofinisher.

Second, those images must be in JPEG format. iPhoto will often accept images in other formats, but the program is designed to work with JPEG images.

And finally, the concept of resolution will arise again and again in your digital imaging endeavors. You'll want big, high-resolution images for good-quality prints, and small, low-resolution images for convenient emailing to friends and family. As described on pages 131 and 140, you can use iPhoto to create low-resolution versions of your images.

Where Digital Images Come From

iPhoto can work with digital images from a variety of sources.

Digital camera

Digital cameras are more plentiful and capable than ever. The key factor that differentiates cameras is *resolution*: how many *pixels* of information they store in each image. Entry-level cameras typically provide two- or three-megapixel resolution; you can get a good-quality 8- by 10-inch print from an uncropped two-megapixel image.

Most digital cameras connect to the Mac's USB port. Images are usually stored on removable-media cards; you can also transfer images into iPhoto by connecting a *media reader* to the Mac and inserting the memory card into the reader.

Scanner

With a scanner, you can create digital images from photographs and other hard-copy originals.

Scanners also connect via USB, although some high-end models connect via FireWire. Film scanners are a bit pricier, but can scan negatives and slides and deliver great image quality (page 140). Save your scanned images in JPEG format, and then add them to iPhoto by dragging their icons into the iPhoto window.

For tips on getting high-quality scans, visit www.scantips.com.

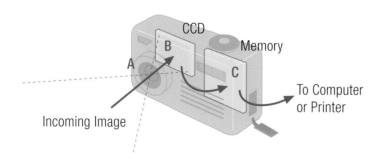

In a digital camera, the image is focused by the lens (**A**) onto the CCD (**B**), where tiny, light-sensitive diodes called photosites convert photons into electrons. Those electrical values are converted into digital data and stored by a memory card or other medium (**C**), from which they can be transferred to a computer or printer.

Compact disc

For an extra charge, most photofinishers will burn your images on a compact disc in Kodak Picture CD format. You get not only prints and negatives, but also a CD that you use with the Mac.

To learn more about Picture CD, go to www.kodak.com and search for *picture cd*.

Internet

Many photofinishers also provide extra-cost Internet delivery options. After processing and scanning your film, they send you an email containing a Web address where you can view and download images. After downloading images, you can drag their icons into iPhoto's window.

A Short Glossary of Imaging Terms

artifacts Visible flaws in an image, often as a result of excessive *compression* or when you try to create a large print from a low-resolution image.

CompactFlash A removable-memory storage medium commonly used by digital cameras. A CompactFlash card measures 43 by 36 by 3.3 mm. The thicker *Type 2* cards are 5.5 mm wide.

compression The process of making image files use less storage space, usually by removing information that our eyes don't detect anyway. The most common form of image compression is *JPEG*.

EXIF Pronounced *ex-if*, a standard file format used by virtually all of today's digital cameras. EXIF files use JPEG compression but also contain

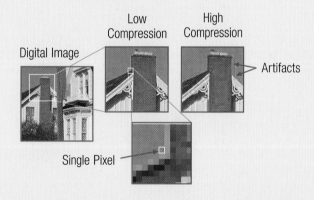

Digital Image — Low Compression — High Compression — Artifacts — Single Pixel

details about each image: the date and time it was taken, its resolution, the type of camera used, the exposure settings, and more. iPhoto retrieves and stores EXIF information when you import images. EXIF stands for *Exchangeable Image File*.

JPEG Pronounced *jay-peg*, the most common format for storing digital camera images, and the format that iPhoto is designed to use. Like MP3, JPEG is a *lossy* compression format: it shrinks

files by discarding information that we can't perceive anyway. And as with MP3, there are varying degrees of JPEG compression; many imaging programs enable you to specify how heavily JPEG images are compressed. Note that a heavily compressed JPEG image can contain *artifacts*. JPEG stands for *Joint Photographic Experts Group*.

megapixel One million pixels.

pixel Short for *picture element*, the smallest building block of an image. The number of pixels that a camera or scanner captures determines the *resolution* of the image.

resolution 1. The size of an image, expressed in pixels. For example, an image whose resolution is 640 by 480 contains 480 vertical rows of pixels, each containing 640 pixels from left to right. Common resolutions for digital camera images are 640 by 480, 1280 by 960, 1600 by 1200, 2048 by 1536, and 2272 by 1704. 2. A measure of the capabilities of a digital camera or scanner.

SmartMedia A commonly used design for removable-memory storage cards. SmartMedia cards measure 45 by 37 by .76 mm.

Importing Photos into iPhoto

The first step in assembling a digital photo library is to import photos into iPhoto.

iPhoto can directly import photos from the vast majority of digital cameras. (See a list at www.apple.com/iphoto/compatibility/.) You can specify that iPhoto delete the images from the camera after importing them, but I don't recommend it. It's always best to erase your memory card using the controls on your digital camera. And as I say on the DVD, I like to verify that my photos imported correctly before wiping them off of my memory card.

You can also import photos by dragging them from the Finder into the iPhoto window, or by using the Import command in the File menu. You might take this approach if you have scanned JPEG images on your hard drive or if you're using a media reader.

Each time you import images, iPhoto creates a new roll (as in roll of film—get it?). Even when you import just one image, iPhoto creates a roll for it. You can use the New Film Roll from Selection command to consolidate a lot of these little rolls into fewer larger ones; see page 99.

After you've finished importing images, you can disconnect your camera or remove your media card from its reader. Before you do, however, check to see if its icon appears on your Finder desktop. If its icon does appear, drag it to the Trash or select it and press ⌘-E.

Importing from a Camera

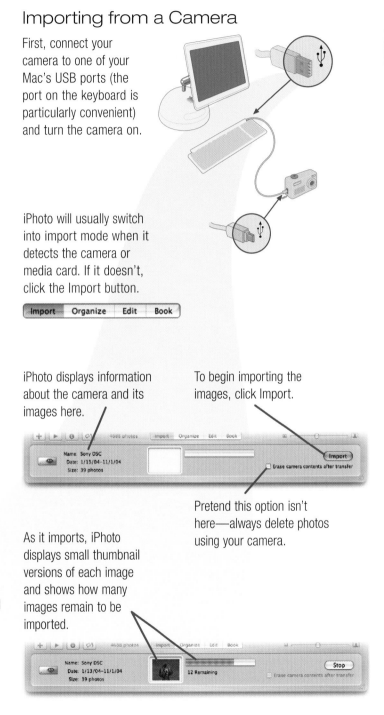

First, connect your camera to one of your Mac's USB ports (the port on the keyboard is particularly convenient) and turn the camera on.

iPhoto will usually switch into import mode when it detects the camera or media card. If it doesn't, click the Import button.

iPhoto displays information about the camera and its images here.

To begin importing the images, click Import.

Pretend this option isn't here—always delete photos using your camera.

As it imports, iPhoto displays small thumbnail versions of each image and shows how many images remain to be imported.

See how to import photos.
◉ **Importing Photos with a Media Reader**
◉ **Importing Photos from the Finder**

Importing from the Finder

To import an entire folder full of images, drag the folder to the Photo Library item or into the viewing area.

iPhoto gives the new roll the same name as the folder that its images came from. You can rename the roll using the technique on page 101.

To import only some images, select their icons and then drag them into the iPhoto window.

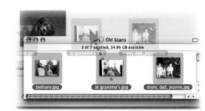

Importing from Email

A friend has emailed some photos to you, and you want to add them to your iPhoto library. Here's how: First, save the photos on your Mac's desktop. Next, drag them into the iPhoto window as shown above. Finally, delete the photos from your desktop.

Note: If you use the Mac OS X Mail program, you don't even have to save the photos on your desktop first. Simply drag them from the email message into the iPhoto window.

Importing from PhotoCDs and Picture CDs

iPhoto can also import images saved on a Kodak PhotoCD or Picture CD. (PhotoCD is an older format that you aren't likely to see too often. Picture CD is a newer format that most photofinishers use.)

With a PhotoCD, you can't simply drag images from the CD into iPhoto's window. Instead, switch iPhoto into Import mode, insert the CD, and then click the Import button in the bottom-right corner of the iPhoto window.

For a Picture CD, choose Import from iPhoto's File menu, locate the Picture CD, and then locate and double-click the folder named Pictures. Finally, click the Open button. Or, use the Finder to open the Pictures folder on the CD and then drag images into iPhoto's window.

Where iPhoto Stores Your Photos

When you import photos, iPhoto stores them in a folder called iPhoto Library, located inside the Pictures folder.

Get in the habit of backing up the iPhoto Library folder frequently to avoid losing your images to a hardware or software problem. iPhoto's burning features are ideal for backing up photos (see page 136).

And whatever you do, don't futz with the files inside this folder—renaming or moving them could cause iPhoto to have problems finding your photos.

When you import images that are already stored on your hard drive, iPhoto makes duplicate copies of them in your iPhoto Library folder. To avoid wasting disk space, you might want to delete the original files after importing them into iPhoto. You can store your iPhoto Library folder elsewhere, such as on an external hard drive. For details, see page 139.

After the Import: Getting Organized

iPhoto forces some organization on you by storing each set of imported images as a separate roll. Even if you never use iPhoto's other organizational features, you're still ahead of the old shoebox photo-filing system: you will always be able to view your photos in chronological order.

But don't stop there. Take the time to use at least some of iPhoto's other organizational aids, which let you give titles to rolls and individual images, and assign comments and keywords to images to make them easier to find.

Titles are names or brief descriptions that you assign to photos and rolls: Party Photos, Mary at the Beach, and so on. iPhoto can use these titles as captions for its Web photo albums and books. Using the View menu, you can have iPhoto display titles below each thumbnail image.

iPhoto 4 introduced a feature that lets you assign titles more or less automatically. It's the Batch Change command, and you can see it in action on the DVD and read about it here and on page 145.

There's one more benefit to assigning titles to photos: when you're working in iDVD, you can search for a photo by typing part of its title in the photo media browser's Search box.

Take advantage of iPhoto's filing features, and you'll be able locate images in, well, a flash.

Assigning Titles to Images

To assign a title to an image, select the image and type a name in the Title box.

With the Batch Change command in the Photos menu, you can also have iPhoto assign titles, dates, and other information to one or more photos for you; see page 145.

Assigning Comments

You can also assign a comment to a photo; think of a comment as the text you'd normally write on the back of a photograph. You can search for photos based on comments, and iPhoto can use comments as captions for the photos in a book.

To display the Comments box, click the ⓘ button.

To assign a comment, select the photo and type the comment in the Comments box. You can also use the Batch Change command to assign the same comment to numerous photos.

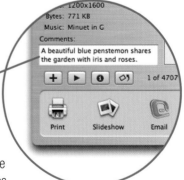

See how to rotate and title images.
◎ Rotating Vertical Photos
◎ Naming a Roll
◎ Assigning Titles to Photos

Assigning Titles to Rolls

iPhoto names rolls as though they were prisoners—
it gives them each a number. Use the Title box to give
rolls names that are more descriptive.

Changing the Date

You can also edit the date of a roll or a single
image. This is handy if your digital camera's
built-in clock wasn't set correctly or if you
want a roll's date to reflect the day you shot
its images, not the day you imported them.

Rotate Verticals as Needed

Some cameras automatically rotate photos
taken in vertical orientation. If yours doesn't,
the job is yours. Select the photo or photos
and then click the rotate button (◎) or
press ⌘-R (to rotate counterclockwise)
or ⌘-Shift-R (to rotate clockwise). You
can also rotate photos while viewing a slide
show; see page 115.

To title a roll, select it by clicking on its
name, then type a title in the Title box.

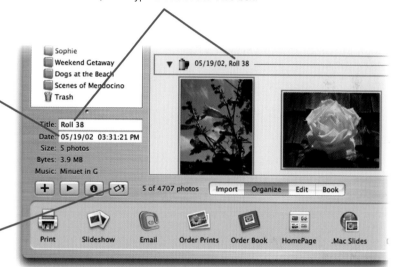

Tips for Working with Rolls

Changing the Sort Order

iPhoto displays rolls chronologically, with the oldest roll at the
top of the window. To have your
newest rolls appear at the top,
choose Preferences from the
iPhoto menu, click Appearance,
and click the Place Most Recent
Photos at the Top check box.

Hide Rolls You Aren't Using

To the left of each roll's name is
a tiny, down-pointing triangle:
click it, and iPhoto collapses the
roll, hiding its images. I like to
collapse every roll whose photos
I don't need to see at the
moment. This clears the clutter
in my iPhoto window and speeds

up scrolling and changing the
size of thumbnails.

A related tip: press the Option
key while clicking on a collapsed
roll's triangle, and iPhoto
expands every roll in your library.
Similarly, to collapse every roll,
Option-click on the down-
pointing triangle of any roll.

Viewing Rolls

If iPhoto isn't displaying individual
rolls, and is instead showing all
the photos in your library, choose
Film Rolls from the View menu.
When this command has a check
mark next to it, iPhoto displays
your library sorted by roll.

Browsing and Working with Rolls

Anxious to start having fun with the photos you've brought in? Go ahead and skip on to page 102, where you can you learn about creating photo albums and much more.

But if you're an obsessive organizer or an iPhoto veteran whose photo library has become cluttered over the years, read on. iPhoto 4 introduced some features that make it easier to navigate and organize a large photo library.

One such feature lets you quickly display photos from a specific year. Instead of scrolling through your library to find those photos from 2002, for example, you can beam yourself back in time with a couple of clicks: click the little triangle next to the Photo Library icon, then click 2002.

Want to quickly view the last set of shots you brought in? Click the Last Roll item. Want to see all the shots you took in the last year? Click the Last 12 Months item. Better still, customize both features to match the way you like to view your photo library.

For real photo neatniks, the best news is that you can move photos from one roll to another and create new rolls containing photos already in your library. Just as you can move prints from one envelope to another after getting them back from the photo lab, you can move your digital photos from one roll to another after bringing them into iPhoto.

If you're just getting started with iPhoto and you have a small photo library, these organizational aids may not mean much to you. But as your photo library grows, you'll grow to appreciate them.

Customizing Your View

To customize the organizational aids in iPhoto's Source area, choose Preferences from the iPhoto menu and click the General button.

To customize the Last Months album, specify the desired number of months. The maximum value is 18 months; I set mine to 1 month to put my most recent photos just a click away.

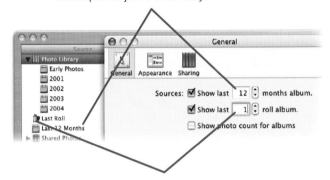

To be able to quickly peruse more than just the last set of photos you imported, customize the Last Roll item. You can specify up to 25 rolls.

Appearance Preferences

While you have the Preferences dialog box open, you might want to click its Appearance button and examine those options.

Want to see your thumbnail photos against a gray background? Drag the Background slider to the left. You can also choose to turn off the shadow effect that iPhoto puts behind each photo in Organize view, and to display a border around each thumbnail photo.

See how to quickly view photos and create new rolls.
◉ **Viewing Photos from Specific Years**
◉ **Customizing the Source List**
◉ **Creating a New Roll**

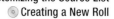

Moving Photos Between Rolls

One of my favorite iPhoto 4 features isn't even mentioned in iPhoto's online help: you can drag photos from one roll to another. It's a great way to keep your photo library organized.

For example, say you take six shots at a party and you import them right away so everyone can look. Then you fire off another 28 shots as the party progresses. When you bring that second set in, iPhoto stores them in their own roll, as always. But for organization's sake, you probably want both sets of photos in the same roll. No problem: just drag one set of photos into the other roll.

To move photos between rolls, you need to view your library by film roll (choose Film Rolls from the View menu). That's the best way to view your library anyway.

Merging Two Rolls

To merge two rolls into one, drag one roll to the other roll.

Step 1. Select the roll by clicking the roll's name.

Step 2. Drag until the name of the destination roll is highlighted by the bold blue bar, then release the mouse button.

Moving Just a Few Photos

To move just a few photos to a different roll, select them and then drag them to the destination. (For tips on selecting photos, see page 103.)

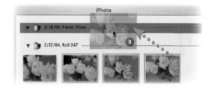

The destination roll's photos don't even have to be visible. Simply drag the photos to the destination roll's name.

Wrong Roll? If you dragged too far (or not far enough) and ended up depositing some photos in the wrong roll, just choose Undo Add to Roll from the Edit menu.

A Roll of Their Own: New Film Roll From Selection

Dragging photos from one part of a large photo library to another can be awkward and wrist-taxing. There's another way to consolidate photos into one roll: the New Roll From Selection command.

Select the photos that you want to put in a roll of their own, then sprint up to the

File menu and choose New Film Roll From Selection.

Have several rolls that each contain just a few photos? This command is a great way to consolidate them into just one roll.

Assigning Keywords and Ratings

Chances are that many of your photos fall into specific categories: baby photos, scenic shots, and so on. By creating and assigning *keywords*, you make related images easier to find.

Keywords are labels useful for categorizing and locating all the photos of a given kind: vacation shots, baby pictures, mug shots, you name it.

iPhoto has five predefined keywords that cover common categories. But you can replace the existing ones to cover the kinds of photos you take, and you can add as many new keywords as you like.

You can assign multiple keywords to a single image. For example, if you have a Beach keyword, a Dog keyword, and a Summer keyword, you assign all three to a photo of your dog taken at the beach in July.

To create and assign keywords, choose Keywords from the Edit menu (or press ⌘-K). This displays the Keywords window.

Keywords are one way to categorize your photos; ratings are another. You can assign a rating of from one to five stars to a photo—rank your favorites for quick searching, or mark the stinkers for future deletion.

For details on searching for photos, see "Searching by Keywords" on page 112 and "Creating Smart Albums" on page 104.

Assigning Keywords

If you're like me, you don't use keywords as often as you should. Let's resolve to change that—as our photo libraries grow, finding specific shots will get harder. Keywords can help.

To assign a keyword, display the Keywords window by choosing Show Keywords from the Photos menu.

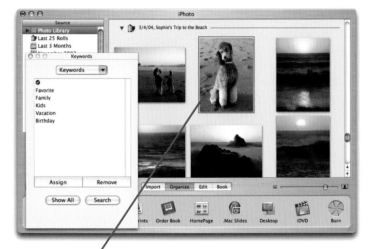

Step 1.
Select the photo or photos to which you want to assign keywords.

Tip: To display keywords below your photos, choose Keywords from the View menu (or press Shift-⌘-K).

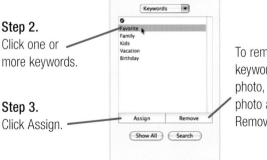

Step 2.
Click one or more keywords.

Step 3.
Click Assign.

To remove a keyword from a photo, select the photo and click Remove.

See how to rate photos.
⊙ **Rating Your Photos**

GO TO DVD

Creating and Editing Keywords

You can create new keywords to describe the types of photos you take.

Step 1. Choose New from the pop-up menu at the top of the Keywords window.

Step 2. Type the new keyword's name.

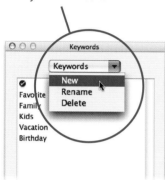

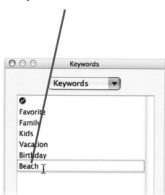

Renaming Keywords

To rename an existing keyword, select it and choose Rename from the Keywords pop-up menu. Then, type a new name.

If you've already assigned a given keyword to some photos, think twice about renaming that keyword. If you do rename it, the photos to which you've assigned that keyword will inherit the new keyword.

For example, say you've assigned a Friends keyword to photos of all your friends. If you later rename the Friends keyword to Enemies, all the photos of your friends will take on the new keyword.

Art Critic: Rating Your Photos

iTunes has allowed us to be music critics for a some time now. Now iPhoto lets us be art critics, too: you can assign a rating of from one to five stars to a photo.

There are a few ways to rate a photo.

With the Photos menu. Choose a rating from the My Rating submenu.

With the keyboard. Press ⌘ along with 0 (zero) through 5. This shortcut pairs up nicely with the arrow keys: rate a photo, press an arrow key to move to the next photo, and repeat.

With the shortcut menu. Control-click on a photo and choose a rating from the My Rating submenu.

In one fell swoop. Want to give a bunch of photos the same rating? Select them, then use one of the previous techniques.

During a slide show. Move the mouse, then click the desired rating. Or just press 0 (zero) through 5 to rate the currently displayed photo.

Viewing Ratings

To see ratings displayed beneath your photo thumbnails, choose My Rating from the View menu (Shift-⌘-R).

You can also use ratings as a search criterion when creating smart albums (page 104).

▼ 📷 3/4/04, Sophie's Trip to the Beach

Creating Albums

Getting photos back from a lab is always exciting, but what's really fun is creating a photo album that turns a collection of photos into a story.

An iPhoto album contains a series of photographs sequenced in an order that helps tell a story or document an event.

Creating albums in iPhoto is a simple matter of dragging thumbnail images. You can add and remove photos to and from albums at any time, and you can sequence the photos in whatever order you like. You can even include the same photo in many different albums.

The photos in an album might be from one roll, or from a dozen different rolls. Just as an iTunes playlist lets you create your own music compilations, an iPhoto album lets you create your own image compilations.

And once you create albums, you can share them in a variety of ways.

Step 1: Create an Empty Album

To create a new album, choose New Album from the File menu or click the Add Album button.

Step 2: Name the Album

iPhoto asks you to name the new album.

Step 3: Add Photos

As you drag, iPhoto indicates how many photos you've selected.

After you've named the album, begin dragging photos into it. You can drag photos one at a time, or select multiple photos and drag them in all at once.

See techniques for working with albums and selecting photos.
⦿ **Creating an Album**
⦿ **Shortcuts for Selecting Photos**
⦿ **Fine-Tuning an Album**

A Shortcut for Creating Albums

You can create an album and add images to it in one step. Select one or more images and choose New Album from Selection from the File menu.

You can also drag the images to a blank spot of the Source area (right). When you use this technique, iPhoto gives the new album a generic name, such as *Album-1*. To rename the album, double-click its name and type a new name.

Tips for Selecting Photos

Selecting photos is a common activity in iPhoto: you select photos in order to delete them, add them to an album, move them around within an album, and more.

When working with multiple photos, remember the standard Mac OS selection shortcuts: To select a range of photos, click on the first one and Shift-click on the last one. To select multiple photos that aren't adjacent to each other, press ⌘ while clicking on each photo.

You can also select a series of pictures by dragging a selection rectangle around them.

Organizing an Album

The order of the photos in an album is important: when you create slide shows, books, or Web photo galleries, iPhoto presents the photos in the order in which they appear in the album.

Once you've created an album, you may want to fine-tune the order of its photos.

To edit an album, double-click its name.

To move an album to a different location in the Source area, drag it up or down.

To change the order of the photos, drag them. Here, the flower close-up is being moved so it will appear after the other two garden shots.

Don't want a photo in an album after all? Select it and press the Delete key. This removes the photo from the album, but not from your hard drive or Photo Library.

Creating Smart Albums

iPhoto can assemble albums for you based on criteria that you specify. The *smart album* feature works much like the smart playlist feature in iTunes: spell out what you want, and your Mac does the work for you.

A few possibilities: Create an album containing every shot you took in the last week. Or of every photo you took in November 2002. Or of every November 2002 photo that has *Sophie* in its title. Or of every photo from 2001 that has *Paris* as a keyword, *croissant* in its title, and a rating of at least four stars.

If you've taken the time to assign titles, comments, and keywords to your photos, here's where your investment pays off. You can still use smart albums if you haven't assigned titles and other information to photos; you just won't be able to search on as broad a range of things.

Smart albums are a great way to quickly gather up related photos for printing, backing up, emailing—you name it. Smart albums are also how you search for photos in iPhoto 4. The Search box that iPhoto 2 provided doesn't exist in iPhoto 4—to find a photo, you must create a smart album.

Note: In iPhoto 4.0, some smart album features didn't work properly. Apple fixed these bugs with an update. Be sure you're using iPhoto 4.0.1 or a later version, if available. Get updates through the Software Update system preference or at www.apple.com/iphoto.

Creating a Smart Album

Step 1. Choose New Smart Album from the File menu (Option-⌘-N).

You can also create a new smart album by pressing the Option key and clicking on the new album button (⬛).

Step 2. Specify what to look for.

Type a name for the smart album.

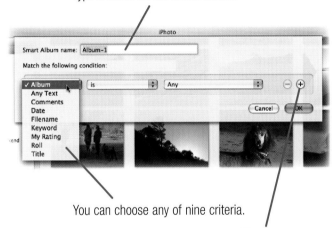

You can choose any of nine criteria.

To add another criterion, click the ⊕ button (see opposite page).

Step 3. Click OK or press Return.

In the Source area, iPhoto indicates smart albums with a special icon (⬛).

Changing a Smart Album

To modify a smart album, select it in the Source area and choose Edit Smart Album from the File menu.

See how to create a smart album.
◎ **Creating a Smart Album**

Be More Specific: Specifying Multiple Criteria

By adding additional criteria, you can be very specific about what you want to find.

To delete a criterion, click the ⊖ button. To add a criterion, click the ⊕ button.

Normally, iPhoto locates photos that meet all the criteria you specify. To have iPhoto locate a photo that meets any one of the criteria, choose any.

Tips for Smart Albums

They're alive. iPhoto is always watching. If you import photos that meet a smart album's criteria, iPhoto adds those photos to the album. iPhoto may also add to a smart album when you edit photo information. For example, if you change a photo's title to *Beach picnic*, iPhoto adds the photo to any smart album set up to search for *beach* in the title.

From smart to dumb. You can't turn a smart album into a static one—unlike iTunes, iPhoto doesn't provide a Live

Updating check box. Here's a workaround. Click the smart album in the Source list, then select all the photos in the album. (Click one photo, then press ⌘-A.) Next, choose New Album from Selection from the File menu. This creates an album containing the photos currently in the smart album.

Rearranging photos. iPhoto doesn't let you drag photos around in a smart album. To rearrange the photos, use the technique described above to

create a "dumb" album from the smart one. Then modify the dumb version.

No trash, please. You can't delete a photo from a smart album. If you don't want a photo in a smart album, edit its information so it no longer meets the album's criteria. Or make a dumb version of a smart album and delete the photo from that album.

Roll your own Find command. Wish iPhoto had a Find command? Make your own. Create a

smart album and name it Find. Specify the criterion you search for most often (for example, *Any Text contains*). When you need to find some photos, edit the Find smart album's criteria and hit Return.

Don't forget about Batch Change. Lack the discipline and strength of character to assign titles and keywords to every single photo? Me too. Don't forget about the next-best thing: the Batch Change command. It's described on page 145.

Basic Photo Editing

Many photos can benefit from some tweaking. Maybe you'd like to crop out that huge telephone pole that distracts from your subject. Maybe the exposure is too light, too dark, or lacks contrast. Or maybe the camera's flash gave your subject's eyes the dreaded red-eye flaw.

iPhoto's edit mode can fix these problems and others. And it does so in a clever way that doesn't replace your original image: if you don't like your edits, choose Revert to Original from the Photos menu.

iPhoto's editing features address many common image problems, but iPhoto isn't a full-fledged digital darkroom—you can't, for example, darken only a portion of an image. For advanced image editing, you'll want a program such as Adobe Photoshop or its less-expensive but still powerful sibling, Photoshop Elements (see page 131).

Editing Essentials

To switch to iPhoto's edit mode, select a photo—either in the Photo Library or in an album—and click the Edit button. Or, simply double-click the photo.

Improve image quality and retouch flaws; see page 108.

Use the size slider to zoom in and out. When zoomed in, you can quickly scroll by pressing ⌘ and then dragging within the image.

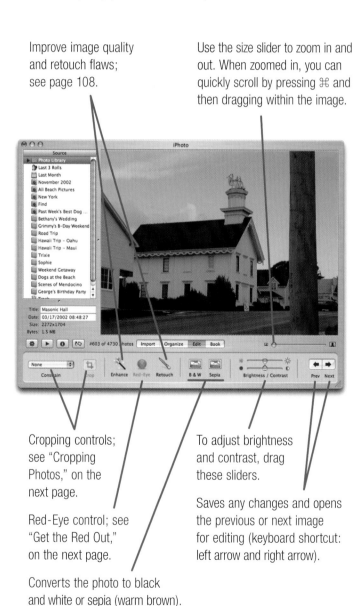

Cropping controls; see "Cropping Photos," on the next page.

Red-Eye control; see "Get the Red Out," on the next page.

Converts the photo to black and white or sepia (warm brown).

To adjust brightness and contrast, drag these sliders.

Saves any changes and opens the previous or next image for editing (keyboard shortcut: left arrow and right arrow).

Cropping Photos

To crop out unwanted portions of a photo, first click and drag within the image to indicate which portion you want to retain.

Drag to create a selection. To move the selection, drag within it. To resize it, drag any corner. To start over, click on the image anywhere outside the selection.

Have a specific output dimension in mind? Choose the most appropriate option from the Constrain pop-up menu. For example, if you plan to order a 4 by 6 print, choose 4 x 6 (Postcard). iPhoto restricts the proportions of the cropping area to match the option you choose. If you're planning a vertically oriented print, choose Constrain as Portrait or press the Option key while dragging. To create a cropping selection of any size, choose None. To override the current constrain setting, press ⌘ while dragging.

Note: When you crop a photo, you throw away pixels, effectively lowering the photo's resolution. If you print a heavily cropped photo, you may notice ugly digital artifacts. There are two morals to this story. First, think twice about cropping the daylights out of a photo. Second, always shoot at the highest resolution your camera provides; this gives you more flexibility to crop later (see page 131).

To apply the crop area to the image, click Crop.

Get the Red Out

Red-eye is a common problem caused by the bright light of an electronic flash reflecting off a subject's retinas and the blood vessels around them.

Be sure the Constrain pop-up menu is set to None, then drag to select the subject's eyes.

To apply the fix, click the Red-Eye button.

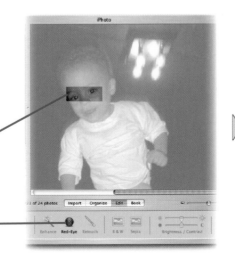
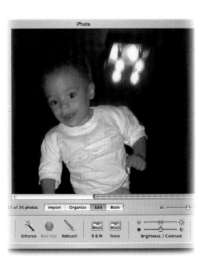

Enhancing and Retouching Photos

Some photos need work. Old photos can appear faded, their color washed out by Father Time. They might also have scratches and creases brought on by decades of shoebox imprisonment.

New photos can often benefit from some enhancement, too. That shot you took in a dark room with the flash turned off—its color could use some punching up. That family photo you want to use as a holiday card—the clan might look better with fewer wrinkles and blemishes.

iPhoto's Enhance and Retouch tools are ideal for tasks like these. With the Enhance tool, you can improve a photo's colors and exposure, and rescue a photo you might otherwise delete. With the Retouch tool, you can remove minor scratches and blemishes, not to mention that chocolate smudge on your kid's face.

Both tools enable you to view before-and-after versions of your work: press the Control key, and iPhoto shows you what the image looked like before you began retouching and enhancing. And you can always backtrack one step by using the Undo command, or return to Square One by choosing Revert to Original from the Photos menu.

As with iPhoto's other editing features, the Enhance and Retouch tools appear in iPhoto's edit mode. If you aren't familiar with how to switch to edit mode, see "Basic Photo Editing" on page 106.

Using One-Click Enhance

To apply one-click enhance, click the Enhance icon in the Edit pane at the bottom of the iPhoto window.

Before: This dimly lit shot is barely visible.

After: iPhoto has let the dogs out.

Tips

As you may have noticed, the Enhance tool improves image quality by adjusting brightness, contrast, and color balance all at the same time. To see what your image looked like before you clicked Enhance, press and hold down the Control key (that's Control, not ⌘).

If at first you don't succeed, click, click again. Each time you click Enhance, iPhoto processes the image again. But too much enhancement can make an image appear grainy and artificial. If that happens, choose Undo Enhance Photo from the Edit menu as many times as needed to backtrack.

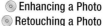

See how to enhance and retouch photos.
- Enhancing a Photo
- Retouching a Photo

Using the Retouch Tool

To use the Retouch tool, click the Retouch icon in the Edit pane.

To remove a flaw, position the crosshair pointer over the flaw and then drag away from the flaw in short strokes.

Before: Cute kid, but a little dirty.

After: We lost the dirt, but kept the freckles.

Tips

As with the Enhance tool, you can temporarily see what your image looked like before you began retouching by pressing and holding down the Control key.

To retouch with more precision, use the size slider to zoom in on the area of the image that you're working on.

When the Retouch tool is active, you can't use the ⌘-drag technique to scroll a zoomed-in photo. Use the scroll bars and scroll arrows to scroll, or deactivate the Retouch tool by clicking its icon again.

You can undo each mouse click by choosing Undo Retouch from the Edit menu. To undo all of your retouching, choose Revert to Original from the Photos menu. Note that you'll also lose any other edits, such as cropping.

Scratches are best removed by rubbing the mouse pointer over a scratch until it disappears. That's because iPhoto learns the pattern on either side of a scratch, and rubbing makes this pattern easier to learn. Also, some scratches disappear faster if you rub at a ninety-degree angle to the scratch. Experiment and undo as needed.

Using the Edit Window

Normally, iPhoto displays the image you're editing within the iPhoto window itself. But iPhoto also provides a separate edit window that you may prefer. One reason to use an edit window is that you can have multiple edit windows open simultaneously, enabling you to compare images. And the edit window has some features that the Edit pane lacks.

Displaying the Edit Window

To open an image in a separate window, press the Option key while double-clicking on the image. You can also use the Preferences command to have iPhoto always use the separate window when you double-click on an image.

Enlarges or reduces the image to fit the size of the edit window.

To customize the edit window toolbar, click Customize.

You can enter a custom constrain dimension here.

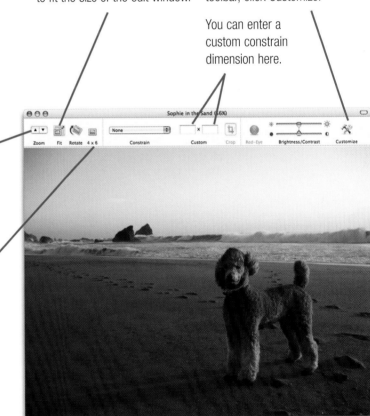

Zoom in and out. When zoomed in, you can quickly scroll by pressing ⌘ and dragging within the image. **Tip:** To zoom in on a specific area, drag to create a crop rectangle, then click the zoom button.

Do you frequently crop to specific constraints? Customize the tool-bar and add those cropping constraints for one-click access.

Using iPhoto with Other Imaging Programs

If you have Adobe Photoshop or another image editing program, you might want to set up iPhoto to work with it: when you double-click an image in iPhoto's Organize view, your Mac will switch to your image editing program, which will open the image.

Choose Preferences from the iPhoto menu, click the General button, and in the area labeled Double-click photo, click the Opens Photo In button. Next, click the Select Application button, and locate and double-click your image editing program.

Don't want iPhoto to always open images in another program? Here's an easy alternative: to open a photo in a different program, simply drag the photo's thumbnail image to the program's icon in your dock. For example, drag a photo to the Photoshop icon to open the image in Photoshop.

Restoring the Original Image

iPhoto also includes iSafetyNet. Actually, there is no feature by that name, but there might as well be: even after you've cropped and otherwise modified an image, you can always revert to the original version by selecting the image and then choosing Revert to Original from the Photos menu.

Customizing the Edit Window Toolbar

To customize the edit window toolbar, click its Customize button or choose Customize Toolbar from the Window menu.

You can then add and remove tools to suit your needs.

To add a tool, drag it to the toolbar. To remove a tool you don't use, drag it off of the toolbar.

You can also rearrange tools by dragging them left and right on the toolbar. And using the Show pop-up menu, you can specify whether the toolbar appears with icons and text, with just icons, or with just text. To display small icons for each tool, check the Use Small Size box.

Searching by Keywords

One way to search for photos is to create a smart album containing the criteria you're looking for (page 104).

If you've assigned keywords to your photos, you have another, more convenient option: the Keywords window, which lets you quickly search for photos to which you've assigned one or more keywords.

To search for photos using the Keywords window, choose Show Keywords from the Photos menu or pressing ⌘-K. When you search for photos, iPhoto displays only those that meet your criteria. You can then do whatever you like with the photos you've found: edit and retouch them, add them to an album, email them, view them as a slide show, print or delete them, and so on.

Doing a lot of searching? Note that you don't have to close the Keywords window. If you like, simply drag the window off to the side so you can see it and your photos at the same time.

Searching by Keywords

Step 1.

To search your entire library, make sure the Photo Library item is selected. To search within a specific album, select it.

Step 2.

Click the keyword you want to search for. You can further narrow your search by selecting additional keywords—for example, ⌘-clicking Dogs to find all photos of dogs taken at the beach. To widen the search, ⌘-click on a highlighted keyword again to deselect it.

Step 3.

Click the Search button.

iPhoto displays the number of photos it found.

iPhoto displays only those photos that have the search keyword or keywords assigned to them. (To view keywords below each photo as shown here, choose Keywords from the View menu or press Shift-⌘-K.)

To display all photos again, click the Show All button in the Keywords window.

EXIF Exposed: Getting Information About Photos

I mentioned earlier that digital cameras store information along with each photo—the date and time when the photo was taken, its exposure, the kind of camera used, and more. This is called the *EXIF* data.

iPhoto saves this EXIF data when you import photos. To view it, select a photo and choose Show Info from the Photos menu (⌘-I).

Much of this information may not be useful to you, but some of it might. If you have more than one digital camera, for example, you can use the window's Photo tab to see which camera you used for a given shot.

If you're interested in learning more about the nuts and bolts of photography, explore the Exposure tab to see what kinds of exposure settings your camera used.

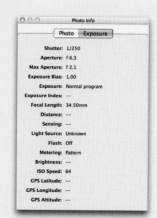

At the very least, you might just want to explore the Photo Info window to see the kind of information iPhoto is keeping track of for you.

Creating Slide Shows

With iPhoto's slide show feature, you can display on-screen slide shows, complete with background music from your iTunes music library. iPhoto even displays a gorgeous transition between each image. With the dissolve effect, for example, one photo fades out as the next one fades in.

Most of the time, you'll want to add photos to an album before viewing them as a slide show. That way, you can arrange the photos in a sequence that best tells your story.

But you don't have to stash photos in an album to view a slide show—just select the photos you want to screen, then set up the slide show as described here. To quickly screen your latest shots, select the Last Rolls album. To relive an entire year, select one of the recent years in Source list. To see a few photos over and over again, just Shift-click on each one.

In iPhoto 4, slide shows also include some housekeeping conveniences. Move your mouse during a slide show, and you get a set of tools for rotating, rating, and deleting photos.

You can view your slide shows on the Mac's screen or, if you're using a PowerBook with an S-video jack, you can connect the computer to a TV set to view the slide show on a television. You can also connect your Mac to a video projector and show your slide show on a big screen.

Somebody get the lights.

Viewing a Slide Show

In a hurry? Select the album or photos you want to screen, click the ▶ button near the lower-left corner of the iPhoto window, and sit back and watch.

Want more control? Follow these instructions to customize your slide show's music, transitions, and more.

Step 1.

Select the photos you want to show.
To show an entire album, select the album.

Step 2.

Click the Slideshow button in iPhoto's Organize pane. The Slideshow dialog box appears.

Choose a transition style.

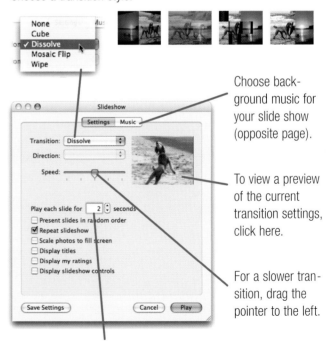

Choose background music for your slide show (opposite page).

To view a preview of the current transition settings, click here.

For a slower transition, drag the pointer to the left.

Type a duration for each image, or click the up and down arrows to set a duration.

See how to adjust slide show settings and review photos.
◉ **Creating a Slide Show**
◉ **Reviewing Photos in a Slide Show**

Step 2 (continued).

When this box is checked, iPhoto repeats the slide show until time itself comes to an end or until you press the Esc key or the mouse button, whichever comes first.

iPhoto can adjust the way it projects each picture to ensure that the screen is always completely filled, with no black borders. Note that vertically oriented shots and photos you've cropped may display strangely.

Display information and do some housekeeping while the slide show plays (below).

Displays the photos in random order instead of in the order they appear in the iPhoto window.

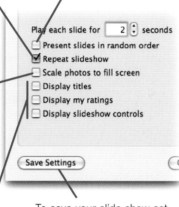

To save your slide show settings but not actually view the slide show, click Save Settings.

For a silent slide show, uncheck the box.

To pick a song from your iTunes music library, choose iTunes Library. To assign an entire playlist to the slideshow, choose the playlist's name.

To hear a song, double-click it or select it and click playbutton ▶.

The currently selected slide show or playlist appears here.

To sort the song list, click a column heading. You can also move the columns (drag their headings) and resize them (drag their boundaries).

To narrow down the list of songs displayed, type part or all of a song or artist name.

Step 3.

Click the Play button (Play) to begin.

Screen Test: Reviewing Photos

If you move the mouse while a slide show plays back, a set of controls appears that lets you rotate, rate, and delete the currently displayed photo. This is a handy way to perform common housekeeping chores on a

freshly imported set of photos: click Last Roll, start the slide show, and get to work.

Note: The workings of the Trash button depend on what you're viewing. If you're viewing a slide show of an album, clicking the

Trash button removes a photo from the album. If you're viewing photos directly from the Photo Library (for example, you clicked

the Last Roll item), clicking the Trash button moves the photo to the iPhoto Trash.

Slide Show Tips

When Just One Song Won't Do

Want more than one song to play back during a slide show? In iTunes, create a playlist containing the songs you want to use. Then, return to iPhoto and choose the playlist's name from the pop-up menu in the Music portion of the Slideshow Settings dialog box.

Slide Show in a Window

Normally, an iPhoto slide show takes over the Mac's screen. But you can have iPhoto display a slide show in a window: just press the Control key when clicking the ► button or the Play button in the Slide Show Settings dialog box.

Note that the slide show controls described on page 114 aren't available in this window.

Assigning Songs to Albums

You can assign a different song to each of your albums. When you view a particular album as a slide show, iPhoto plays the song you've assigned to it.

To assign a song to a specific album, start iTunes and position its window so you can see it and your iPhoto albums. Then, simply drag a song to an album.

The song you've assigned to the album appears in iPhoto's information area.

Tip: You can also drag a song to the Photo Library, Last Rolls, and Last Months items. When you drag a song to the Photo Library item, iPhoto asks if you want to make that song the default slide show music. If you click OK, iPhoto will assign that song to all future albums you create. (You can always change this song assignment manually.)

Expand the List

If you're choosing music and you have a very large iTunes library, enlarge the Slide Show dialog box by dragging its lower-right corner. You won't have do to quite as much scrolling to locate a song.

To Each Its Own

Every album can have its own slide show settings—and not just for music. All of the other options that you can adjust in the Slide Show Settings dialog box—transition style, photo scaling, and so on—can also apply on an album-by-album basis. Just select the album whose settings you want to adjust, click the Slideshow button in the Organize pane, make your adjustments, and click Save Settings.

Videotaping a Slide Show

Many PowerBooks have S-video jacks that enable you to display their screen images on a TV set, or record them using a camcorder or videocassette recorder. You can take advantage of these TV-savvy Macs to record a slide show on tape.

First, connect the PowerBook's S-video connector to a camcorder or VCR, open System Preferences, and use Displays to turn on video mirroring. Next, press your video deck's Record button, and begin playing back the slide show. To record the background music, too, connect the Mac's speaker jack to your video deck's audio-input jacks.

Creating Special Effects

You can add some interesting special effects to your slide shows by duplicating photos, modifying the duplicates, then sequencing them in an album.

For example, you can have a photo start out in black and white and then dissolve into a color version. Or create a few duplicates of a photo, and then crop each one progressively tighter. When iPhoto dissolves from one to the next, you'll get a zoom-in effect.

To duplicate a photo, select it, then choose Duplicate from the Photos menu (⌘-D).

Slide Show Keyboard Controls

To Do This	Do This
Pause the slide show	Spacebar
	(If the slide show has music, the music continues to play but the images won't change. To resume the slide show, press the spacebar again.)
Adjust the speed of the slide show	The up arrow and down arrow keys
Manually move through the slide show	The left arrow and right arrow keys
Rate the currently displayed photo	0 (zero) through 5
Rotate the currently displayed photo	⌘-R (clockwise) or Option-⌘-R (counterclockwise).
Stop the slide show	Esc (or click the mouse button)

Choosing Display Preferences

Using the Slideshow Settings dialog box, you can have iPhoto display additional items during a slide show.

Display Titles. Each photo's title appears in the upper-left corner of the screen.

Display My Ratings. Each photo's rating appears centered at the bottom of the screen.

Display Slideshow Controls. The rotation, rating, and deletion tools described on page 115 appear immediately—no need to move the mouse first.

Exporting a Slide Show as a QuickTime Movie

Want to email a slide show to someone or post it on a Web site? Configure the slide show settings as desired, then use the Export command to create a QuickTime movie as described on page 134.

Sharing Photos via Email

Email takes the immediacy of digital photography to a global scale. You can take a photo of a birthday cake and email it across the world before the candle wax solidifies. It takes just a few mouse clicks—iPhoto takes care of the often tricky chores behind creating email photo attachments.

iPhoto can also make images smaller so they transfer faster. Take advantage of this feature, and you won't bog down your recipients' email sessions with huge image attachments.

Normally, iPhoto uses the Mac OS X Mail program to email photos. If you use a different email program, you can configure iPhoto to use it, as described on the next page.

Step 2.
Click the Email Button

iPhoto displays the Mail Photo dialog box.

Step 3.
Specify the Image Size

iPhoto can make the images smaller before emailing. (This doesn't change the dimensions or file sizes of your original images, which iPhoto always stores in all their high-resolution glory.)

After you've specified mail settings, click Compose.

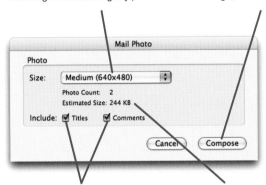

Step 1:
Select the Photos

Select the photos you want to email. Remember that you can select multiple photos by Shift-clicking and ⌘-clicking.

You have the option to include titles and comments along with the images—another good reason to assign this information when organizing your photos.

After iPhoto creates smaller versions, it starts Mac OS X's Mail program. Your photos are added to a new email, which you can complete and send on its way.

iPhoto estimates the size of the final attachments. If you're sending images to someone who is connecting using a modem (as opposed to a high-speed connection), try to keep the estimated size below 300KB or so. As a rule of thumb, each 100KB will take about 15 seconds to transfer over a 56kbps modem.

Tips for Emailing Photos

Setting Email Preferences

You don't use Mac OS X's email program? Me neither—I prefer Microsoft Entourage. You can use iPhoto's Preferences command to tell iPhoto to use a program other than Mail to send your photos. Besides Mac OS X's Mail program, iPhoto can work with Microsoft Entourage, Qualcomm's Eudora, or America Online.

To change your email program preference, choose Preferences from the iPhoto menu and click the General button. Then, choose your preferred email program from the pop-up menu at the bottom of the Preferences window.

Exporting Photos By Hand

When you email a photo using iPhoto's Email button, iPhoto uses the name of the original photo's disk file as the name of the attachment. Problem is, most of your photos probably have incomprehensible filenames, such as 200203241958.jpg, that were assigned to them by your digital camera.

You might want an attachment to have a friendlier file name, such as holidays.jpg. For such cases, export the photo "by hand" and then add it to an email as an attachment. Choose Export from iPhoto's File menu, and be sure the File Export tab is active.

Export the photo as described at right. Finally, switch to your email program, create a new email message, and add the photo to it as an attachment.

Note: iPhoto 4.0 can erroneously report a photo's size to be in the billions of bytes, causing an error when you try to export. Be sure you're using iPhoto 4.0.1 or a later version, if available.

To make the images smaller and thus faster to transfer, type a dimension in the Width or Height box. You need type only one dimension; iPhoto will calculate the other dimension for you.

If your original image is stored in a format other than JPEG, consider choosing JPEG from this pop-up menu.

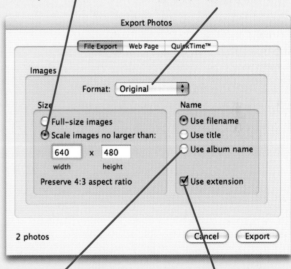

You can have iPhoto name the exported file according to its title or album name. If you're exporting just one photo, you can also type a name after clicking the Export button.

Leave this box checked to improve compatibility with Windows computers.

Sharing Photos on a HomePage

Email is a fun way to share photos, but this method isn't always rosy. When you attach more than a few photos to a single email, you create a large message that can bog down your recipients' Internet connections. And some people just can't seem to receive attachments correctly.

There's another way to get your photos around the world: publish them on a Web site, specifically on an Apple HomePage. iPhoto works together with Apple's .Mac service to make Web photo albums easy to create—it takes only a couple of mouse clicks to make your images available to a global audience. You can also password-protect albums so only certain people can see them.

Note that you must have an Apple .Mac account to create a HomePage. To register for an account, go to www.mac.com. And be sure you're using the latest iPhoto before you start—4.0.1 or a later version, if available. In the original iPhoto 4.0 (and its predecessors), HomePage images could have visible compression artifacts.

Creating a HomePage

You can create a HomePage containing just one photo, a selection of photos, or an entire album. You don't even have to create an album to create a HomePage—you can select some images in the Photo Library and proceed directly to the HomePage button. But it's smarter to create an album, so you can control the order in which the photos appear on the HomePage. Creating an album also makes it easier to revise the HomePage later, as described on the opposite page.

Organize the album's photos in the order you want them to appear. To publish only a few photos, select them first.

To begin the publishing process, be sure you're connected to the Internet, then click the HomePage button.

See a few of my HomePage albums.
http://homepage.mac.com/jimheid

iPhoto connects with Apple's .Mac service and, after a few moments, displays a preview of your HomePage.

iPhoto uses the album name for the name of the HomePage, and uses the title you assigned to each photo as its caption. You can edit any text item in the HomePage preview.

You can change the order of photos by dragging them.

Be sure your .Mac account name appears here.

A two-column layout displays larger thumbnail images.

To hide the list of themes, click Hide Themes.

You can choose from more than a dozen design themes.

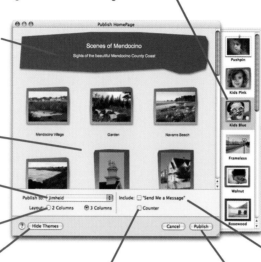

Check this box to add a counter that shows how many times your HomePage has been viewed.

After iPhoto has transferred your photos, a dialog box displays the address of your new HomePage.

You can copy this address to the Mac's Clipboard by dragging across it, then pressing ⌘-C. Paste the address into an email message to notify people that you've published the album.

To see the new HomePage album, click Visit Page Now.

Check this box to add a button that enables visitors to send you a message via Apple's iCard electronic greeting card service.

When you've finished previewing the HomePage, click Publish.

Editing a HomePage Album

What if you publish a HomePage album and then decide to make changes? You have a few options. If the photos you published came from an iPhoto album, simply make the desired changes in iPhoto—add and remove photos, change their order, edit their titles, and so on. Then, select the album and click the HomePage button. iPhoto displays a message containing three options.

Note: If the HomePage isn't based on an album—if you just selected some photos in the library and then clicked

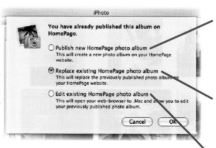

HomePage—this dialog box doesn't appear. This is another good reason to add photos to an album before publishing a HomePage.

Creates a new HomePage album, leaving the existing one unchanged. Choose this option if you want two versions of the HomePage album.

Replaces the existing HomePage album. Choose this option if you just want to update the original HomePage.

Opens your Web browser and the HomePage editing program on .Mac. You might choose this option if you need to perform only a minor edit, such as fixing a typo in a caption or switching from a two-column to a three-column layout.

More Internet Sharing Options

Chances are most of the Internet sharing you do will be through email and Home-Page albums. But when you're in the mood for something completely different, iPhoto is ready. You can also create custom Web photo albums as well as slide shows that are shared through Apple's .Mac service.

.Mac slide shows are a fun way to share photos with other Mac users. Publish some photos as .Mac slides, and other Mac OS X users can configure their Macs to use those photos as their screen savers.

You might create a custom Web album if you're a Web jockey and you already have your own Web site, perhaps one that is served by your local Internet provider rather than Apple's .Mac service. You can also burn a set of Web photo pages onto a CD and send it to anyone who has a Mac or Windows computer.

If you're a Web publisher, you can modify these pages as you see fit. You might open them in a program such as Macromedia Dreamweaver, embellish them with additional graphics or other tweaks, and then upload them to a Web site.

iPhoto's Web pages are on the bland side. To spice up iPhoto's HTML export-ing, try Simeon Leifer's BetterHTMLExport, available from software download sites. BetterHTMLExport provides numerous design templates for you to choose from and modify.

Exporting Web Pages

You can export photos and albums as Web pages to post on sites other than an Apple HomePage. iPhoto creates small thumbnail versions of your images as well as the HTML pages that display them. (HTML stands for *HyperText Markup Language*—it's the set of codes used to design Web pages.)

To export a Web page, select some photos or an album, choose Export from the File menu, then click the Web Page tab. Specify the page appearance and dimensions of the thumbnails and the images, then click Export. In the Export dialog box, click the New Folder button to create a new folder. If you'll be publishing the pages on a Web server, I recommend naming the new folder *index*. This causes iPhoto to create a home page named *index.html,* as required by most Web servers.

Creating a .Mac Slide Show

Step 1.

Select the photos you want to publish. To select an entire album, click its name.

Step 2.

Click the .Mac Slides button.

iPhoto connects to .Mac, then displays a message asking if you're sure you want to publish the slide show.

Step 3.

Click the Publish button.

iPhoto transfers your images to your iDisk. When the transfer is complete, a message appears enabling you to send an announcement email. The announcement contains instructions on how users can access the slide show.

Viewing the Slide Show

Anyone using version 10.2 or later of Mac OS X can view your slide show. You don't have to have a .Mac subscription to view .Mac slides.

Step 1.

Open System Preferences, then open the Desktop & Screen Saver item and click its Screen Saver tab. (In Mac OS X 10.2, open the Screen Effects system preference.)

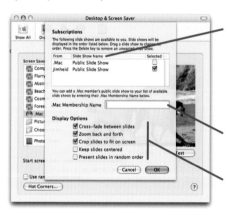

Step 2.

Click the .Mac option in the Screen Savers list, then click Options. (In OS X 10.2, click Configure.)

Slide shows you've subscribed to appear here. To remove a slide show from the list, select it and press the Delete key. To temporarily disable one, uncheck its box. To change the order in which the slide shows display, drag them up and down in the list.

To subscribe to a user's .Mac slide show, type the user's .Mac name here—for example, *jimheid*.

Fine-tune display options.

Step 3.

Click OK.

To view the slide show, click the Test button or activate the screen effects. (Use the Hot Corners button to specify how and when the screen effects activate.)

Burning HTML Albums on a CD

Even if you aren't a Web jockey, there's a good reason to consider exporting an album as a set of Web pages: you can burn the exported pages onto CDs, and then mail them to others. They can view the album on their Macs or PCs using a Web browser—no attachment hassles, no long downloads.

After exporting the Web page, use the Mac OS X Finder to copy its folders and HTML pages to a blank CD-R disc. Burn the disc, eject it, and you have a photo Web site on a disc.

To view the site, simply double-click on the site's home page file. (If you followed my recommendation on the opposite page, this file is named *index.html*.)

And by the way, resist the urge to rename the site's home page file. If you change the name, the links in the Web album won't work. If you want a different name for the home page file, export the Web pages anew.

Similarly, don't rename any image files or move them from their folders.

Sharing Photos on a Network

If you have more than one Mac on a network, you can share each Mac's photo library and make it accessible to the other Macs on the network.

Network photo sharing leads to all kinds of possibilities. Keep your "master" photo library on one Mac, and then access it from other Macs when you need to—no need to copy the library from one Mac to another and worry about which library is the most current.

Don't like centralization? Embrace anarchy: Let everyone in the family have his or her own photo library, and then use sharing to make the libraries available to others.

Have an AirPort-equipped PowerBook or iBook? Sit on the sofa (or at poolside) and show your photos to friends and family. Or take your laptop to their house and browse their libraries. Network sharing, a PowerBook or iBook, and AirPort form the ultimate portable slide projector.

You can choose to share an entire photo library or only some albums. And you can require a password to keep your kids (or your parents) out of your library.

Activating Sharing

To share your photo library with other Macs on a network, choose Preferences from the iPhoto menu, then click the Sharing button.

To have the Mac automatically connect to shared libraries it finds on the network, check this box.

You can share your entire library or only selected albums. To share a specific album, click its check box.

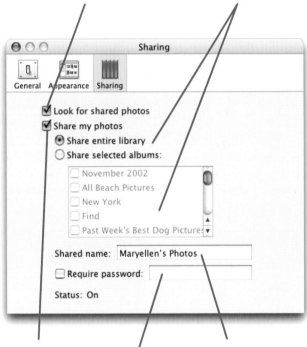

To share your photos, check this box.

To password-protect your shared photos, check this box and specify a password.

The name you specify here appears in other users' iPhoto Source lists.

See how to share photos and access shared photos.
◉ **Sharing Photos on a Network**

Accessing Shared Photos

To access shared photos, choose Preferences from the iPhoto menu and be sure the Look for Shared Photos box is checked. iPhoto scans your network and if it finds any shared photo libraries, it adds their names to the Source list.

To view a shared library, click its name in the Source list.

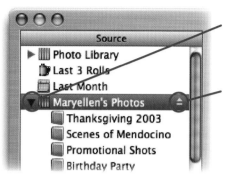

To view albums in a shared library, click the little triangle next to the library's name.

To disconnect from a shared library (perhaps to reduce traffic on your network), click the Eject button.

Working with Shared Photos

No Keywords or Info

Unfortunately, iPhoto ignores any keywords, titles, or comments that you may have assigned to the photos in a shared library, even if you copy those photos to your local photo library.

As a result, you can't use smart albums or keyword searches to find photos in a shared library.

If you want to copy some photos to your local library *and* pre-serve this information, burn the photos to a CD or DVD using the techniques described on page 136. Then, insert the CD in your Mac and copy the pho-tos to your library.

Slide Show Music

You can view a slide show of a shared album, but if the shared album has music assigned to it, you won't hear that music. Instead, iPhoto plays its default music—the rockin' *Minuet in G*, unless you've assigned a differ-ent song to your library.

But here's an interesting twist: you can temporarily assign a song or playlist from *your* local iTunes library to a *shared* album. Just use the techniques described on pages 115 and 116.

When you assign local music to a shared album, iPhoto doesn't save your assignment. If you disconnect from the shared

album and then reconnect, it's back to *Minuet in G* or whatever your default song happens to be.

Exporting Shared Photos

Normally, the Export command is unavailable when you're view-ing a shared photo, even when in edit mode. Thus, you can't export a photo located in a shared library.

Or can you? Here's the secret: open the shared photo in the iPhoto edit window (described on page 110). Now you can export the photo. Open several photos in the editor window, and you can even export them as a QuickTime movie or Web page.

Just Looking

You can view and print shared photos and order prints of them. You can also email them and create a HomePage album or a .Mac slide show.

But you can't edit shared photos. To crop, retouch, or perform other digital darkroom work, copy the shared photos you want to edit to your local iPhoto library: select the photos, then drag them to the Photo Library item in the Source list or to an album.

Printing Photos

Internet photo sharing is great, but hard copy isn't dead. You might want to share photos with people who don't have computers. Or, you might want to tack a photo to a bulletin board or hang it on your wall—you'll never see "suitable for framing" stamped on an email message.

iPhoto makes hard copy easy. If you have a photo-inkjet printer, you can use iPhoto to create beautiful color prints in a variety of sizes. This assumes, of course, that your photos are both beautiful and in color.

When printing your photos, you can choose from several formatting options, called *print styles*, by using the Style pop-up menu in the Print dialog box. For example, if you choose the Sampler style, you can print pages that contain the same photo in several different sizes. With the style named N-Up, you can print up to 16 photos per page.

Printing with iPhoto is straightforward, but to get the best results and avoid wasting pricey photo paper and ink, there are a couple of fine points to be aware of.

And to get the best results, you'll want to use images with a resolution high enough to yield sharp results at your chosen print size. You'll find more details on this aspect of printing on the following pages.

Step 1 (optional).

Crop the photo you want to print so that its proportions match that of the paper size you want to print. For details on cropping, see page 107.

You don't have to crop before printing, but if you don't crop your print will probably have wildly uneven borders. If you choose the Standard Prints print style, iPhoto may even refuse to print the photo (see "When iPhoto Balks," on page 129).

Tip: If you want to retain an uncropped version of the photo, make a duplicate before cropping: select the photo and press ⌘-D.

Step 2.

Be sure that the photo you want to print is selected or displayed in the iPhoto edit mode. To print multiple photos, be sure that iPhoto is in Organize mode, then select the photos.

Step 3.

If you're using a paper size other than letter—for example, 5 by 7 inch photo paper—choose Page Setup from the File menu and select the appropriate settings.

To enable iPhoto to display paper size options that pertain to your printer, choose your printer model.

Choose the paper size that you plan to use.

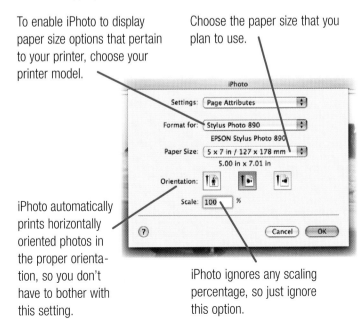

iPhoto automatically prints horizontally oriented photos in the proper orientation, so you don't have to bother with this setting.

iPhoto ignores any scaling percentage, so just ignore this option.

See the basics of photo printing.
◉ **Printing Your Photos**

Step 4.

Choose Print from the File menu, and choose the appropriate settings.

The Full Page style is the most versatile and reliable. Other styles include Contact Sheet, Standard Prints, N-Up, Sampler, and Greeting Card (see page 128).

Be sure your printer is selected here.

iPhoto includes presets for many popular inkjet printers. Choose the preset that best matches the type of paper you're using.

iPhoto displays a preview of your first page. To see a preview of all pages, click Preview.

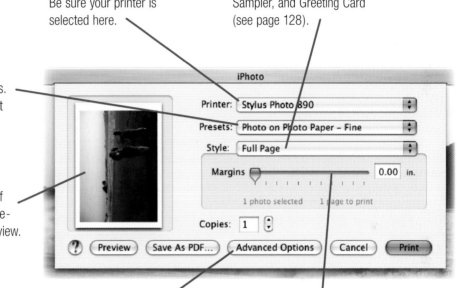

Access additional printing options specific to your printer—for example, to fine-tune paper or print-quality settings.

When you've chosen the Full Page style, you can adjust margin dimensions here. To print a borderless image, specify a margin of 0 (zero).

Note: To create borderless prints, your printer must support borderless printing and you must choose a borderless paper-size option in the Page Setup dialog box.

Printing Tips and Troubleshooting

Other Print Styles

When you want to make more than just a simple print, investigate iPhoto's other print styles.

The Greeting Card style formats the page so you can fold it into a card.

The N-Up style prints multiple copies of a single photo on each page. You can choose to print as few as two copies per page, or as many as 16.

The Sampler style mixes and matches sizes on a single sheet—much like the combination of print sizes you might get from a portrait studio. This style provides two templates, which you can choose using the Template pop-up menu.

The Contact Sheet style, described at right, lets you print numerous shots on a single sheet—handy for reference purposes or to simply squeeze a lot photos out of a sheet of paper.

Printing a Contact Sheet

Photographers often create contact sheets—quick-reference prints containing small versions of multiple photos, usually an entire roll's worth on each *contact sheet*. (The term derives from the traditional technique: a contact sheet is created by sandwiching negatives between a piece of glass

Specify how many images you want to appear on each row of the contact sheet.

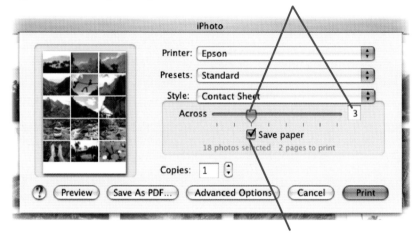

and photographic paper, and then exposing the sandwich to light.)

To include only certain photos on a contact sheet, select them before choosing the Print command. You can use contact sheets to provide an at-a-glance reference for a series of photos.

But you can also use a contact sheet to squeeze several images onto a single sheet of paper.

Check the Save paper box to have iPhoto print vertical images in horizontal orientation, even if you rotated them. You'll have to turn the sheet sideways to view some images, but you'll get more images on each sheet of paper.

Tip: You can use contact sheets to print multiple copies of one photo. Simply select only one photo before choosing Print.

When iPhoto Balks

You've selected a photo, chosen the Print command, and selected the Standard Prints style. You choose the 4x6 print size, and all seems right with the world.

Then you glance at the little preview area of the Print dialog box where, instead of your photo, you see red text proclaiming, "The selected print size will not fit on the current paper size."

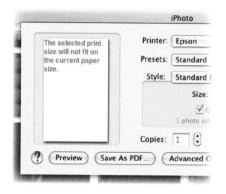

Here are a few remedies to try.

Check page setup options. Choose the Page Setup command and make sure that you've chosen your printer and the paper size that corresponds to the desired print size.

Click the One Photo Per Page box. You'll find it under the Size pop-up menu in the Print dialog box.

Give up. When all else fails, give up. Specifically, choose the Full Page print style instead. It's much less finicky.

When Prints Disappoint

When your prints aren't charming, read on.

Verify paper choices. In iPhoto's Print dialog box, be sure to choose the preset that matches the type of paper you're using and the quality you're seeking. It's easy to overlook this step and end up specifying plain paper when you're actually using pricey photo paper.

Check ink. Strange colors? Check your printer's ink supply. Many printers include diagnostic software that reports how much ink remains in each cartridge.

Clean up. The nozzles in an inkjet printer can become clogged, especially if you don't print every day. If you're seeing odd colors or a horizontal banding pattern, use your printer's cleaning mode to cleaning your ink nozzles. Most printers can print a test page designed to show when the nozzles need cleaning. You may have to repeat the cleaning process a few times.

Preserving Your Prints

After all the effort you put into making inkjet prints, it may disappoint you to learn that they may not last long.

Many inkjet prints begin to fade within a year or two—even faster when displayed in direct sunlight. Some printer manufacturers now offer pigment-based inks and archival papers that last for decades, but pigment-based printers are pricier than the more common dye-based printers.

If you have a dye-based printer, consider using a paper rated for longer print life. Epson's ColorLife paper, for example, has a much higher permanence rating than Epson's Premium Glossy Photo Paper.

To prolong the life of any print, don't display it in direct sunlight. Frame it under glass to protect it from humidity and pollutants. (Ozone pollution, common in cities, is poison to an inkjet print.)

Allow prints to dry for at least a few (preferably 24) hours before framing them or stacking them atop each other. For long-term storage, consider using acid-free sleeves designed for archival photo storage.

Finally, avoid bargain-priced paper or ink from the local office superstore. Print preservation guru Henry Wilhelm (www.wilhelm-research.com) recommends using only premium inks and papers manufactured by the same company that made your printer.

Is all this necessary for a print that will be tacked to a refrigerator for a few months and then thrown away? Of course not. But when you want prints to last, these steps can help.

To learn more about digital printing, read Harald Johnson's *Mastering Digital Printing* (Muska & Lipman, 2003).

Ordering Prints

Inkjet photo printers provide immediate gratification, but not without hassles. Paper and ink are expensive. Getting perfectly even borders is next to impossible, and getting borderless prints can be equally frustrating.

There is another path to hard copy: ordering prints through iPhoto. Click the Order Prints button, specify the print sizes you want, and iPhoto transmits your photos over the Internet to Kodak's Ofoto print service. The prints look great, and because they're true photographic prints, they're much more permanent than most inkjet prints.

You can also order prints from other online photofinishers, many of whom also offer free online photo albums and other sharing services. Using these services isn't as straightforward as clicking a button in iPhoto, but it isn't difficult, either. Many services, such as Shutterfly (www.shutterfly.com), offer software that simplifies transferring your shots. And some services offer output options that iPhoto doesn't, such as calendars, mouse pads, and even photo cookies. For links to some online photofinishers, see www.macilife.com/iphoto.

Ordering Prints

Step 1.

Select the photos you want prints of, then click the Order prints button in iPhoto's Organize pane.

Order Prints

Step 2.

Specify the sizes and quantities you want.

The yellow triangle of doom (⚠) indicates that the photo doesn't have enough resolution for good quality at that size; see the sidebar at right for details.

Want a 4 by 6 of every photo you selected? Specify the quantity here.

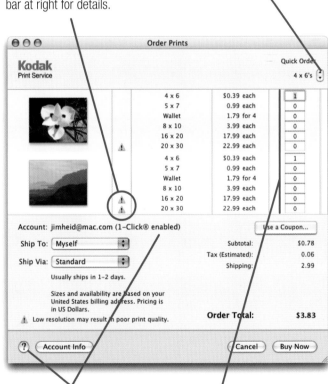

To order prints, you must have an Apple ID account with 1-Click ordering enabled. For help, click the help button.

Specify how many prints you want for each size.

Create a Temporary Album

If you're ordering prints from many differ-ent rolls, create an album and use it to hold the photos you want to print. Give the album an obvious name, such as *Pix to Print*. This makes it easier to keep track of which photos you're printing. After you've placed your order, you can delete the album.

Cropping Concerns

The proportions of most standard print sizes don't match the proportions of a typical digital camera image. As a result, Kodak automatically crops a photo to fill the print size you've ordered.

The problem is, automatic cropping may lop off part of the image that's important to you. If you don't want your photos cropped by a machine, do the cropping

yourself using iPhoto's Edit mode before ordering. Use the Constrain pop-up menu to specify the proportions you want.

If you plan to order prints in several sizes, you may have even more work to do. A 5 by 7 print has a different *aspect ratio* than a 4 by 6 or an 8 by 10. If you want to order a 5 by 7 *and* one of these other sizes, you need to create a sepa-rate version of each picture—for exam-ple, one version cropped for a 5 by 7 and another cropped for an 8 by 10.

To create versions of a picture, make a duplicate of the original photo for each size you want (select the photo and press ⌘-D), and then crop each version appropriately.

If you crop a photo to oddball propor-tions—for example, a narrow rectan-gle—Kodak's automatic cropping will yield a weird-looking print. If you have

an image-editing program, such as Adobe Photoshop Elements, here's a workaround. In the imaging program, create a blank image at size you plan to print (for example, 5 by 7 inches). Then open your cropped photo in the imaging program and paste it into this blank image. Save the resulting image as a JPEG file (use the Maximum quality setting), add it to iPhoto, and then order your print.

No Questions, Please

Kodak can't print a photo whose file name contains a question mark (?). No digital camera creates files that are so named, but if you scan and name images yourself, keep this restriction in mind.

Resolution's Relationship to Print Quality

If you're working with low-resolution images—ones that you've cropped heavily or shot at a low resolution, for example—you may see iPhoto's dreaded low-resolution warning icon when ordering prints or a book (⚠).

This is iPhoto's way of telling you that an image doesn't have enough pixels—enough digital information—to yield a good-quality print at the size that you've chosen.

Don't feel obligated to cancel a print job or an order if you see this warning. But do note that

you may see some artifacts in your prints.

The table here lists the minimum resolution an image should have to yield a good print at various sizes.

Print Sizes and Resolution

For This Print Size (Inches)	Image Resolution Should be Least (Pixels)
Wallet	640 by 480
4 by 6	768 by 512
5 by 7	1075 by 768
8 by 10	1280 by 1024
16 by 20 or larger	1600 by 1200

131

Creating Books

With iPhoto's Book button and Apple's help, you can turn an album of photos into a hard-bound, linen-covered book. iPhoto books make spectacular gifts and are ideal for promotional portfolios and other business applications, too.

To create a book, first create an album containing the photos you want to publish, in the order you want them to appear. Then, click iPhoto's Book button to display the Book pane.

Next, choose a theme design from the Theme pop-up menu. Finally, arrange the photos and text captions on each page as described here.

To order your finished book, click the Order Book button in the Book pane or in iPhoto's Organize pane. At this phase, you can choose a color for the book's linen cover. Color options include black, burgundy, light gray, or navy.

You can also print a book using your own inkjet printer. Just choose the Print command while in book mode.

One last note: Because of the printing method used to create iPhoto books, Apple recommends against including black-and-white photos in a book. This restriction doesn't apply if you plan to print a book's pages using your own inkjet printer.

Browsing Books

Catalog
Places up to eight photos on a page, with room for captions and descriptions.

Classic
Symmetrical page designs with up to four photos per page, with captions in the elegant Baskerville typeface.

Collage
Positions photos askew on the page and allows for up to six photos per page. Some page designs allow for text.

Picture Book
Positions photos as bleeds—the photos extend to the edges of the page. This theme provides no captions or titles.

Portfolio
Allows up to four photos per page and provides for captions and titles.

Story Book
Positions photos askew on the page and leaves room for storytelling.

Year Book
Allows for up to 32 photos per page—ideal for a class yearbook or a collection of police mug shots.

Designing a Book

You design a book one page at a time. iPhoto displays a thumbnail version of the current page; to zoom in on the thumbnail, use the size slider. You can edit the text on each page and choose a different design from the Page Design pop-up menu.

Each theme has a variety of page designs; choose a design here. Some designs place more photos on each page than others, and some have large text areas that can accommodate your prose.

Tips: To apply a page design to all subsequent pages in the book, press the Option key while choosing the design. And if you're working with low-resolution images, use a design that puts several images on a page. Each image will be smaller, and thus more likely to print with acceptable quality.

To work on a different page, select it. To move a page within the book, drag it left or right.

Note: Moving a page also changes the order of the photos in your album.

The Portfolio theme is my favorite; I like its contemporary, elegant look.

To hide the faint lines that iPhoto draws on-screen around title and comment boxes, uncheck this box. Either way, these lines will not print.

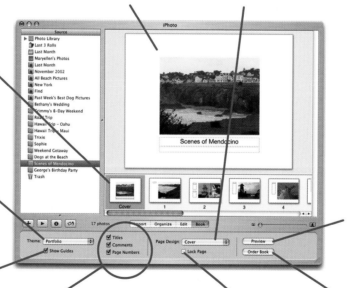

To preview the book, click Preview. You can also use the book preview window to edit captions.

You can include titles, comments, and page numbers in your book.

Tip: You can change the formatting of these items by selecting the text you want to change, and then using the Font command in the Edit menu.

When you change the number of photos on a page, iPhoto changes the placement of all photos on subsequent pages. To ensure that the photos on the page you're working on will remain on that page, click Lock Page.

When you're ready to order your book, click Order Book.

More Ways to Share Photos

By using the Export command in the File menu, you can turn a photo album—or any set of photos that you've selected—into a portable slide show.

iPhoto can combine a series of photos into a QuickTime movie, complete with a music soundtrack from your iTunes library. You can publish the resulting movie on a Web site, burn it to a CD, or bring it into iDVD and burn it to a DVD.

Looking for still more ways to share? Redecorate your Macintosh desktop with your favorite photo. Or, use a set of photos as a screen saver.

It's obvious: If your digital photos aren't getting seen, it isn't iPhoto's fault.

Exporting Photos as Movies

Why export still images in a movie format? Because iPhoto will add a music soundtrack and dissolve transitions between images. Think of an iPhoto QuickTime movie as a portable slide show. Email it, post it on a Web site, or burn it to a CD or DVD—it will play back on any Mac or Windows computer that has QuickTime installed.

Portable slide show: An iPhoto-created QuickTime movie playing back in the QuickTime Player program.

Note: In an iPhoto QuickTime movie, each image is always separated by a dissolve transition. You can't use the other transitions, such as cube, that iPhoto slide shows provide.

Step 1.

Select a set of images or switch to an album, then choose Export from the File menu.

Step 2.

To access movie-export options, click QuickTime.

Specify the duration for each image to display.

You can specify that iPhoto add a background color or background image to the movie. The color or image appears whenever the dimensions of the currently displayed photo don't match that of the movie itself. (For example, in a 640 by 480 movie, the background will be visible in photos shot in vertical orientation.) The background will also be visible at the beginning and end of the movie—before the first image fades in and after the last image fades out.

Specify the desired dimensions for the movie, in pixels. The preset values shown here work well, but if you specify smaller dimensions, such as 320 by 240, you'll get a smaller movie file—useful if you plan to distribute the movie over the Internet.

Export Photos

File Export | Web Page | QuickTime™

Images

Width: 640
Height: 480
Display image for 2.00 seconds

Background

◉ Color ▇
○ Image [   ] (Set...)

Music

☑ Add currently selected music to movie.

28 photos   (Cancel) (Export)

iPhoto uses the song or playlist assigned to your photo library or to the current album (see page 115). To create a silent movie, uncheck this box.

Step 3.

To create the movie, click Export and type a name for the movie.

Using Photos as Desktop Images and Screen Savers

The Organize pane's Desktop button lets you share photos with yourself. Select a photo and click Desktop, and iPhoto replaces the Mac's desktop with the photo you selected.

If you select multiple photos or an album, your desktop image will change as you work, complete with a cross-dissolve effect between images. It's an iPhoto slide show applied to your desktop.

Another way to turn an iPhoto album into a desktop screen saver is to use the Desktop & Screen Saver system preference—choose the album in the Screen Savers list (right).

Warning: Using vacation photos as desktop images has been proven to cause wanderlust.

Burning Photos to CDs and DVDs

The phrase "burning photos" can strike terror into any photographer's heart, but fear not: I'm not talking about open flames here. If your Mac has a CD or DVD burner, you can save, or burn, photos onto CDs or DVDs. You can burn your entire photo library, an album or two, just a few photos, or even just one.

iPhoto's burning features make possible all manner of photo-transportation tasks. Back up your photo library: burn the entire library and then stash the disc in a safe place. Move photos and albums from one Mac to another: burn a selection, then insert the disc in another Mac to work with them there. Or send a few high-resolution photos to a friend who has a slow modem connection: burn the photos and pop the disc into the mail.

iPhoto doesn't just copy photos to a disc. It creates a full-fledged iPhoto library on the disc. That library contains the images' titles and keywords, any albums that you burned, and even original versions of images you've retouched or cropped. Think of an iPhoto-burned disc as a portable iPhoto library.

iPhoto's burning features are compatible with any CD or DVD burner supported by Mac OS X. If you can burn with iTunes, you can burn with iPhoto, too. To burn to DVD discs in iPhoto, however, you must use Mac OS X version 10.2 (Jaguar) or a later version.

Now back away from that fire extinguisher—we've got some burning to do.

Burning Basics

Burning photos involves selecting what you want to burn, then clicking the Burn button a couple of times.

Step 1. Select photos.

Use the selection techniques discussed on page 103 to specify which photos to burn. Remember that you can also select multiple albums by Shift-clicking or ⌘-clicking on each one.

Step 2. Click the Burn button.

iPhoto asks you to insert a blank disc.

Step 3. Insert a blank disc and click OK.

iPhoto displays information about the pending burn in its information area. You can add or remove photos to or from the selection, and iPhoto will update its information area accordingly.

Tip: Give your disc a descriptive name by typing in the Name box.

Step 4. Click the Burn button again.

iPhoto displays another dialog box. To cancel the burn, click Cancel. To proceed, click Burn.

iPhoto prepares the images, then burns and verifies the contents of the disc.

Working with Burned Discs

When you insert a disc burned in iPhoto, the disc appears in iPhoto's photo library list. To see its photos, select the disc's name. Note that the disc's photos aren't in the iPhoto library on your hard drive— they're in the iPhoto library on the disc.

If the disc contains multiple albums, a small triangle appears next to the disc's name. To view the disc's albums, click the triangle.

You can display photos on a disc using the same techniques that you use to display photos stored in your iPhoto library. You can also order prints, display slide shows, create desktop images, and export images and QuickTime movies.

However, you can't crop, retouch, or otherwise edit photos stored on a CD or DVD. To edit a photo, add it to your library by dragging it to the Photo Library item or to an album.

Copying an Album from a Burned Disc

You've burned an album to disc, and now you want to copy the entire album to your hard drive (or someone else's) in order to work on the photos. Here's how.

Step 1. Select the album in the photo library list.

Step 2. Select all the photos in the album. (A quick way to do this: select one photo then press ⌘-A.)

Step 3. Drag the selected photos into a blank area of the photo album list. iPhoto creates a new album, which you'll probably want to rename, and adds the photos to it.

Burning CDs for Windows Computers

The burning feature in iPhoto creates a disc intended to be used by iPhoto. Among other things, that means that the disc contains a convoluted folder structure that can only be deciphered by iPhoto.

If you want to burn some photos for a friend who uses Windows— or to send to a photofinisher— you need to use a different procedure. You can also use these steps to burn a disc for a fellow Mac user who doesn't use iPhoto.

Step 1. Prepare a disc.
Insert a blank CD or DVD in your Mac's optical drive. The dialog box below appears.

Type a name for the CD and click OK. The blank disc's icon appears on your desktop.

Step 2. Copy the photos.
Position the iPhoto window so that you can see it and the blank disc's icon. Drag the photos that you want to burn to the icon of the blank disc.

As an alternative to dragging photos, you can also select them and use the File menu's

Export command to export copies to the blank disc. This approach gives you the option of resizing the photos and changing their file names.

Step 3. Burn. To burn the disc, drag its icon to the Burn Disc icon in your dock. (The Burn Disc icon replaces the Trash icon when you've selected a blank disc.) In the dialog box that appears next, click the Burn button.

Creating and Managing Photo Libraries

As your photo library grows to encompass thousands of photos, locating specific images can be cumbersome. A huge photo library is also more difficult to back up, since it may not fit on a CD or even a DVD.

The answer: more photo libraries. iPhoto lets you have multiple photo libraries and switch between them. If your photo library has reached gargantuan proportions, back it up and create a new, empty one.

How often should you create a new library? That depends. You might base your decision on disk space: if you back up your library by burning it to a CD-R, create a new library each time the size of your current library reaches about 650MB. That way, you can always be sure your library will fit on a CD. (To see how much space your library uses, select the Photo Library item, then look in the information area below the albums list.)

Or, you might prefer a chronological approach. If you take hundreds of photos every month (or more), consider creating a new library each month. Then again, maybe a subject-oriented approach is best for you. Use one iPhoto library to hold your family shots, and another to hold work-related shots.

You get the idea: by taking advantage of iPhoto's ability to work with multiple photo libraries, you make it easier to organize your photos—and to back them up.

Creating a New Library

Before creating a new library, you may want to back up your existing library by dragging your iPhoto Library folder to another hard drive or to a blank CD or DVD. For some backup strategies, see the sidebar on the opposite page.

Step 1. Quit iPhoto.

Step 2. Locate your iPhoto Library folder and rename it.

To quickly locate the folder, choose Home from the Finder's Go menu, then double-click the Pictures folder, where you'll find the iPhoto Library folder.

Step 3. Start iPhoto.

iPhoto asks if you want to locate an existing library or create a new one.

Step 4. Click Create Library.

iPhoto proposes the name iPhoto Library, but you can type a different name if you like.

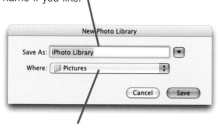

You don't need to store your library in the Pictures folder; see the sidebar below.

iPhoto creates the new, empty library.

Switching Between Libraries

There may be times when you want to switch to a different iPhoto library—for example, to access the photos in an older library. Here's how.

Step 1. Quit iPhoto.

Step 2. Locate your current iPhoto library folder and change its name.

Step 3. Start iPhoto.

iPhoto asks if you want to find an existing library or create a new one.

Step 4. Click Find Library. The Open Photo Library dialog box appears.

Step 5. Select the library you want to use and click the Open button.

Managing and Backing Up Your Library

Storing Photos Elsewhere

Normally, iPhoto stores your photo library in the Pictures folder. You might prefer to store your library elsewhere, such as on an external FireWire hard drive.

To store your photo library elsewhere, quit iPhoto, then simply move the iPhoto Library folder wherever you like. If you're copying the library to a different disk,

delete the original library folder after the copy is complete. Restart iPhoto, click the Find Library button, and use the Open Photo Library dialog box to aim iPhoto in the right direction.

Backing Up

In the film days, you had to fall victim to a fire or other disaster in order to lose all your photos. In the digital age, it's much easier to lose photos. All it

takes is a hardware failure or software glitch.

Please don't let photo loss happen to you. Take the time to back up your iPhoto libraries.

If your Mac contains a burner and your library will fit on a single blank disc, use iPhoto's burning features to back up.

If you don't have a burner or your library won't fit on a single disc, buy an external FireWire hard

drive and drag your iPhoto Library folder over to it. Repeat this procedure every now and then.

If you don't want to buy a hard drive, use backup software. Apple's own Backup, included with a .Mac membership, can copy photos to CDs, DVDs, or hard drives. Many other backup programs are available, including Dantz Development's powerful Retrospect and Econ Technologies' friendly ChronoSync.

Getting Old Photos into iPhoto

You love your digital camera and the convenience of iPhoto, and it would take an act of Congress to force you to use film again.

And yet the past haunts you. You have boxes of negatives and slides that you haven't seen in years. If you could get them into iPhoto, you could organize them into albums and share them through HomePage albums, slide shows, prints and books, and even movies and DVDs.

To bridge the gap between pixels and print, you need a scanner. Here's an overview of what to look for, and some strategies for getting those old photos into iPhoto.

Scanning the Options

Before you buy a scanner, take stock of what types of media you'll need to digitize. Do you have negatives, prints, slides, or all three? Not all scanners are ideal for every task.

Flatbed scanners. If you'll be scanning printed photos, a *flatbed scanner* is your best bet. Place a photo face down on the scanner's glass, and a sensor glides beneath it and captures the image.

Repeating this process for hundreds of photos can be tedious. If you have a closet full of photos, you may want to look for a scanner that supports an automatic document feeder so you can scan a stack of photos without having to hand-feed the scanner. Some of Hewlett-Packard's flatbeds include photo feeders that can handle up to 24 prints in sizes up to 4 by 6 inches. Other scanners accept optional document feeders. Just be sure to verify that the document feeder can handle photos—many can't.

Film scanners. A print is one generation away from the original image, and may have faded with time or been poorly printed to begin with. Worse, many photos are printed on linen-finish paper, whose rough texture blurs image detail when scanned. Bottom line: you'll get better results by scanning the original film.

Many flatbed scanners include a film adaptor for scanning negatives or slides. With some scanners, the adaptor snaps on to the scanner's bed. A more convenient option is a scanner with the adaptor built into the lid, such as Epson's Perfection 3170 Photo. The Perfection 3170 can scan negatives, mounted slides and, unlike many flatbeds, medium-format film, such as the 120 format popular in old cameras.

A flatbed scanner with a film adaptor is a versatile scanning system, but a *film scanner* provides much sharper scans of negatives and slides. Unfortunately, this quality will cost you: film scanners cost more than flatbeds.

Many film scanners provide a dust- and scratch-removal option called Digital ICE (short for *image correction/enhancement*). Developed by Applied Science Fiction (www.asf.com) and licensed to numerous scanner manufacturers, Digital ICE does an astonishingly good job of cleaning up color film. However, it doesn't work with black and white negatives.

Scanning Right

Whether you use a flatbed or film scanner, you'll encounter enough jargon to intimidate an astronaut: histograms, tone curves, black points, white points. Don't fret: all scanners include software that provides presets for common scanning scenarios, such as scanning for color ink-jet output. Start with these presets. As you learn about scanning, you can customize settings to optimize your exposures.

The right resolution. A critical scanning setting deals with how many dots per inch (dpi) the scanner uses to represent an image. Volumes have been written about scanning resolution, but it boils down to a simple rule of thumb: If you're using a flatbed scanner and you plan to print your scans on a photo inkjet printer, you can get fine results with a resolution of 180 to 240 dpi. If you plan to order photographic prints from your scans, scan at 300 dpi. Scanning at more than 300 dpi will usually not improve quality—but it will definitely use more disk space.

Film scanners are different. A film scanner scans a much smaller original— for example, a 35mm negative instead of a 4 by 6 inch print. To produce enough data for high-quality prints, a film scanner must scan at a much higher resolution than a flatbed. The film scanner I use, Minolta's Scan Elite 5400, scans at up to 5400 dpi.

This difference in approach can make for even more head scratching when it comes time to decide what resolution to use. Just do what I do: use the presets in the scanning software. I typically choose my film scanner's "PhotoCD 2048 by 3072" option, which yields a file roughly equivalent to a six-megapixel image.

Special circumstances. If you plan to apply iMovie's Ken Burns effect to an image, you'll want a high-resolution scan so you can zoom in without encountering jagged pixels. Experiment to find the best resolution for a specific image and zoom setting.

In a related vein, if you plan to crop out unwanted portions of an image, scan at a higher resolution than you might normally use. Cropping discards pixels, so the more data you have to begin with, the more cropping flexibility you have.

Format strategies. Which file format should you use for saving images? iPhoto works best with JPEG images, but the JPEG format is *lossy:* it sacrifices quality slightly in order to save disk space. If this is the last time you plan to scan those old photos, you may not want to save them in a lossy format.

When scanning my old slides and negatives, I save the images as TIFF files. Then, I use Photoshop Elements' Batch Processing command to save a second set of photos in JPEG format. This gives me JPEGs that I can use in iPhoto, while my original, uncompressed scans are safely archived.

(If you don't have Photoshop Elements, you can perform this automation chore using a utility such as Yellow Mug Software's EasyBatchPhoto, available at www.yellowmug.com.)

Photos, Meet iPhoto

Once you've scanned and saved your photos, you can import them into iPhoto.

Filing photos. To take advantage of iPhoto's filing features, you may want to have a separate iPhoto roll for each set of related photos. In the Finder, move each set of related photos into its own folder, giving each folder a descriptive name, such as *Vacation 1972*. Next, drag each folder into the iPhoto window.

iPhoto gives each roll the same name as its corresponding folder.

You can delete the folders after you've imported their shots, since iPhoto will have created duplicates in its iPhoto Library folder.

Turn back the clock. To make your iPhoto library chronologically accurate, change the date of each roll to reflect when its shots were taken, not when you imported them. First, click on the roll's name (if you can't see it, choose Rolls from the View menu). Next, type the desired date in the Date box near the lower-left corner of the iPhoto window. Press the Return key after typing the date, and iPhoto immediately sorts the roll into the proper position.

Beware of black and white. It'd be fun to assemble black and white photos into an iPhoto book, but according to Apple, black and white photos print poorly because of the process used to print iPhoto books. You can, however, order prints from black and white shots.

Time for retouching. You can use iPhoto's Retouch tool to fix scratches and dust specks, and its Enhance button to fix color and exposure problems. For serious retouching, though, use Photoshop Elements or Photoshop. To learn more about digital retouching, I recommend Katrin Eisman's *Photoshop Restoration and Retouching* (New Riders, 2003).

iPhoto Tips

Dealing with Duplicates

Here's a common scenario: you use iPhoto to import some photos from your camera, and you don't delete the photos from the camera after importing. Then, you shoot another dozen or so photos and prepare to import them. iPhoto is smart enough to know that you've already imported some of the photos, and it will ask you if you want to skip those duplicates.

The photo about to be imported appears here.

The photo already in your library appears here.

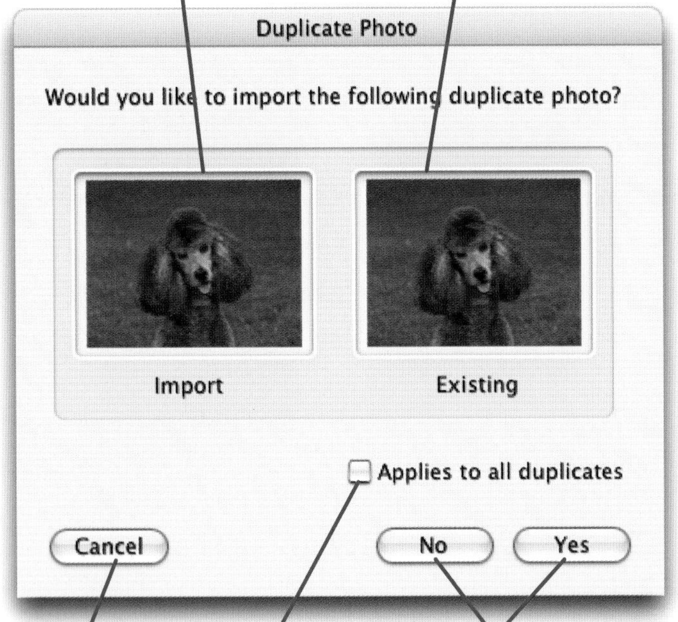

Duplicate Photo

Would you like to import the following duplicate photo?

Import

Existing

Applies to all duplicates

Cancel   No   Yes

Cancel the entire import session.

To have iPhoto apply your "no" or "yes" choice to all duplicates it finds, check this box. Your choice here applies to the current importing session only.

To import the duplicate anyway, click Yes. To skip this photo (that is, to not import it), click No.

AppleScripts for iPhoto

Like iTunes and iDVD, iPhoto supports the AppleScript automation technology that is part of Mac OS X. A large collection of iPhoto scripts is available, and some of the best come from Apple. You can download scripts that simplify the process of assigning keywords to photos, scripts that automate iPhoto and Photoshop, and much more. For links to my favorite iPhoto scripts, visit this book's companion Web site.

Controlling the Camera Connection

You can use the Image Capture program, included with Mac OS X, to control what happens when you connect a digital camera to your Mac. By choosing the Preferences command from the Image Capture menu, you can have the Mac start up iPhoto, start up Image Capture or a different program, or do nothing at all.

Get links to iPhoto add-ons and
additional online photo services.
www.macilife.com/iphoto

Importing Only Some Images

Speaking of Image Capture, it's the program to use when you want to import only some photos from a camera. Say you've shot twenty photos but you know only five of them are going to be keepers. Rather than import all twenty into iPhoto and then delete fifteen of them, use Image Capture.

After connecting your camera and turning it on, start up Image Capture and click its Download Some button. A window appears containing thumbnail versions of each photo.

Next, you need to tell Image Capture where to store the downloaded photos. I like to store them in a temporary folder

that I create on my desktop. From the Download Folder pop-up menu in Image Capture's toolbar, choose Other. Press ⌘-D to jump to your desktop and then click the New Folder button. Name the folder anything you like—I use the name *Import Me.* Then click the Open button.

Finally, click the Download button to download the photos you selected. Quit Image Capture, drag those photos into your iPhoto window, and delete the temporary folder.

Yes, it's a bit of work, but it's a good technique to use if your camera contains dozens of images and you know you'll only be keeping a small selection of them.

Use the Download Folder pop-up menu to specify where you want downloaded items to be stored.

Select the photos you want to download, remembering to Shift-click and ⌘-click to select multiple photos.

Many digital cameras can also take short movies; you can use Image Capture to download them.

The Options dialog box contains some useful features, including the ability to set your camera's built-in clock to match your Mac's.

Another way to be selective. Many cameras *mount* on the Mac's desktop as though they were storage devices (which, in a way, they are). If your camera does, you have another way to selectively import photos into iPhoto.

To determine if your camera mounts on the desktop, turn the camera on and connect it. Switch to the Finder and see if a new icon appears on your desktop and in the sidebar area of the Finder's windows. If it does, you can examine the photos on its memory card. Double-click the camera's icon, then double-click the folder named DCIM. Inside *that* folder are one or more folders containing your photos. To preview them, double-click their icons. To copy a photo into iPhoto, drag its icon from the Finder into the iPhoto window.

When your memory card contains many images but you want to copy only a few of them, this method can be faster than the Image Capture technique.

You can even use the Finder to help you determine which images to bring in: choose Show View Options from the Finder's View menu, and check the Show Icon Preview box. Now enlarge the preview icons by dragging the slider at the top of the View Options window.

And by the way, *all* memory readers mount on the desktop, so even if your camera doesn't, you can still use this technique: just pop your memory card into a reader.

More iPhoto Tips

Sharing Your Camera on a Network

When you use the sharing features in iTunes and iPhoto, you're using a Mac OS X networking technology called *Rendezvous*. Rendezvous lets devices on a network work together without you having to fuss with networking settings.

In Mac OS X 10.3 (Panther), the humble Image Capture program also supports Rendezvous, and you can use it to share your camera on a network—or even on the Internet. These may not be the most practical tasks in the world, but they're fun geek experiments.

To share your camera, connect it to your Mac and turn it on. If iPhoto starts, either hide it or quit it—you won't be using it for this game.

Next, start Image Capture and choose Preferences from the Image Capture menu. Click the Sharing button, then check the Share My Devices box and the box next to your camera's name.

To also share the camera on the Internet, check the Enable Web-Sharing box. Jot down the address that appears below this box, or select it and copy it to the Clipboard—you'll need it later.

Now you can access your camera from another Mac on your network. Start its copy of Image Capture, choose the Preferences command, and check the Look for Shared Devices box.

Next, choose Browse Shared Devices from the Devices menu. Click the triangle next to your camera's name, click the check box, then click OK. An Image Capture window appears—now you can copy images from the camera, just as if it was connected directly to your Mac.

It gets better. Fire up Apple's Safari Web browser and choose its Preferences command. Click the Bookmarks button in the Preferences dialog box, and in the Bookmarks Bar area, check the Include Rendezvous box.

Now click on the Rendezvous pop-up in the bookmarks bar, and choose the item that begins *Digital Cameras on.* In a few moments, your browser window displays the contents of the camera along with buttons for downloading and deleting pictures.

With some cameras, you can even take a picture by remote control: click the Take Picture button in the browser window. Finally, you have a way to see what the dog does when you leave the house.

For the ultimate geek exercise, have your friends in a distant city access your camera over the Internet. (Assuming you both have broadband connections—modems won't do.) Send them the address you jotted down when you turned on Web sharing. Now they'll able to browse your camera's memory card and take pictures, too, at least until your camera's battery dies or you decide to switch it off.

Note that some cable and DSL Internet providers supply combined modem/routers that may require reconfiguration for this trick to work. Specifically, you or your provider may need to configure port 5100 to forward its traffic to the host computer.

See the Batch Change command in action.
Using the Batch Change Command

Including Photos in Documents

You may want to include photos in documents that you're creating in Microsoft Word or other programs. It's easy: just drag the image from iPhoto into your document.

If you drag an image to the Finder desktop or to a folder window, iPhoto makes a duplicate copy of the image file. Use this technique when you want to copy a photo out of your library.

To Experiment, Duplicate

You have a photo that appears in multiple albums, but you want to edit its appearance in just one album, leaving the original version unchanged in other albums.

Time for the Duplicate command: select the photo and choose Duplicate from the Photos menu (⌘-D). Now edit the duplicate.

From Import to Album

If you have photos on your Finder desktop—whether on your hard drive, a Picture CD, or a digital camera's memory card—you can import them and create an album in one fell swoop. Simply drag the photos from the Finder into a blank area of the Source list. iPhoto imports the photos, storing them in their own roll. iPhoto also creates an album and add the photos to it.

Duplicating an Album

There may be times when you'll want several versions of an album. For example, you might have one version with photos sequenced for a slide show and another version with photos organized for a book. Or you might simply want to experiment with several different photo arrangements until you find the one you like best.

iPhoto makes this kind of experimentation easy. Simply duplicate an album by selecting its name and choosing Duplicate from the Photos menu (⌘-D). iPhoto makes a duplicate of the album, which you can rename and experiment with.

You can make as many duplicates of an album as you like. You can even duplicate a smart album—perhaps as a prelude to experimenting with different search criteria.

Stay Out of the Library

I've mentioned it before, but it bears repeating: *never* add files to or remove them from the folders inside the iPhoto Library folder. Indeed, I recommend that you don't even venture inside this folder. Renaming, moving, or otherwise modifying files inside your iPhoto Library folder is a great way to lose photos. Let iPhoto manage the library for you—add and remove photos only by dragging them into and out of the iPhoto window.

Batch Changing

With the Batch Change command in the Photos menu, you can change the title, date, or comments for an entire set of photos at once.

Select the photos, then choose Batch Change. Use the pop-up menu to choose the tidbit of information you want to change. If you're changing the date, it's a good idea to add an interval between each photo. This helps iPhoto sort the photos.

If you're like me and you're too lazy to assign titles and comments to individual photos, the Batch Change command is a good compromise: assign a phrase to a set of related photos, and you can search for that phrase when creating smart albums.

Mastering Your Digital Camera

Resolution Matters

Always shoot at your camera's highest resolution. This gives you maximum flexibility for cropping, for making big prints, and for iMovie's Ken Burns effect. You can always use iPhoto to make photos smaller (for example, for emailing or Web publishing).

Shutter Lag

Many digital cameras suffer from a curse called *shutter lag*—a delay between the time you press the shutter button and the moment when the shutter actually fires.

Shutter lag occurs because the camera's built-in computer must calculate exposure and focus. If you're shooting fast-moving subjects, it's easy to miss the shot you wanted.

The solution: give your camera a head start. Press and hold the shutter button partway, and the camera calculates focus

and exposure. Now wait until the right moment arrives, then press the button the rest of the way.

ISO Speeds

In the film world, if you want to take low-light shots, you can buy high-speed film—ISO 400 or 800, for example. Fast film allows you to take nighttime or indoor shots without the harsh glare of electronic flash.

Digital cameras allow you to adjust light sensitivity on a shot-by-shot basis. Switch the camera into one of its manual-exposure modes (a common mode is labeled *P*, for *program*), and then use the camera's menus to adjust its ISO speed.

Note that shots photographed at higher ISO speeds—particularly 400 and 800—are likely to have digital *noise*, a slightly grainy appearance. For me, it's a happy trade-off: I'd rather have a sharp, naturally lit photo with some noise than a noise-free but blurry (or flash-lit) photo.

Higher ISO speeds can also help you capture fast-moving action by day. The higher speed forces the camera to use a faster shutter speed, thereby minimizing blur. That shot on this page of Mimi leaping into the air? Shot at ISO 400.

White Balance

Few light sources are pure white; they have a color cast of some kind. Incandescent lamps (light bulbs) cast a yellowish light, while fluorescent light is greenish. Even outdoors, there can be light-source variations—bluish in the morning, reddish in the evening. Each of these light sources has a different *color temperature.*

Our eyes and brains compensate for these variances. Digital cameras try to do so with a feature called *automatic white balance*, but they aren't as good at it. That's why many cameras have manual white balance adjustments that essentially let you tell the camera, "Hey, I'm shooting under incandescent (or fluorescent) lights now, so make some adjustments in how you record color."

White balance adjustments are usually labeled WB, often with icons representing cloudy skies ☁, incandescent lamps ☀, and fluorescent lighting ☵. You'll probably have to switch to your camera's manual-exposure mode to access its white balance settings.

Sharpness and Color Settings

Digital cameras do more than simply capture a scene. They also manipulate the image they capture by applying sharpening and color correction (including white balance adjustments).

Some photographers don't like the idea of their cameras making manipulations like these. If you're in this group, consider exploring your camera's menus and tweaking any color and sharpness settings you find.

For example, one of my cameras—Sony's 8-megapixel F828—has two color modes: "standard" and "real." The "standard" mode is the default mode, and it punches up the color in a way that I find artificial. One of the first things I did when I got this lovely machine was to switch its color mode to "real."

Another of my cameras (I collect them, or so it sometimes seems) is Canon's 5-megapixel S50. It has several sharpening modes, and the default mode is too sharp for my tastes. I took its sharpening mode down a couple of notches. If I feel that an image needs a bit of sharpening, I'll bring it into Photoshop and sharpen it there.

Going RAW

Many advanced digital photographers are embracing the *Camera RAW* format, which is supported by a growing number of mid-range and high-end cameras. RAW images contain the exact data captured by the camera's CCD—without performing any in-camera color or sharpness adjustments. A RAW image isn't necessarily *superior* to a JPEG. It's simply more malleable—you can alter its appearance with much more flexibility. With JPEG or TIFF files, the camera has already manipulated the original CCD data—there's no turning back.

But working with RAW *greatly* complicates your workflow, especially with iPhoto in the mix. iPhoto doesn't support RAW. So you must import your photos using other means (such as a media reader), process them in Photoshop or elsewhere, save them as Photoshop files, export them as JPEGs, and then bring those JPEGs into iPhoto to order books, prints, make slide shows, and the like. Whew.

For many digital camera users, RAW offers no great advantage. Today's cameras do a better job of image enhancement than an inexperienced user could do with RAW post-processing in Photoshop. Still, there's an appeal to having access to *exactly* what the CCD originally captured, especially for photographers who know their way around Photoshop.

If you aren't ready to go RAW, go partway: master your camera's manual exposure modes and white balance settings, and tweak any settings relating to color vividness and sharpening to take them down a notch or two.

Learning More

To learn more about digital photography and Photoshop, I heartily recommend *Real World Digital Photography* by Katrin Eisman, Seán Duggan, and Tim Grey (Peachpit Press, 2004).

And if you like to learn by watching, I humbly recommend a few instructional DVDs that I helped to produce: *Making Your Photos Look Great with Photoshop Elements* and *Secrets of the Photoshop Masters, Volumes I and II*. You can order them online at www.avondalemedia.com.

Tips for Better Digital Photography

Get Up Close

Too many photographers shy away from their subjects. Get close to show detail. If you can't get physically closer, use your camera's zoom feature, if it has one. If your camera has a macro feature, use it to take extreme close-ups of flowers, rocks, seashells, tattoos—you name it. Don't limit yourself to wide shots.

Vary Your Angle

Don't just shoot from a standing position. Get down into a crouch and shoot low— or get up on a chair and shoot down. Vary your angles. The LCD screen on a digital camera makes it easy—you don't press your eye to the camera to compose a shot.

Changing your angle can be a great way to remove a cluttered background. When photographing flowers, for example, I like to position the camera low and aim it upwards, so that the flower is shot against the sky.

Avoid Digital Zooming

Many digital cameras supplement their optical zoom lenses with digital zoom functions that bring your subject even closer. Think twice about using digital zoom—it usually adds undesirable artifacts to an image.

Position the Horizon

In landscape shots, the position of the horizon influences the mood of the photo. To imply a vast, wide open space, put the horizon along the lower third of the frame and show lots of sky. (This obviously works best when the sky is cooperating.) To imply a sense of closeness— or if the sky is a bland shade of gray— put the horizon along the upper third, showing little sky.

This rule, like others, is meant to be broken. For example, if you're shooting a forlorn-looking desert landscape, you might want to have the horizon bisect the image to imply a sense of bleak monotony.

Crop Carefully

You can often use iPhoto's cropping tool to fix composition problems. But note that cropping results in lost pixels, and that may affect your ability to produce high-quality prints. Try to do your cropping in the camera's viewfinder, not iPhoto.

Kill Your Flash

I turn off my camera's built-in flash and rarely turn it on. Existing light provides a much more flattering, natural-looking image, with none of the harshness of electronic flash. Dimly lit indoor shots may have a slight blur to them, but I'll take blur over the radioactive look of flash any day.

Beware of the Background

More accurately, *be aware* of the background. Is a tree growing out of Mary's head? If so, move yourself or Mary. Are there distracting details in the background? Find a simpler setting or get up close. Is your shadow visible in the shot? Change your position. When looking at a scene, our brains tend to ignore irrelevant things. But the camera sees all. As you compose, look at the entire frame, not just your subject.

Embrace Blur

A blurred photo is a ruined photo, right? Not necessarily. Blur conveys motion, something still images don't usually do. A photo with a sharp background but a car that is blurred tells you the car was in motion. To take this kind of shot, keep the camera steady and snap the shutter at the moment the car crosses the frame.

You can also convey motion by turning this formula around: If you pan along with the moving car as you snap, the car will be sharp but the background will be blurred.

Indoor shots taken without a flash will often have some motion blur to them, too, since the camera will have to take a longer exposure. I'd rather see a somewhat blurry shot of dancing partygoers than a tack-sharp, harshly lit one.

Compose Carefully

Following a couple of rules of thumb can help you compose photos that are more visually pleasing.

First, there's the age-old *rule of thirds*, in which you divide the image rectangle into thirds and place your photo's subject at or near one of the intersections of the resulting grid.

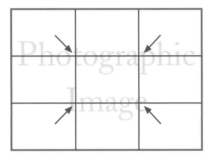

Place your photo's subject at or near these intersections.

This composition technique yields images that are more visually dynamic.

A second technique is to draw the viewer's eyes to your subject and add a sense of dynamism by using diagonal lines, such as a receding fence.

No Tripod?

If you want to take sharp photos in low light, mount your camera on a tripod. If you don't have a tripod handy, here's a workaround: turn on your camera's self-timer mode—the mode you'd usually use when you want to get yourself in the picture—then set the camera on a rigid surface and press the shutter button. Because you won't be holding the camera when the shutter goes off, you won't risk getting a blurred shot.

iMovie:
Editing Video

The Macintosh
iLife '04

iMovie at a Glance

Video can be a powerful vehicle for communicating an idea, setting a mood, selling a product, or recalling a memory. It can also be great way to put people to sleep.

Video editing is the process of assembling video clips, still images, and audio into a finished package that gets your message across and keeps your audience's eyes open. Video editing is what iMovie is all about.

With iMovie, you can import video from a miniDV camcorder connected via FireWire. iMovie controls your camcorder during the importing process, stashing incoming clips on its Clips pane.

Then, you edit clips and sequence them by dragging them to the timeline, optionally adding music from your CD collection or iTunes music library and creating titles, effects, and scene transitions. When you're finished, a few mouse clicks send your efforts back out to tape or to iDVD.

You can use iMovie to edit interminable home movies, but you can also use it to assemble montages of photos from iPhoto, promotional videos, and anything else that belongs on the small screen.

Quiet on the set.

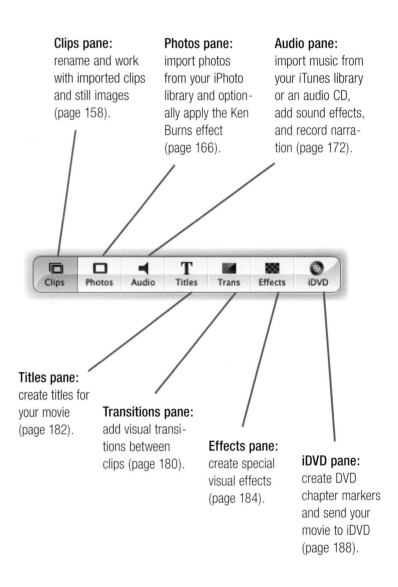

Clips pane: rename and work with imported clips and still images (page 158).

Photos pane: import photos from your iPhoto library and optionally apply the Ken Burns effect (page 166).

Audio pane: import music from your iTunes library or an audio CD, add sound effects, and record narration (page 172).

Titles pane: create titles for your movie (page 182).

Transitions pane: add visual transitions between clips (page 180).

Effects pane: create special visual effects (page 184).

iDVD pane: create DVD chapter markers and send your movie to iDVD (page 188).

See the movie-making process from start to finish.
iMovie: Making Movies

GO TO DVD

The monitor displays video as you import it or play it back.

Switch between the clip viewer and the timeline viewer (page 161).

The scrubber bar lets you move through and crop a clip (page 158).

Rewind, start and stop playback, and play back in full-screen mode.

Adjust the speaker's volume as you work in iMovie.

Video clips and still images that you import are stored in the Clips pane until you add them to the timeline.

The playhead indicates the current playback location. Drag it left and right to quickly move backward and forward within your movie or within a single clip.

These buttons switch between iMovie's panes, each of which lets you work with a different kind of element.

Create bookmarks to aid in editing and trimming clips (page 162).

You can sequence clips by dragging them from the Clips pane to the timeline (page 160).

Display a track's audio waveform to be able to see changes in the audio (page 178).

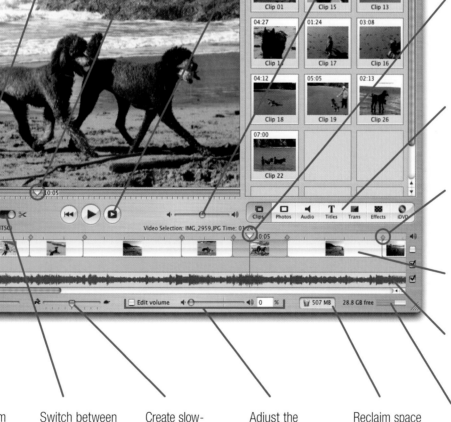

Drag the zoom slider to zoom in and out on the timeline.

Switch between camera mode (to import video) and edit mode (page 156).

Create slow- and fast-motion effects (page 185).

Adjust the audio levels of individual clips (page 176).

Reclaim space by emptying the iMovie trash now and then (page 159).

iMovie displays remaining free disk space here.

The Essentials of Movie Making

Editing video is one of the most complex tasks you will perform in iLife. Not that it's technically difficult—iMovie, FireWire, and the miniDV video format have made it easier than ever.

But editing video can be time consuming and labor intensive. Bringing media into iMovie, fine-tuning the length of clips, timing shots to match a music track, adding transitions and effects—it all takes time. But as a creative exercise, video editing is hard to beat.

If you're new to video editing, start small. Create a short movie—between 30 and 90 seconds. Try your hand at a simple music video, like the one I create on the DVD: some video, some still photos from iPhoto, and a music soundtrack from iTunes. Your first effort shouldn't be an epic; it should be a short story, or even a single well-wrought paragraph. That's the best way to learn the art and science of editing—and to appreciate its magic.

Video Editing: The Big Picture

Import Assets

Bring in video from a camcorder and, optionally, add photos and music from iTunes or from a compact disc.

Trim the Fat

Use iMovie's crop markers and Crop command to discard unwanted portions of clips.

Sequence Clips

Drag clips to the timeline viewer and clip viewer to add them to your final movie. Trim clips as needed to fine-tune their length.

Add Eye Candy

Create transitions between clips, and add titles and any special effects.

Polish

If you've added music or other audio tracks, you'll want to fine-tune audio levels for each track.

Export

Record your movie back to tape, send it to iDVD, or export it as a QuickTime movie to publish on a Web site.

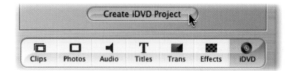

A Short Glossary of Video Terms

aspect ratio The relationship of height to width in an image. A TV image has an aspect ratio of 4:3—four units of width for each three units of height.

clip A piece of video footage or a still image. A finished movie generally contains multiple clips, sequenced on the timeline.

FireWire The high-speed interface used to connect video gear, such as a miniDV camcorder, to the Mac. Also used for other devices, including hard drives and, of course, the iPod.

frame A single still image in a movie clip, and the smallest unit of a movie clip you can work with. One second of video contains 30 frames.

miniDV Often abbreviated DV, a video format that stores high-quality video and stereo audio on a tiny cassette. The miniDV format has been a major factor in the digital video revolution.

In a DV camcorder, circuitry converts video and audio into digital data, which is recorded on the tape. When you import or export DV video, you're simply transferring bits across a FireWire cable. By contrast, older video formats, such as VHS and Hi-8, store audio and video in analog form.

playhead iMovie's equivalent to the blinking cursor in a word processor. As a clip plays back, the playhead moves to show where you are in relation to the entire movie or video clip.

rendering The process of creating frames for a transition, title, or effect.

transition A special effect that acts as a segue between two clips.

track An independent stream of audio or video. iMovie lets you have one video track and two separate audio tracks.

Importing Video

In video production, *assets* are the building blocks that you assemble into a finished product. The type of asset you work with most is usually video—clips from a DV camcorder. But you may also work with photos from your iPhoto library, music from your iTunes library, narration that you record, and audio files extracted from compact discs.

Because a finished movie can comprise a large number of assets, it's a good idea to store them all in one folder. This makes it easier to back up your project and copy it to other drives.

iMovie helps you in this regard: When you create a new movie project, iMovie creates a folder and gives it the name of your movie.

Inside your project's folder is another folder called Media; this is where iMovie stores imported video clips, as well as other files it creates as you work. Don't move or rename any files within the Media folder; if you do, iMovie may not be able to open your project correctly. As a general rule, you shouldn't put any files in the Media folder yourself—let iMovie manage this folder.

Digital video requires about 200MB of disk space per minute, so be sure you have plenty of free hard drive space before importing. You might want to buy an external hard drive and use it for your video endeavors.

Importing Video

Connect your DV camcorder to your Mac's FireWire jack.

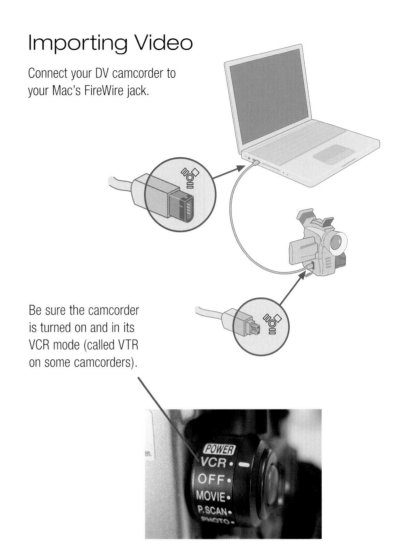

Be sure the camcorder is turned on and in its VCR mode (called VTR on some camcorders).

Tip: To store imported video on an external hard drive, simply create your project on the external drive. If you've already started the project and it's on your internal drive, quit iMovie, copy the project to the external drive, then open that copy.

See the process of importing assets.
⊚ **Importing a Music Track**
⊚ **Importing Photos**

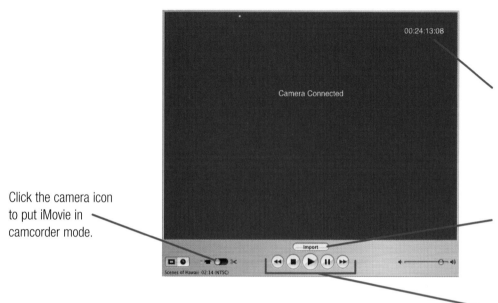

Click the camera icon to put iMovie in camcorder mode.

iMovie displays the time code that your camera recorded on the tape. This can help you keep track of where you are on a tape as you fast-forward or rewind.

To start and stop importing, click Import or press the spacebar while the tape is playing back.

When iMovie is in camcorder mode, the playback buttons control your camcorder.

iMovie displays each clip you import on the Clips pane.

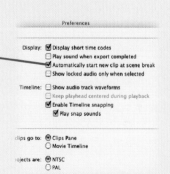

Using iMovie's Scene-Detection Feature

To make your imported video easy to work with, use iMovie's scene-detection feature, which causes iMovie to begin a new clip each time it detects a scene break. (Your camcorder generates a scene break automatically each time you press its Record button.)

To turn on scene detection, choose Preferences from the iMovie menu, and click the check box labeled Automatically Start New Clip at Scene Break.

If you don't use scene detection, iMovie still divides your video into separate clips as you import. iMovie can't create a file larger than 2GB, so it starts a new clip after every nine minutes or so. Locating a specific scene in a nine-minute clip is tedious—use scene detection instead.

Working with Clips

After you import video and other assets, the real work (and fun) of building your movie begins.

All building projects require advance preparation, and video editing is no exception. You might begin by renaming your clips to give them descriptive names. You don't have to rename clips, but doing so can make them easier to sort out and manage.

Next, you might crop a clip to remove footage you don't want. iMovie defines cropping differently than imaging programs, such as iPhoto. When you crop a clip in iMovie, you change its length, not its dimensions—you remove seconds or minutes, not pixels. After cropping a clip, you might add it to the movie by dragging it to the timeline at the bottom of the screen.

As you perform these tasks, you'll often work with iMovie's playhead, moving it to the start of a clip, or dragging it back and forth—a process called *scrubbing*—to find the portion you want to retain.

Naming and cropping—these are the chores that prepare clips for their screen debut. And that debut occurs when you drag the clips to the timeline.

Rename Your Clips

iMovie automatically names imported clips, giving them names, such as Clip 01 and Clip 02, that aren't exactly descriptive. Give your clips descriptive titles, such as Bird Close-up or Beach Long Shot, to help you identify them. To rename a clip in the Clips pane, simply click its name and type a new name. Or, double-click on a clip and type a new name in the Clip Info dialog box. You can also rename clips in the clip viewer (described on page 161).

Cropping Clips

Any clip you import may have extraneous junk at its beginning and end. By cropping the clip to remove this excess, you'll make a better movie and will reclaim disk space as a bonus.

If you're planning to add a transition before or after a clip, make the clip a bit longer than you otherwise would.

Step 1. Select the clip you want to crop. You can also crop a clip that you've already added to the timeline.

Step 2. Click in the dashed ruler area beneath the monitor, then drag the triangular crop markers left and right to mark the footage you want to keep. To review your selection, drag the playhead left and right.

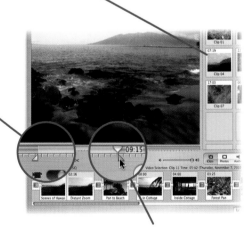

Step 3. To perform the crop, choose Crop from the Edit menu (or press ⌘-K).

As you adjust the crop markers, iMovie tells you how long the cropped clip will be.

Controlling What Plays Back

You already know that clicking the play button or pressing the spacebar begins playback. You may have noticed that *what* iMovie plays back depends on what is selected.

You can choose to play just one item—a clip, a title, a transition, and so on—by selecting that item, then clicking on the play button or hitting the spacebar. This can be a handy way to check out a title or transition you've just added. Along the same lines, to play back a portion of your project, select those items by Shift-clicking, then start playback.

To play an entire project, press your keyboard's Home key to move the playhead to the beginning of the movie, and then begin playback.

Emptying the Trash

When you crop a clip, iMovie puts its discarded portion in the Trash—not the same Trash the Finder provides for discarding unwanted files, but a separate, iMovie-specific Trash. Reclaim disk space by emptying iMovie's Trash as you work (choose Empty Trash from the File menu). But if you've done a lot of cropping, emptying the Trash can take a few minutes, so wait until you're ready to take a break. And note that once you empty iMovie's Trash, you can't reclaim footage that you've cropped out.

Reclaiming the Past

You're working on your movie and realize that a shot you cropped really needs to be longer after all. If you haven't emptied the Trash, you can restore the cropped footage. Select the clip, then choose Restore Clip from the Advanced menu.

The Keys to Precision

To fine-tune a crop marker's position, select the crop marker and press the keyboard's left and right arrow keys to move the marker in one-frame increments. To move in 10-frame increments, press Shift along with the arrow key. These keyboard controls work throughout iMovie.

Trimming Clips (and the Pros and Cons of Jump Cuts)

Trimming is the opposite of cropping. When you crop, you use the crop markers to indicate which portion of a clip you want to keep. When you trim, you use the crop markers to indicate what you want to delete. Drag the crop markers left and right to mark the footage that you want to toss to the cutting room floor. Then, press your keyboard's Delete key or choose Clear from the Edit menu.

It's best to use trimming to remove footage from the very beginning or very end of a clip. If you delete footage from the middle of a video clip, you'll end up with an awkward, visually jarring jump in the action. This kind of sloppy splice is called a *jump cut,* and it's usually a sign of shoddy movie-making.

Then again, one director's flaw might be another's effect. Jump cuts are common special effects in music videos and other "arty" productions.

To avoid a jump cut, put a cutaway or reaction shot at the point where the jump cut would be (see page 164). If you don't have a cutaway or reaction shot, put a three- to five-frame cross-dissolve transition at the jump cut point. This is called a *soft cut,* and it's common in documentaries and newscasts.

There's one more way to trim clips: the direct-trimming feature that debuted in iMovie 4. Direct trimming is a great way to fine-tune clips that you've already added to the timeline (see page 162).

Timeline Techniques: Adding Clips to a Movie

A clip in the Clips pane is like a baseball player on the bench. To put the clip on the playing field, you must add it to the timeline.

Select the clip, then drag it to the timeline.

Tip: Want to insert a clip between two clips that are already on the timeline? Just drag the clip between them, and the two existing clips separate to make room for the addition. (If a transition is between the two clips, you need to delete it first; see page 181.)

Other Ways to Add Clips

Usually, you work with one clip at a time, dragging it to the timeline after you've cropped it as described on the previous pages.

But there's more than one way to work with clips.

Drag several at once. You can add multiple clips to the timeline at once. Select each clip by Shift-clicking on it, then drag the clips to the timeline as a group. You can also select multiple clips by dragging a selection rectangle around them; click the narrow gray border between clips to begin drawing the selection.

Paste from the Clipboard. You can also add a clip to the timeline using the Paste command. Select a clip in the Clips pane—or a clip that's already in the timeline—and cut or copy, then paste. If the playhead is at the end of the timeline, that's where the pasted clip appears. If you select a clip that's already in the timeline before you paste, the pasted clip appears immediately to the right of that clip.

Timeline Versus Clip: Which Viewer to Use?

You can view your project's march of time in either of two ways: using the timeline viewer or the clip viewer. Each viewer has its strengths, and you're likely to switch between them frequently as you work on a movie. To switch between views, click the clip viewer button or the timeline viewer button, or press ⌘-E.

The Clip Viewer: Basic Sequencing

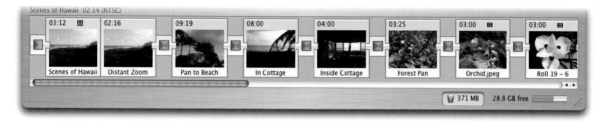

The clip viewer shows large thumbnail versions of each clip. In this viewer, you can change the order of clips by dragging them left and right. You can also rename clips here. However, this viewer does not show audio tracks or provide audio controls. The clip viewer is ideal when you're first assembling a movie or you want to experiment with different clip sequences. When it's time for audio fine-tuning and other precise work, switch to the timeline viewer.

The Timeline Viewer: Audio, Trimming, and More

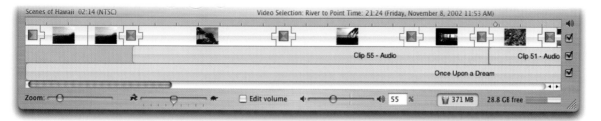

The timeline viewer adds two audio tracks and controls for adjusting audio levels and creating slow- or fast-motion effects. You can't drag to change the order of clips in this view. Use the timeline viewer to work with sound, trim clips directly, and speed up or slow down video. To swap the order of clips around, switch to the clip viewer.

Advanced Timeline Techniques

In a well-edited video, the cuts between scenes occur at exactly the right moments. In movies, the action cuts between two actors as they converse, enforcing both the dialog and the drama. Every moviegoer has experienced this, probably without even thinking about it.

In music videos, scenes change in rhythm with a piece of music, turning the visuals and the soundtrack into a unified performance. Every MTV viewer has seen this, probably without even thinking about anything at all. (I'm kidding, kids—music videos are among the most tightly edited productions on the planet.)

Where precise editing is concerned, iMovie was always a bit of a blunt instrument. You could crop and trim clips with single-frame accuracy, but precisely positioning them on the timeline was cumbersome. And timing cuts to a piece of music was like trying to fix a Swiss watch with a jackhammer.

In iMovie 4, several features work together to make the timeline viewer more precise. You can set *bookmarks*, visual guideposts that aid in trimming and positioning clips. You can trim clips directly in the timeline, much as you can in high-end programs, such as Apple's Final Cut Pro. And *timeline snapping* makes it easy to move clips to the desired location as you drag them to and within the timeline viewer.

To see these features in action, watch the iMovie segment of the DVD. Then try them out for yourself.

Setting Bookmarks

A bookmark is a virtual Post-It note that you can tack onto the timeline. Want to go back and refine a section later? Set a bookmark so you don't lose your place. Want to time edits to music? Create bookmarks at each beat, measure, or other musical milestone.

To create a bookmark, position the playhead where you want the bookmark to be, then choose Add Bookmark from the Bookmarks menu or press ⌘-B. A bookmark appears as a small green diamond on the timeline.

Tips: You can set a bookmark while your movie is playing. The ⌘-B keyboard shortcut is ideal for this, as you can see on the DVD.

You can use the Bookmarks menu or keyboard shortcuts to jump from one bookmark to the next. Press ⌘-[to move to the previous bookmark and ⌘-] to move to the next one.

Trimming Clips in the Timeline

With iMovie's direct trimming feature, you can remove footage from a clip after you've added it to the timeline. Video editors often describe this process as changing a clip's *in point* or *out point.*

To trim a clip, move the pointer near one end of the clip and then drag toward the center.

See techniques for working with the timeline.
⊙ **Creating Bookmarks**
⊙ **Activating Timeline Snapping**
⊙ **Using Direct Trimming**

Tips for Trimming

Resurrecting trimmed footage.

Need to bring back some footage that you trimmed away? Provided you haven't emptied iMovie's Trash, you can. Just drag the edge of the clip again. For example, to bring back some footage from the end of a clip, drag to the right.

Recognizing trimmed clips.
You can tell whether a clip has been trimmed by looking at it.

A clip that has been trimmed has square corners.

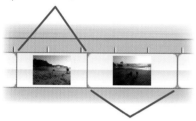

A clip that hasn't been trimmed has slightly rounded corners.

Note: When you empty iMovie's Trash, all clips appear untrimmed.

Trimming and adjacent clips. What happens if you trim a clip that already has a clip next to it? It depends.

If you lengthen a clip, the clips to its right move to the right, extending the total length of your project. Videographers call this a *ripple* edit.

What if you don't want to change the position of the remaining clips? For example, maybe you've already timed them to music or narration, and a ripple edit would ruin your work. Easy: just press ⌘ while lengthening the clip. When you ⌘-drag to lengthen a clip, iMovie also trims the clip directly next to the clip you're stretching, making it shorter. All other clips stay in place, and the overall length of your project stays the same. This is called a *rolling* edit.

Why the Drag? If you've watched the DVD included with this book, you may have noticed that I dragged a clip to the right before trimming its in point. Why? Because I had turned on timeline snapping (described at right). When snapping is on, the playhead often wants to jump to the clip to its left, making in-point adjustments cumbersome.

I could have simply turned off snapping, but sometimes it's easier to temporarily put a bit of space around a clip. It just goes to show how there are often multiple approaches to an editing task.

It's a Snap: Timeline Snapping

You've probably encountered snapping features in other Mac programs: when you drag one item near another, it snaps toward the second item as though the two shared a magnetic attraction.

iMovie's timeline-snapping feature brings this magnetism to your movies. Use the Preferences command to turn on timeline snapping, and the playhead snaps to various elements as you drag: to the beginning and end of clips, to bookmarks, to DVD chapter markers, and to silent portions of audio tracks (page 178).

Better still, clips themselves snap to these same elements as you drag them. And so does the mouse pointer when you're using direct trimming.

As you can see on the DVD, timeline snapping pairs up beautifully with bookmarks and direct trimming.

Tip: You can temporarily activate (or deactivate) timeline snapping: just press the Shift key while dragging an element.

Creating Cutaways

A *cutaway* is a common video-production technique. Think of Barbara Walters nodding solemnly while Fabio describes what kind of tree he'd like to be. Or maybe the video changes to show a close-up of Grandma's garden as she talks about it. To create edits like these, use the Advanced menu's Paste Over at Playhead command.

Try it yourself. The Extras folder of the DVD contains footage you can use to experiment with cutaways. Open the folder named Cutaway Footage and read the instructions inside.

Step 1. Get Your Shots

Begin planning cutaway shots when shooting your video. After Grandma talks about her garden, shoot some close-ups of the plants she talked about. While you're shooting the school play, grab a couple of shots of the audience laughing or clapping. Or after you've shot an interview, move the camera to shoot a few seconds of the interviewer nodding. (In TV news, this kind of shot is called a *noddie*.)

Tip: Still have an old VHS or 8mm camcorder? Dust it off, pop it on a tripod, and use it to shoot short cutaway shots. Dub the footage to your miniDV camcorder, then import it into iMovie. The video quality won't match exactly, but your viewers may never notice. And your cutaways will be authentic rather than staged.

Step 2. Set Up for the Edit

With your footage imported, you're ready to set up for the edit. With cutaway shots, you retain the audio from the primary clip and discard the audio from the cutaway shot. iMovie does this for you: choose Preferences from the iMovie menu and be sure the Extract Audio in Paste Over box is checked.

Step 3. Crop the Cutaway.

Using the crop markers as described on page 158, crop the cutaway footage so that it begins at the first frame you want to use as the cutaway. Don't bother specifying the exact end of the cutaway at this point—you'll do that in Step 5.

Step 4. Copy the Cutaway.

In the Clips pane, select the cutaway and choose Copy from the Edit menu (⌘-C).

Make sure your primary and cutaway footage exist as separate clips.

Try your hand at some cutaways
with the footage in the Extras folder.

Step 5. Mark the Footage You Want to Replace.

With your primary footage in the timeline, navigate to the spot where you want the cutaway to begin (tip: a bookmark can be a handy way to indicate where you plan to insert a cutaway). Select the clip in the timeline, then drag crop markers to indicate the area you want to replace.

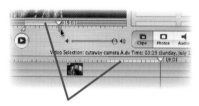

As you drag the crop markers, iMovie highlights the region that will be replaced by the cutaway. The cutaway will be inserted where the yellow bar starts, and it will end where the yellow bar ends. iMovie also indicates how long the cutaway will be.

Step 6. Insert the Cutaway.

Choose Paste Over at Playhead from the Advanced menu (Shift-⌘-V).

The pushpin icons indicate the audio is locked to the video above it. If you move the video, the audio moves along with it, maintaining synchronization between sound and picture.

iMovie pastes the cutaway footage into the timeline, beginning at the location of the first crop marker.

iMovie mutes the audio of the cutaway clip so you don't hear it.

iMovie extracts the audio from the primary clip and puts it in Audio Track 1.

Cutaway Notes and Tips

When you choose Paste Over at Playhead, iMovie uses as much footage from your cutaway clip as is needed to fill the region you highlighted. For example, if the cutaway clip is five seconds long and you highlighted a three-second region with the crop markers, iMovie uses the first three seconds of the cutaway clip.

On the other hand, if the cutaway clip isn't long enough—if you highlight five seconds but your cutaway clip is only three seconds long—iMovie pads out the extra time with blank footage called a *color clip* (see page 194).

(The one exception to the previous paragraph occurs if your cutaway clip is a still image. In this case, iMovie simply extends the length of the still image to fill the region you highlighted.)

For those times when you want precise control over the contents of the cutaway clip, use a different technique to insert the cutaway. In Step 3, crop the cutaway clip to the *exact* length you want it to be. Copy the cropped clip to the Clipboard, then position the playhead at the spot where you want

to insert it—don't highlight an area with the crop markers. Now choose Paste Over at Playhead. iMovie pastes the entire cutaway clip, replacing an equal amount of footage in the timeline.

Whew. Got all that? It's actually easier than it sounds. Experiment with the footage on the DVD, and you'll be cutting away in no time.

Adding Photos to Movies

Photographs are mainstays of many types of movies, especially montages and documentaries. With the iPhoto browser in iMovie, you can add photos from your iPhoto library to your movies. You can also add photos that aren't stored in your iPhoto library by dragging them into iMovie or by using the File menu's Import command.

When adding photos to movies, consider taking advantage of iMovie's *Ken Burns effect* to add a sense of dynamism to your stills. Why name a feature after a filmmaker? Think about Ken Burns' documentaries and how his camera appears to move across still images. For example, a shot might begin with a close-up of a weary face and then zoom out to reveal a Civil War battlefield scene.

That's the Ken Burns effect. Now, Ken Burns himself would probably call it by its traditional filmmaking terms: *pan and scan* or *pan and zoom*. These terms reflect the fact that you can have two different kinds of motion: panning (moving across an image) and zooming (moving in or out).

Whatever the effect's name, its result is the same: it adds motion and life to otherwise static images.

Note: iMovie 4.0 had a bug that caused the Ken Burns effect to yield poor-quality results when zooming out. Be sure you're using iMovie version 4.0.1 or a later version, if available.

Adding a Photo from Your iPhoto Library

Step 1.

Click the Photos button.

To import the photo as a static image, uncheck the Ken Burns Effect box.

Tip: If you plan to fine-tune the duration of the photo by trimming it in the timeline, turn off the Ken Burns effect when importing the photo, then add the effect later, as I do on the DVD.

To view a specific album, choose its name from the pop-up menu.

Step 2.

Select the photo. You can select multiple photos by Shift-clicking or ⌘-clicking on them.

See how to work with photos.
⊙ **Using the iPhoto Browser**
⊙ **Applying the Ken Burns Effect**

Step 3.

Adjust the duration and zoom settings as desired.

To pan-zoom a photo, you must specify the start and finish settings for the move: that is, how you want the photo to look when it first appears, and how you want it to look at the end of its duration.

Reverses your settings— for example, turns a zoom in into a zoom out.

When zoomed in on a photo, drag the photo using the hand pointer to specify which part of it you want to see.

Displays the results of your settings in the preview monitor.

iMovie applies the settings and adds the photo or photos to the timeline.

Note: The Ken Burns effect is sticky. That is, iMovie remembers the last set of pan and zoom settings that you used and applies them to future photos.

To specify the length of time you want the image to appear, drag the slider or type in the box. (Values are in seconds and frames. For example, for a 5½ second duration, type 5:15.)

Specify the desired start and finish zoom settings by dragging the slider or by typing in the box. To change the starting zoom setting, click the Start button before adjusting the zoom setting. Similarly, to change the ending zoom setting, first click Finish.

Photo Tips

Photos from elsewhere. You can also use photos that aren't stored in your iPhoto library. Click the Clips button, then drag the photos into the Clips pane.

You can also import photos using the Import command in the File menu. You can even drag a photo's icon directly to the timeline.

When you import a photo using any of these techniques, iMovie applies the current Ken Burns effect settings to the photo. To change those settings, see the next page. Alternatively, if you know what Ken Burns settings you want, you can set them up first and then import the photo.

Trimming photo clips. If you've applied the Ken Burns effect to a photo, you can trim its duration in the timeline, but you can't extend it. If you haven't applied Ken Burns, you can trim *and* extend a photo's duration. If you anticipate changing a photo's duration as you work, wait to apply the Ken Burns effect until *after* you've laid out your clips in the timeline.

Cropping a photo. Want to show just part of a photo? Be sure that the Ken Burns Effect box is checked, then select a photo in the Photos pane. Click the Start button and use the pan and zoom controls to crop the photo. Next, press the Option key and click the Finish button. (Pressing Option tells iMovie to copy the Start settings to the Finish settings.) Specify a duration for the clip, then click Apply.

167

Working with the Ken Burns Effect

There's more to Ken Burns than meets the eye. Here are some tips to help you get more out of this powerful effect.

Changing Settings

You've applied the Ken Burns effect and now decide that you want to change the clip's pan, zoom, or duration settings. Select the clip in the timeline and click the Photos button. Now make the desired adjustments and click Update.

Tip: As an alternative to clicking the Photos button, you can also Control-click on the clip in the timeline and choose Edit Photo Settings from the shortcut menu.

Note: If there's a transition on either side of the clip, iMovie will need to recreate it, since it contains frames that will no longer match the new clip. iMovie displays a message warning you that the transition will have to be "re-rendered."

To always have iMovie re-render transitions, check this box.

To cancel the new Ken Burns settings and keep the old clips, click Cancel.

To re-render adjacent transitions, click OK.

Watch Your Proportions

If you plan to show a photo at actual size (that is, a zoom setting of 1.00), be sure the photo's proportions match the 4:3 aspect ratio of television—otherwise, the image won't completely fill the screen.

Most digital camera images have these proportions. You can use iPhoto to crop those that don't: in the Constrain pop-up menu in iPhoto's Edit pane, choose the option 4 x 3 (DVD).

A standard TV image has an aspect ratio of 4:3—four units of width for every three units of height.

If you don't want to crop the image, here's a quick workaround: use the Zoom slider to zoom in just enough so that the image fills the preview area. That way, you won't end up with unsightly black borders around part of the photo.

Image Resolution and Zooming

iMovie imports photos at their full resolution. This enables you to zoom in on part of a photo and still retain image sharpness.

However, if you zoom in on a low-resolution image or one that you've cropped heavily in iPhoto, you will probably notice some chunky-looking pixelation. So think twice about zooming in on low-resolution images unless you want that pixelated look.

Zoom to Tell a Story

Creative use of zooming can help tell your story. When you zoom in, you gradually focus the viewer's attention on one portion of the scene. You tell the viewer, "Now that you have the big picture, this is what you should pay attention to."

When you zoom out, you reveal additional details about the scene, increasing the viewer's sense of context. You tell the viewer, "Now that you've seen that, look at these other things to learn how they relate to each other."

Go Slow

Unless you're after a special effect, avoid very fast pans and zooms. It's better to pan and zoom slowly to allow your viewers to absorb the changes in the scene.

Generally, a zoom speed of 0.05 to 0.1 per second gives a pleasing result. For example, a five-second clip should have a difference between start and finish zoom of about 0.5.

Vary Your Zoom Direction

Variety is the spice of zooming. If you're creating a photo montage and zooming each image, consider alternating between zooming in and zooming out. For example, zoom in on one image, then zoom out on the next.

A fine example of this technique lives within Mac OS X itself: Mac OS X's screen saver alternates between zooming in and zooming out.

Tip: iMovie provides a shortcut that makes it easy to obtain this variety. Select more than one photo in the Photos pane, specify Ken Burns settings, and then press the Option key while clicking the Apply button. iMovie adds the photos to the timeline and alternates between zooming in and zooming out.

The Need to Render

When you import a photo or apply the Ken Burns effect, iMovie must create the video frames that represent your efforts. This is called rendering, and is described in more detail on page 181.

You can continue to work in iMovie while a clip is rendering, but you may notice that the program's performance is a bit slower.

Advanced Ken Burns Techniques

Ken Burns has some limitations. One is that you can't "hold" on a certain frame. You might want to have a 10-second clip in which the photo zooms for the first eight seconds and then remains static for the last two. Or maybe you want to zoom in part way, freeze for a couple of seconds, and then continue zooming.

Ken can't do that.

Another limitation is that you can't combine multiple moves in a single clip. For example, you might want to pan across a photo and then zoom in on part of it.

Ken can't do that, either.

At least not without a little finessing. It's actually possible to accomplish both of these tasks in iMovie. Here's how.

Holding on a Frame

To hold on a frame, save a frame from a Ken Burns-generated clip, then add it to the timeline.

Step 1.

Set up the Ken Burns effect as desired and then apply it, as described on page 168.

Step 2.

Select the clip that iMovie has rendered, then move the playhead to its last frame.

Step 3.

Choose Create Still Frame from the Edit menu (Shift-⌘-S).

Step 4.

Locate the still frame in the Clips pane, drag it to the timeline and, if necessary, trim it to the desired length.

Tip: You can also adjust the still frame's duration by double-clicking the clip, then entering a new duration in the Clip Info dialog box.

Variations

You can also start by holding on a frame, and then panning and zooming. First, apply the Ken Burns effect, then navigate to the first frame of the resulting clip and create a still frame from it. Position the still-frame clip before the Ken Burns clip.

Another variation involves inserting a still image in the middle of a Ken Burns move so that panning and zooming stops and then resumes. For this trick, apply the Ken Burns effect and then split the resulting clip where you want to hold on a frame. (To split a clip, position the playhead at the desired split point and choose Split Video Clip at Playhead from the Edit menu.)

Next, move the playhead to the last frame of the first half of the clip (or to the first frame of the second half). Create a still frame, and drag the resulting clip between the two halves.

Try out Photo to Movie in the Extras folder.

GO TO DVD

Combining Moves

Combining two kinds of moves involves importing the same photo twice and applying different Ken Burns settings each time.

Step 1.

Set up the first Ken Burns move as desired and then apply it.

Step 2.

In the iPhoto browser, select a different photo, and then select the same photo that you selected for Step 1.

This tricks iMovie into preparing to create a new clip instead of updating the one you just created.

Step 3.

In the Ken Burns Effect area of the Photos pane, click the Reverse button.

Reverse

This reverses the Ken Burns settings that you set up for Step 1: its end point becomes the new start point.

Step 4.

Specify the Finish settings for the second Ken Burns move and then apply it.

Beyond Ken Burns: Other Pan-Zoom Tools

Ken Burns isn't the only game in town. Several companies offer pan-zoom tools that work with iMovie.

Photo to Movie. A trial version of this excellent program from LQ Graphics is included on the DVD. Photo to Movie makes it very easy to create pan-zoom effects. Create your effect in Photo to Movie, export it as a QuickTime movie, and then bring it into iMovie and add it to your project.

Photo to Movie's results are superior to those created by Ken Burns effect. Photo to Movie supports what animators call

ease in and *ease out*: rather than motion abruptly starting and ending, as it does with the Ken Burns effect, the motion

starts and ends gradually. The results have a more professional appearance.

SlickMotion. This simple program is included with GeeThree's Slick Transitions and Effects Volume 4, an extensive library of iMovie effects. SlickMotion also supports ease-in/ease-out, and adds the ability to rotate images.

Virtix Zoom & Pan. This program is an effect plug-in that runs directly within iMovie. It also supports image rotation.

Motion Pictures. This scaled-down version of Photo to Movie is included with Roxio's Toast 6 Titanium.

Adding Audio to Movies

In movie making, sound is at least as important as the picture. An audience will forgive hand-held camera shots and poor lighting—*The Blair Witch Project* proved that. But give them a noisy, inaudible soundtrack, and they'll run for the aspirin.

Poor quality audio is a common flaw of home video and amateur movies. One problem is that most camcorders don't have very good microphones—their built-in mikes are often located on the top of the camera where they pick up sound from the camera's motors. What's more, the microphone is usually far from the subject, resulting in too much background noise. And if you're shooting outdoors on a windy day, your scenes end up sounding like an outtake from *Twister*.

If your camcorder provides a jack for an external microphone, you can get much better sound by using one. On the following pages, you'll find some advice on choosing and using microphones.

If you've already shot your video or you can't use an external mike, there is another solution: don't use the audio you recorded. Instead, create an audio *bed* consisting of music and, if appropriate, narration or sound effects.

iMovie provides several features that you can use to sweeten your soundtracks. Take advantage of them.

Importing Music from an Audio CD

Click the Audio button.

Simply insert the CD. If your Mac is connected to the Internet, iMovie will access CDDB (described on page 21) to retrieve the disc and track names.

To add a track, select it and click Place at Playhead, or simply drag the track to one of the timeline's audio tracks.

Note: Depending on how you've set up your iTunes preferences, your Mac may also start iTunes when you insert the audio CD. If that happens, simply click the iMovie icon in the dock or click anywhere in the iMovie window to make iMovie the active program again.

Importing Music from Your iTunes Library

Use the iTunes browser to bring in music from your iTunes library.

Step 1.

Position the playhead where you want the music to begin playing.

Step 2.

Click the Audio button.

Step 3.

Locate the song you want to import.

You can choose a specific playlist from this pop-up menu.

You can sort the list of songs by clicking on a column heading. Drag columns left and right to move them. Resize columns by dragging the vertical line between their headings.

Use the Search box to quickly locate a song based on its name or its artist's name.

To play a song, select it and click this button, or simply double-click the song's name.

To add a song to the movie, click Place at Playhead.

Step 4.

Click the Place at Playhead button.

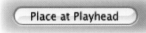

iMovie adds the music to the timeline's second audio track.

Tip: As an alternative to clicking Place at Playhead, you can also click and drag a song to any location on the timeline.

Recording an Audio Narration

If you connect a microphone to your Mac, you can record narration directly within iMovie.

To begin recording, click the red button ◉ next to the volume meter in iMovie's Audio pane. To stop recording, click the red button again.

As you record, iMovie adds your narration to the first audio track, positioning it at the playhead's location and giving it the name *Voice 01.*

Tip: For the best sound, you want to record loud but not too loud. At its loudest, your voice should illuminate the yellow portion of iMovie's volume meter. If you illuminate the red portions, your sound will be distorted.

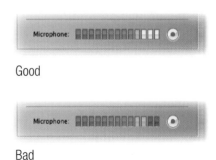

Good

Bad

Also, position the mike carefully to avoid the "popping p" syndrome—bursts of breath noise. Record the phrase "pretty poppies" as a test, and back off if the results sound like a hurricane. (Audio trivia: those breathy, percussive consonants are aptly called *plosives.*)

Tips for Recording Better Sound

Upgrade Your Microphone

To get better sound, get a high-quality external microphone and place it close to your subject.

Before you buy an external mike, determine whether your camcorder can accept one. Some inexpensive camcorders don't provide a jack for an external mike; others may require an adapter that connects to the bottom of the camera. Most mid-range and all high-end camcorders have external mike jacks. On most cameras, it's a ⅛-inch stereo minijack.

Clip-on. Microphones come in all sizes and designs. Some are specialized—for example, a *lavaliere* mike, which clips to a lapel or shirt, is great for recording a single voice, such as that of a teacher (or DVD host). But a lav mike is unsuitable for recording a musical performance.

Shotgun approach. When you can't get the mike close to your subject but still want to reduce extraneous noise, consider a *shotgun* mike. In a shotgun mike, the microphone capsule is mounted within a long barrel designed to reject sound coming from the side of the mike. Shotgun mikes are popular in TV news and movie making. They're sensitive enough to be located out of the video frame, and their highly directional sensitivity means they won't pick up noise from cameras and crew members.

A shotgun mike works best when mounted on a *boom*, a long pole (often hand-held)

that allows the mike to point down at the subject. When you see a video crew with one person who appears to be holding a fishing pole with a long tube on the end of it, you're seeing a shotgun mike (and a sound technician) in action.

Two in one. The most versatile mike you can buy is a *single-point stereo* mike. A stereo mike crams two microphone capsules into a single package. Each capsule is precisely positioned relative to its companion, thus eliminating one of the biggest challenges of stereo recording: getting accurate balance and separation between the left and right channels. I use the AT822 from Audio-Technica (www.audio-technica.com). You can see this mike in the GarageBand segment of the DVD.

With high-quality extension cables, the mike and camera can be up to about 25 feet apart. At greater distances, you risk losing some high frequencies and picking up hum and other electrical noise.

A balanced alternative. When you need to run cables longer than 25 feet or so—or when you want the best possible quality and are prepared to pay for it—

consider a *balanced* mike. All of the aforementioned mikes are available in balanced and unbalanced versions. A balanced mike is wired in a way that reduces electrical noise and allows for cable runs of up to 100 feet or so. Balanced mikes cost more than unbalanced ones, but pros and serious amateurs prefer balanced mikes due to their resistance to electrical noise and their support for longer cable runs.

A balanced mike typically uses an *XLR* connector, and only high-end camcorders have XLR jacks. But there is a way to connect a balanced mike to an unbalanced miniplug jack: the DXA-2 adaptor from BeachTek (www.beachtek.com). A compact metal box that attaches to your camera's tripod mount, the DXA-2 requires no external power supply and has built-in knobs for adjusting volume levels.

Placement is Everything

To do justice to any mike, position it properly. For that school play or recital, use a mike stand and position the mike high, pointing down toward the stage at about a 45-degree angle. If you can't set up your own mike stand, just try to get the mike at least a few feet off the stage and as close to center stage as possible.

How close should the mike be? That depends on what you're recording (see the table at right). The closer the mike is to a sound source, the less room noise and reverberation it picks up.

But if the mike is too close, stereo separation is exaggerated—some sounds come only from the left speaker, others only from the right, and sounds in the center are louder than they should be. Move the mike too far away, and you get a muddy sounding recording with too much room reverb.

When recording a live performance, try to show up for rehearsals so that you have time to experiment with different mike distances. If your camera has a headphone jack, connect a good pair of headphones—ones whose cups surround your ears and thus block out external sounds. Record a test, play it back, and listen.

For recording narrations, consider assembling a makeshift sound booth that will absorb room echo and block computer and hard drive noise. Glue some sound-absorbing acoustical foam onto two sheets of plywood or foamcore. (See www.soundsuckers.com for a wide selection.) Position the two sheets in front of you in a V shape, with the mike at the narrow end. If you're on a tight budget, use blankets, pillows, carpet remnants, or even a coat closet. The idea is to surround yourself, and the mike, with sound-absorbing material.

Another major microphone manufacturer, Shure, has published some excellent mike-placement tutorials. Download them at www.shure.com/booklets.

A Field Guide to Mike Placement

Scenario	Ideal Mike Position
Solo piano	About a foot from the center of the piano's harp, pointed at the strings (open the piano's recital lid).
Wedding ceremony	As close to the lovebirds as possible. Many wedding videographers attach a wireless lavaliere mike to the groom or the officiator. (Bridal gowns tend to rustle too much.) A mike hidden in a flower arrangement may also work.
Narrator	6 to 9 inches from the speaker's mouth, angled downward. To avoid plosive problems, use a windscreen and position the mike just off to the side, pointing at the mouth. Alternative: a lavaliere mike.
Choral group	1 to 3 feet above and 2 to 4 feet in front of the first row of the choir.
Birthday party around a table	On an extended floor stand, angled downward. Alternative: on a tabletop desk stand, pointing at the birthday kid.

Creating an Audio Bed

If you weren't able to get good audio when you originally shot your video, consider muting your video's audio track and just putting a music bed behind your shots. Create a montage of shots, using bookmarks and direct trimming to help you time your edits to the music.

And finally, a related tip: If you're shooting scenes where the audio is mostly ambient sound—the waves at the beach, the din of a party—shoot a few minutes of uninterrupted video, keeping the camera stationary. After importing the video, delete the video track and keep the audio. (In iMovie, drag the video clip to the timeline, then choose Extract Audio from the Advanced menu.) Now you have an audio bed upon which you can put a series of video shots. After you add those shots, mute their audio. This technique eliminates jarring sound changes between shots.

Working with Audio Tracks

Adjusting the volume of an audio track is a common task. And when you combine audio in any way—mixing music, sound effects, dialog, and background sounds—you almost always need to adjust the relative levels of each sound to create a pleasing mix.

iMovie provides several ways to work with sound levels. You can reduce the volume of an entire sound clip. You might do this if you're mixing music with the sound of the surf, and don't want the waves to drown out the music.

You can also vary a track's volume level over time. When combining music and narration, you might want the music to start at full volume, fade when the narrator talks, then return to full volume when she stops.

The timeline viewer provides several controls for adjusting volume levels. Many of them are easier to use when you have iMovie display audio track *waveforms*. Choose Preferences from the iMovie menu, and click the Show Audio Track Waveforms check box.

A waveform looks a bit like the penmanship of an earthquake seismograph. Back-and-forth lines indicate the intensity of the shaking—in this case, of the sound wave. Being able to see your sound instead of just a horizontal colored bar is a big help when trimming audio tracks, adjusting volume, and creating audio fades.

Adjusting the Volume of a Clip

To adjust the volume of an entire audio clip, select the clip and then drag the volume slider located below the timeline.

You can also type a value in the text box.

To Fade Out or Fade In

Creating an audio fade involves working with *volume markers* in the timeline.

Step 1.

Select the audio clip and click the Edit Volume checkbox below the timeline.

Step 2.

Click the horizontal line in the audio track to create and adjust volume markers.

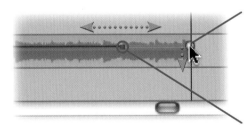

To lower the volume, drag the marker down. To move the marker earlier or later in time, drag it left or right.

To adjust the duration of the fade, drag the beginning point of the marker left or right.

The completed fade.

Conversely, to create a fade-in, drag the beginning point of a volume marker all the way down, then drag the end point up.

Adjusting Volume Over Time

Here's how to adjust a track's volume level to accommodate narration or dialog in another track.

Step 1.

Click the Edit Volume check box below the timeline.

When the Edit Volume box is checked, iMovie displays a volume level bar on each track.

Step 2.

Click on the audio track's volume level bar at the point where you want to adjust the volume. A volume marker appears.

Step 3.

To lower the volume, drag the marker down. To increase the volume, drag the marker up. To move the point at which the volume changes, drag the marker left or right.

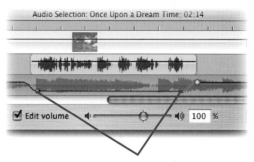

Here, the volume of a music track has been tweaked so that the music gets softer during a narration passage.

To delete a marker, select it and press the Delete key.

Step 4.

When you've finished tweaking volume levels, uncheck the Edit Volume box.

More Sound Advice

Waveform Tips

When you've used the Preferences command to display audio waveforms, iMovie's timeline snapping feature snaps the playhead to silent portions of clips (specifically, when you scroll to within three frames of silence).

To work with more precision when viewing waveforms, zoom in on the timeline. If the audio in a track is on the quiet side, the waveform may be hard to see. Solution: select the audio clip and press the up-arrow key. This accentuates the spikes in the waveform. To make the spikes smaller, press the down-arrow key.

When you empty the iMovie Trash after trimming an audio clip, iMovie must re-render the track's waveform—a red progress bar appears at the bottom of the audio track, and the waveform appears a bit blurry until iMovie renders it. Because this process takes some time, you may want to leave the waveform display turned off unless you need it for precise editing or volume adjustments.

Trimming Audio

You can trim the start and end of an audio clip using the same direct-trimming techniques described on page 162. As with video clips, emptying the iMovie Trash discards audio that you've trimmed.

Scrubbing Audio

Here's a handy way to locate the exact spot to trim or split an audio clip. Zoom in on the timeline, then press the Option key while slowly dragging the iMovie playhead. Your audio plays back, but is slowed down. The sound even plays backwards when you drag the playhead to the left. (Beatles fans: import some *White Album* songs from your iTunes library and have fun.)

Extracting Audio

At times, you may want to use only the audio portion of a clip. For example, you're making a documentary about your grandmother's childhood and you'd like to show old photographs as she talks.

To do this, drag the video clip to the timeline, then select the clip and choose Extract Audio (⌘-J) from the Advanced menu. iMovie copies the audio, places it in Audio Track 1, and mutes the audio in the video clip.

Next, select the video clip in the timeline and press the Delete key. The video vanishes but its audio lingers on, and you can now position still images and other clips in the video's place. You can also drag the audio elsewhere in the timeline.

Overlapping Audio in the Timeline

iMovie may provide just two audio tracks, but that doesn't mean you're limited to two simultaneous sounds. You can overlap multiple audio clips in the timeline's audio tracks: simply drag one audio clip on top of another.

Repeating Sound Effects

You might want some sound effects to play for a long period of time. For example, iMovie's Hard Rain sound effect is less than 10 seconds long, but maybe you need 30 seconds of rain sounds for a particular movie.

For cases like these, simply repeat the sound effect by dragging it from the Audio pane to the timeline as many times as needed. You can also duplicate a sound by Option-dragging it in the timeline. If the sound effect fades out (as Hard Rain does), overlap each copy to hide the fade.

You can build magnificently rich sound effect tracks by overlapping sounds. To create a thunderstorm, for example, drag the Thunder sound effect so that it overlaps Hard Rain. Add the Cold Wind sound while you're at it. And don't forget to use iMovie's audio controls to fine-tune the relative levels of each effect.

GO TO WEB

Camcorder Sound Settings

Most miniDV camcorders provide two sound-recording settings: 12-bit and 16-bit. Always record using the 16-bit setting. If your sound and picture synchronization drift over the course of a long movie, it's probably because you recorded using 12-bit audio.

Muting an Audio Track

You can mute an audio track entirely by unchecking the box to its right in the timeline viewer. If you uncheck the box next to the video track, iMovie mutes the video's sound. This can be handy when you're replacing the audio in a series of clips with an audio bed—a segment of background audio that will play across multiple clips—as I do on the DVD.

Splitting Audio Clips

You can divide an audio clip into two or more separate clips whose position and volume you can adjust independently. First, select the audio clip you want to split. Next, position the playhead where you want to split the clip. Finally, choose Split Selected Audio Clip at Playhead from the Edit menu or press ⌘-T.

Sources for Sound Effects and Music

Sound Effects

iMovie's library of built-in sound effects, accessed through the Audio pane, covers a lot of aural ground.

But there's always room for more sound, and the Internet is a rich repository of it. One of your first stops should be FindSounds, a Web search engine that lets you locate and download free sound effects by typing keywords, such as *chickadee*. SoundHunter is another impressive source of free sound effects and provides links to even more audio-related sites.

Most online sound effects are stored as WAV or AIFF files, two common sound formats. To import a WAV or AIFF file, use the File menu's Import command or simply drag the file directly to the desired location in the timeline viewer.

Managing Sound Effects

If you assemble a large library of sound effects, you might find yourself needing a program to help you keep track of them. You already have such a program: it's called iTunes. Simply drag your sound effects files into the iTunes window. Use the Get Info command to assign descriptive tags to them, and you can use iTunes' Search box to locate effects in a flash. You might even want to create a separate iTunes music library to store your sound effects.

Music Sources

As for music, if you're a .Mac subscriber, you'll find a symphony's worth of clips on your iDisk. Open the Software folder on your iDisk, then the Members Only folder. The music is in the Freeplay Music folder. (Don't miss the additional sound effects in the Skywalker Sounds folder, too.)

Plenty of royalty-free music is also available online from sites such as SoundDogs and KillerSound. These sites have powerful search features that enable you to locate music based on keywords, such as *acoustic* or *jazz*.

Loopasonic is another cool music site. It offers hundreds of music loops—repeating riffs—that you can assemble into unique music tracks and use in GarageBand (which, of course, you can use to compose your own movie music).

And for building custom-length music tracks, you can't beat SmartSound's Movie Maestro software. Movie Maestro provides an expandable library of songs, each of which is divided into blocks that the Music Maestro software can assemble to an exact length.

Adding Transitions

Visual transitions add a professional touch to your project. Transitions also help tell a story. For example, a cross-dissolve—one clip fading out while another fades in—can imply the passage of time. Imagine slowly dissolving from a nighttime campfire scene to a campsite scene shot the following morning.

Similarly, iMovie's Push transition, where one clip pushes another out of the frame, is a visual way of saying "meanwhile..." Imagine using this transition between a scene of an expectant mother in the delivery room and a shot of her husband pacing in the waiting room, chainsmoking nervously. (Okay, so this is an old-fashioned maternity movie.)

iMovie 4 added a convenient transition-related enhancement. You can apply the same transition to multiple clips in one step: select the clips in the timeline, select a transition, then click the Apply button. You can also update multiple transitions at once: select them in the timeline (⌘-click on them), adjust transition settings, then click Update.

Adding Transitions

To add a transition between two clips, first click iMovie's Transitions button to display the Transitions pane.

If you've selected two or more clips in the timeline, you can apply the transition to all of the clips by clicking Apply.

To preview the transition in iMovie's monitor, click Preview.

When you select a transition, a preview appears here.

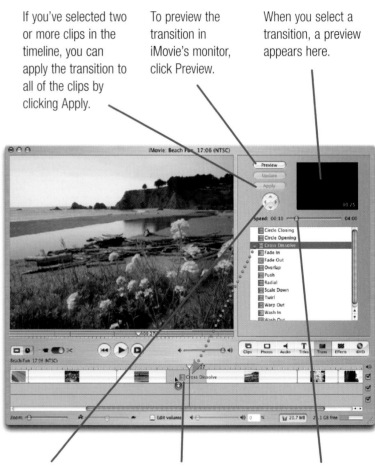

Some transitions, such as Push, allow you to specify a direction (for example, to push from left to right or from top to bottom).

To add the transition, drag it between two clips in the timeline or clip viewer.

To change the transition's duration, drag the Speed slider. The current duration appears in the lower-right corner of the preview box.

Testing the Transition

To see the finished transition, select it and press the spacebar.

If you aren't happy with the transition, you can delete it (press the Delete key) or choose Undo.

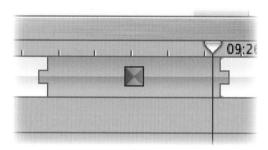

Inserting a Clip at a Transition

When you create a transition between two clips, you establish a connection between those clips.

If you need to insert a new clip between those two clips, you must first delete the transition: select it and hit Delete. Now you can insert the new clip.

Updating a Transition

Change your mind about using a particular transition style? To change an existing transition, first select it in the clip viewer or timeline viewer. Make the desired changes, and click the Update button in the Transitions pane.

Some Background on Rendering

When you create a transition, title, or effect, iMovie must create the video frames that represent your efforts. This rendering process takes time and memory; you'll notice iMovie slows down a bit during rendering.

You can continue to work while rendering takes place. You can even play back your movie, although you may notice stuttering playback when iMovie reaches areas it hasn't finished rendering.

Although you can work during rendering, you might want to avoid adding multiple transitions or titles in rapid-fire succession, as doing so slows iMovie to a crawl. To gauge how long rendering will take, look at the transitions, titles, or effects that you've added: a little red progress bar shows how far along rendering is.

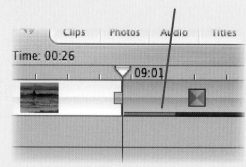

Creating Titles

What's a movie without titles? Incomplete. Almost any movie can benefit from text of some kind: opening and closing credits, the superimposed names of people and places, or simply the words "The End" at, well, the end.

iMovie's Titles pane is your ticket to text. You have nearly 50 title styles from which to choose, with customizing opportunities aplenty.

Many of iMovie's title styles are animated, and it isn't difficult to transcend the bounds of good taste and enter the terrain of tackiness. Use restraint and lean toward classic title styles like Centered and Scrolling.

Regardless of the style you choose, you'll get the best results with sturdy fonts that remain legible despite the limited resolution of television. For example, at small text sizes, Arial Black often works better than Times, which has ornamental serifs that can break up when viewed on a TV set.

iMovie's titling features are improved in version 4. Not only do you get more styles (including Far, Far Away, a big hit among *Star Wars* fans), but you can change the settings of multiple titles at once, much as you can with transitions.

Roll the credits.

To Create a Title

Creating a title involves choosing the title style, specifying title settings, and then dragging the completed title to the timeline.

Step 1. Click the Titles button to display the Titles pane.

Step 2. Choose the title style you want by clicking its name. Some title styles are grouped together in a category; to view them, click the triangle next to the category name.

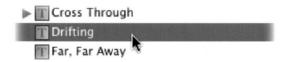

Step 3. Specify the title settings.

See the opposite page for an overview of title settings.

Step 4. Add the title by dragging it to the timeline.

Notes: To add a title to the middle of a clip, split the clip first (position the playhead where you want the title to appear, then press ⌘-T). To superimpose title text over a specific clip, drag the title to the immediate left of that clip.

Changing a Title

Need to change an existing title? In the timeline, select the title. Next, display the Titles pane and make your changes. Finally, click the Update button in the Titles pane. You can also Control-click on a title and choose Edit Title Settings from the shortcut menu.

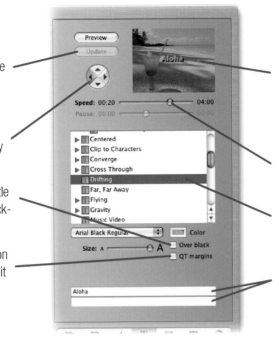

To edit an existing title, select it in the timeline, make your changes, and apply the changes by clicking the Update button.

With some title styles, you can specify text position and scrolling direction.

Normally, iMovie superimposes the title text over a clip. For a simple black background instead, check Over Black.

If you won't be viewing your movie on a TV—perhaps you'll be publishing it on a Web site—you can check this box to have iMovie position titles closer to the edges of the screen.

This is a preview of the title. To update it, click the current title style. To view a large preview in the monitor, click the Preview button.

Use this slider to adjust the title's duration. For some title styles, this slider adjusts scrolling speed.

To add the title, drag its name to the timeline viewer or clip viewer.

Type or paste the title's text here. In title styles that provide multiple text boxes, you can jump from one box to the next by pressing the Tab key.

Tips for Titling

Choosing Colors

You can choose the color for title text by clicking the Color button in the Titles pane. Click on the color palette to choose your hue. To match a color that appears in a clip, click the magnifying glass icon, position the pointer over the color you want to pick up, and then click.

When superimposing text over a clip, choose a text color that contrasts with the clip's contents. And lean toward larger font sizes—they'll be more legible.

Photoshop Titles

You can use Adobe Photoshop or Photoshop Elements to make gorgeous, full-screen titles. You can add photos, create color gradients, shadow effects, and more.

To create a title in Photoshop, specify an image size of 640 by 480 pixels. Create your title, and avoid putting any text in the outer ten percent of the screen.

(It might get cut off when the title appears on a TV set.) And to avoid flicker, make the thickness of any horizontal lines an even number of pixels (for example, 2, 4, 6).

To add the title to your movie, simply drag the Photoshop file's icon into the Clips pane or directly to the timeline. You can even apply the Ken Burns effect to the title if you like.

You can combine Photoshop and iMovie's built-in titling to create titles with text superimposed over a moving textured background. Create the textured

background in import it into iMovie, and apply the Ken Burns effect as desired (a horizontal pan works nicely). Finally, superimpose a text title over the resulting clip.

Color Backgrounds

To create a title over a colored background, create a color clip as described on page 194, then add the title to the color clip.

Adding Effects

Special effects are the spice of the movie world. When used sparingly, they enhance a movie and add appeal. When overused, they can make your audience gag.

iMovie's Effects pane is the gateway to a full spice rack of special effects. The Aged Film effect makes a clip look like old movie film, complete with scratches and jitter. The Lens Flare effect simulates the glare of bright light entering a camera's lens. Fairy Dust gives you that Tinkerbelle look, while Electricity creates *faux* lightning bolts. And the Earthquake effect creates a fast, back-and-forth blur that may tempt you to duck beneath a desk.

You can also apply speed effects to your clips. Slow a clip down to get slow motion, or speed it up for a chuckle.

In iMovie 4, you can apply effects to multiple clips at once: Shift-click to select a range of clips, or ⌘-click to select clips that aren't next to each other in the timeline.

Have fun with iMovie's effects. But remember: too much spice is worse than none at all.

To Add an Effect

Adding an effect involves selecting one or more clips, specifying effect settings, then applying the effect.

Step 1. Select the clip or clips to which you want to apply an effect.

Step 2. Click the Effects button to display the Effects pane.

Step 3. Choose the desired effect by clicking its name. iMovie displays a preview of the effect in the Effects pane.

Step 4. Specify the desired settings for the effect.

To preview the effect in the monitor, click Preview.

To apply the effect to the selected clip or clips, click Apply.

The preview box shows the results of the current effect and its settings.

iMovie can apply or remove an effect over time; see "Effects Over Time" on the opposite page.

Each effect has its own controls; they appear in this area.

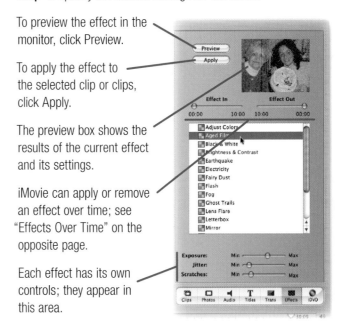

Step 5. To apply the effect, click the Apply button. iMovie renders the video frames required to create the effect.

See how to apply slow motion to a clip.
⊙ Slowing a Clip's Speed

Effects Over Time

Effects aren't an all-or-nothing proposition—iMovie can apply or remove an effect gradually. Apply the Black and White effect over time to make a clip start in black and white and turn into Technicolor. Animate the Soft Focus effect to make a clip start out blurry and come into focus, or vice versa.

To animate effects, use the Effects pane's Effect In and Effect Out sliders.

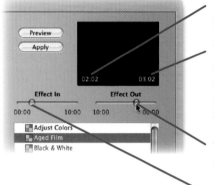

This value indicates how much time will elapse until the effect is fully visible.

This value shows when the effect will start to fade. The time is measured from the end of the clip—in this example, the effect will begin to fade 3 seconds and two frames from the end of the clip.

To make an effect go away over time, drag the Effect Out slider to the left.

To have the effect appear over time, drag the Effect In slider to the right.

Effective Tips

Being selective. Another way to control where an effect begins and ends is to apply the effect to only a portion of a clip. To do this, select the clip in the timeline and then drag crop markers to highlight the range of footage to which you want to apply the effect. Now specify the effect settings and click Apply.

Updating effects. To change a clip's effects, Control-click on the clip in the timeline, then choose Edit Effect Settings from the shortcut menu. Make your tweaks, then click Update.

Removing effects. To remove effects from a clip, select the clip and choose Restore Clip from the Advanced menu. Note: this command isn't available if you've emptied the iMovie Trash.

Speed Effects

That video of Junior's winning soccer game could use some slow-motion instant replays. iMovie provides them. Just select a clip in the timeline, and adjust the clip speed slider at the bottom of the timeline viewer.

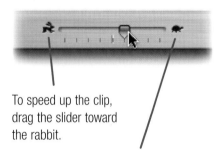

To speed up the clip, drag the slider toward the rabbit.

To slow down the clip, drag the slider toward the tortoise. (You knew that, didn't you?)

Because slowing down or speeding up a clip alters its audio playback, you'll want to mute the audio of a clip when you change its playback speed: select the clip and drag its volume slider to its leftmost position.

Slowing down a clip can also be a nice way to smooth out jerky camera movement. If you had too much coffee before shooting that flower close-up, slow the shot down a bit.

When you export a project containing slowed clips, iMovie may display a dialog box advising you to render those clips for best quality and giving you the option to proceed with or without rendering. Choose the Render and Proceed option, and iMovie performs additional processing that blends adjacent frames to smooth out the slow motion.

It's a Wrap: Exporting to Tape

You've finished your epic—now what? You decide. With iMovie's Share command, you can record your movie back to videotape or save it as a QuickTime movie that you can burn to a CD or post on a Web site for all the world to see. With the tools in the iDVD pane, you can add DVD chapter markers and send your movie to iDVD.

If you don't have iDVD and a SuperDrive DVD burner, chances are you'll export many of your movies back to tape. Once you export a movie to tape, you can connect your camcorder to your TV and screen your efforts. Or, connect the camcorder to a videocassette recorder to make VHS cassette dubs of your movie.

Exporting to Camera

Connect your miniDV camcorder to your Mac's FireWire jack and put the camcorder in VTR mode. Be sure to put a blank tape in your camcorder, or fast-forward until you're at a blank spot in the tape. Don't make the mistake of recording over your original footage—you may need it again in the future.

Step 1.

Choose Share from the File menu (Shift-⌘-E).

Step 2.

Click the Videocamera button.
Adjust settings as desired (see below).

Videocamera

Step 3.

Click Share; iMovie puts your camcorder in record mode and plays back your movie, sending its video and audio data over the FireWire cable to the camcorder.

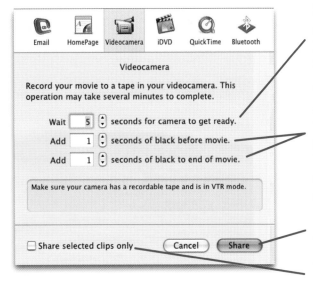

iMovie gives your camcorder five seconds to crank up and prepare to record. Feel free to lower this value—at least until you find you're cutting off the beginning of the movie.

iMovie will add some black footage before and after your movie, eliminating the jarring jump from and to the camcorder's blue standby screen. The preset values of one second probably won't be long enough—add a few seconds of black before the movie, and at least five to 10 seconds of black after it.

Be sure your camcorder is on and in VTR mode, then click Share.

To export only part of your movie, select the clips before choosing Share, then check this box.

Making VHS Dubs

To make a VHS dub of a movie, connect your camcorder's video and audio outputs to the video and audio inputs of a video-cassette recorder.

Your camcorder included a cable that probably has a four-conductor plug on one end, and three RCA phono plugs on the other. Connect the four-conductor plug to the camcorder's output jack (it will be labeled A/V In/Out or something similar). Connect the yellow RCA plug to your VCR's video input jack, the red plug to the audio input jack for the right channel, and the white plug to the audio input jack for the left channel.

You may have to adjust a setting on the VCR to switch input from its tuner to its video and audio input jacks.

Once you've made the connection, put a blank tape in the VCR, press its Record button, and then play back your movie.

If your camcorder and VCR each provide S-video jacks, use them for the video signal. S-video provides a much sharper picture. If you use an S-video cable, use only the audio plugs of the camcorder's cable; just let the yellow one dangle behind the VCR.

Tip: If you'll be doing a lot of dubbing, look for a VCR that has front-panel audio and video input jacks, which eliminate the need to grope around the VCR's back panel.

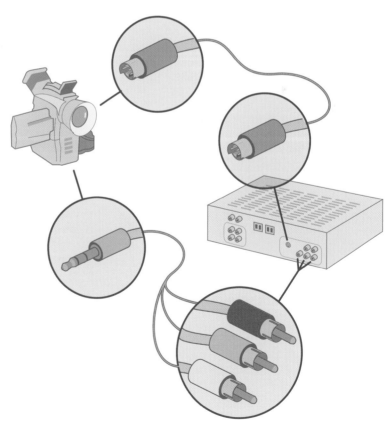

Creating Chapter Markers for iDVD

DVD chapters let you view video on your own terms. Whether you're watching a Hollywood blockbuster or the DVD that accompanied this book, you can use on-screen menus to instantly access scenes of interest. You can also use the Next and Previous keys on your DVD player's remote control to jump to the next chapter or to return to the beginning of a chapter and watch it again.

By adding chapter markers to your movies, you give your viewers this same freedom of movement and spare them the tedium of fast-forwarding and rewinding. You can create up to 99 markers in iMovie, and iDVD will create menus and buttons for them.

Even if you don't have a SuperDrive DVD burner, chapter markers can be handy. You can use them as bookmarks to enable you to quickly navigate through a lengthy movie: when you click a chapter in the iDVD pane, iMovie immediately moves the playhead to that location in the timeline. (You can, of course, also use bookmarks as bookmarks. But iMovie doesn't display a list of bookmarks in one place as it does with chapters markers.)

You don't have to create chapter markers in sequential order. If you add a marker to a movie that already contains some markers, iMovie automatically renumbers any markers that are located to its right.

Adding Chapter Markers

Step 1.

Position the playhead at the location where you want the chapter marker. Note that you can't have a chapter marker within the first one second of a movie, and that there must be at least one second between chapter markers.

You can drag the playhead there or use the keyboard shortcuts described in "The Keys to Precision" on page 159.

Step 2.

Click the iDVD button .

The iDVD pane appears.

Step 3.

Click the Add Chapter button.

Repeat these steps for each chapter marker you want to create.

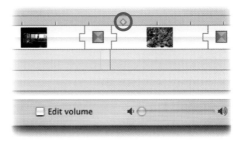

In the timeline viewer, iMovie displays a yellow diamond ◈ at each chapter marker's location.

Naming Chapters

For movies containing chapter markers, iDVD creates a "Scene Selection" menu button. When your DVD's viewers choose that button, they get an additional menu or set of menus that enable them to view each scene.

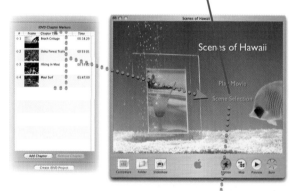

Each marker becomes a button, and each button's name corresponds to the chapter title. Notice that iMovie automatically creates a marker for the very beginning of the movie.

Tip: To quickly rename a chapter marker, select it and press Return. You can move from one marker to the next by using the up-arrow and down-arrow keys. By combining the arrow keys with the Return key, you can rename markers without having to reach for the mouse.

When you add a chapter marker, its name appears in the Chapter Title area of the iDVD pane. iMovie automatically names a chapter after the clip that appears at the marker's location. When you use that movie in an iDVD project, iDVD names buttons according to the chapter titles.

If you haven't named your clips as I recommend on page 158, you can wind up with meaningless chapter titles and button names, such as *Clip 03* or, for iPhoto images, *Roll 86-2*.

Even if you have named your clips, you might still want different button names. You can always edit button names in iDVD, but you can also edit chapter titles in iMovie: simply double-click on the chapter title and then type a new name.

Tips for Creating Chapters

How might you use DVD chapters? That depends on what's in your video. Here are some scenarios to give you ideas.

A wedding video
Create chapters for each of the day's main events: the bridesmaids beautifying the bride, the groom arriving at the church, the ceremony, the reception.

A kid's birthday party
Create chapters for each phase of the party: the arrival of the guests, the games, the opening of presents, the fighting, the crying.

A vacation video
Create chapters for each day or for each destination you visited.

A documentary
Create chapters for each of the main subjects or periods of time that you're documenting.

A training video
Create chapters for each subject or set of instructions.

Sharing Movies via the Internet

First things first: the Internet isn't the best medium for sharing digital video. The huge size of digital video files means that anything but a very short movie will take a long time to transfer, particularly over a modem line.

But if you have made a very short movie—or you have a fast Internet connection and expect that your viewers will, too—you can use iMovie to prepare your work for cyberspace.

With the Share command, you can email a movie or share it through a .Mac HomePage. iMovie compresses the movie heavily to make its file size smaller. In the process, you get an introduction to The Three Musketeers of Internet video: jerky, grainy, and chunky.

A movie compressed for the Internet contains fewer frames per second, so motion may appear jerky. The movie's dimensions are also much smaller—as small as 160 by 120 pixels, or roughly the size of a matchbook. And depending on the options you choose, the sound quality may not be as good as the original.

The best way to share a movie is to drop a DVD or a videocassette in the mail. But if you're willing to trade some quality for the immediacy of email or the world-wide reach of the World Wide Web, iMovie is ready.

To Email a Movie

Step 1.

Choose Share from the File menu (Shift-⌘-E), then click the Email button. Specify the settings shown below, then click Share.

Name your shared movie.

Like iPhoto, iMovie lets you use any of several popular email programs. Choose yours here.

Read it and weep: iMovie tells you just how much your movie will be mangled and how big the mangled version will still be. (Of course, your original movie is still stored in its full DV glory.)

To share only some clips, select them before choosing Share, then check this box.

Step 2.

iMovie compresses the movie and attaches it to a new email message. Compose and address the message, then send it on its way.

Tips

If your movie is short and your connection is fast, you might want to email a larger version of the movie than iMovie creates. Click QuickTime in the Share dialog box, then choose the Web option from the pop-up menu (see page 192). Export the movie, then attach it to an email message.

Many Internet providers restrict the size of attachments—often to 4MB or thereabouts. If your compressed movie is that large, it's better to share it on a HomePage.

Learn more about QuickTime compression.
www.macilife.com/imovie

To Share on a .Mac HomePage

To publish a movie on a .Mac HomePage, you must have a .Mac account.
(Go to www.mac.com to sign up.)

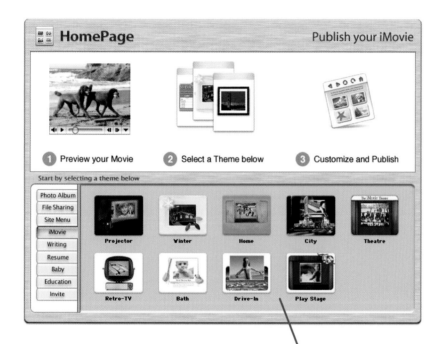

Step 1.

Choose Share from the File menu and click the HomePage button.

Type a name for the movie and click Share.

After iMovie compresses the movie, it copies the movie to your .Mac iDisk and then switches to your Web browser, where you complete the publishing process.

Step 2.

To choose a theme design for the HomePage, click the desired theme.

Step 3.

To choose a different theme, click Themes. To edit the HomePage, click the Edit button. You can edit the HomePage's name, add a caption, turn on a page counter, and turn on a Send Me a Message button that will allow your page's viewers to send you an Apple iCard electronic greeting card.

To finish the publishing process, click Publish. After a few moments, your browser announces that your page is on the Web.

More Ways to Share Movies

In the rightmost hinterlands of the Share dialog box are two buttons that represent iMovie's geekier sharing features—ones you're less likely to use than the others.

With the QuickTime button, you can export your project as a QuickTime movie. You might export a QuickTime movie in order to publish it on a Web site or burn it on a CD (page 196). Or you might want to email a movie to someone but use your own compression settings instead of those applied by iMovie's Email preset.

With the Bluetooth button, you can transfer your movie to a cell phone or other gizmo equipped with Bluetooth wireless technology. A cell phone isn't exactly the best venue for a movie, but it's great geek fun and it allows you to take a movie on the road.

Just remember to switch off your movie theater when the aircraft is not stopped at the gate.

Exporting a QuickTime Movie

To export your project as a QuickTime movie, choose Share from the File menu (Shift-⌘-E), then click the QuickTime button.

Choose a preset from the pop-up menu.

To specify custom compression settings, choose Expert Settings.

Expert advice. You can often improve on the picture quality provided by iMovie's Email, Web, and CD-ROM presets by using the Sorenson Video 3 compression scheme. To access it, hack through the following thicket of dialog boxes. In the Save dialog box that appears after you click Share, choose Movie to QuickTime Movie from the Export pop-up menu, then click the Options button. The Movie Settings dialog box appears; click Settings. In the next dialog box, choose Sorenson Video 3 from the pop-up menu. Now OK your way back to safety. If you like, explore the rest of the Movie Settings dialog box—it's where you can specify the movie's pixel dimensions and sound settings.

To learn about compression, see Clifford VanMeter's QuickTiming Web site (www.quicktiming.org) and *iMovie 4 Visual Quickstart Guide*, by Jeff Carlson (Peachpit Press, 2004). For more QuickTime resources, see www.macilife.com/imovie.

See a movie play on a cell phone.
◉ **Sharing a Movie via Bluetooth**

Exporting to a Bluetooth Device

Bluetooth is a wireless technology that connects devices over distances of up to about 30 feet. You can buy cell phones, printers, palmtop computers, keyboards, and mice that use Bluetooth's radio waves instead of cables to talk to each other and to the Mac.

Many Mac models have built-in Bluetooth. If yours doesn't, you can add Bluetooth using a tiny and inexpensive adapter such as the D-Link Bluetooth USB Adapter, which plugs into any free USB port on your Mac.

Mobile multimedia. Having Bluetooth is just one part of the mobile movie equation. Another part is a multimedia standard called 3GPP, which is supported by a growing number of cell phones and other gadgets. QuickTime supports 3GPP, too, and it's this support, combined with Bluetooth, that makes it possible to play a movie on a phone.

To play a 3GPP movie, you need a 3GPP media player for your device.

On the DVD, I'm using a Nokia 3650 running RealNetworks' free RealPlayer Mobile, which you can download at www.realnetworks.com/mobile.

Making the transfer. Be sure your phone is on, then choose Share from the File menu. In the Share dialog box, click the Bluetooth button, then click Share. iMovie compresses your movie, then displays a dialog box for transferring it.

To have your Mac search for nearby Bluetooth devices, click Search.

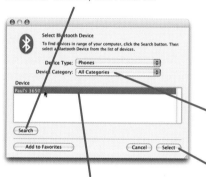

Select the device to which you want to transfer the movie.

Your phone may display a message asking if you want to receive the movie. Choose Yes.

After the transfer is complete, navigate to your phone's messages menu, choose the new message, and watch the show.

Tip: iMovie saves the compressed movie on your hard drive; you can use Mac OS X's Bluetooth File Exchange program to transfer the movie again. In your movie's project folder is a folder named Shared Movies. Inside that folder is a folder named Bluetooth. Your compressed movie is there; its name ends with the file extension .3gp.

If you have numerous Bluetooth devices, you can narrow down the list of devices displayed by choosing the device category.

After choosing a device, click Select.

A Movie In Your Palm

Palm OS-based handhelds can also play movies, but not the 3GPP kind that iMovie creates. To play movies on a Palm, you need to compress them into a format that can be played by a Palm OS movie player.

A first-rate movie player for Palm devices is the free Kinoma

Player, from Kinoma Inc. (www.kinoma.com). With Kinoma's inexpensive Kinoma Producer, you can compress an iMovie for Kinoma Player.

Open your movie's project folder and locate the reference movie that iMovie creates. (It has the same name as your project, but

ends with the extension .mov.) Drag this icon into Kinoma Producer, choose the desired audio and video settings, and click the Convert Files button. You can use Bluetooth File Exchange to transfer the compressed movie to your Palm.

Tips for Clips

Moving Clips from the Timeline

On occasion, you may want to remove a clip from the movie but keep it on the Clips pane to use later. If you're working in the clip viewer, this is easy: simply drag the clip back to the Clips pane.

But the more powerful timeline viewer, where you probably do most of your work, doesn't let you drag clips back to the Clips pane. Here's a workaround: In the timeline, select the clip you want to move to the Clips pane, and choose Cut from the Edit menu. Then select any clip on the Clips pane and choose Paste.

Copying and Pasting Clips

Speaking of the Edit menu, it's worth noting that you can make additional copies of a clip by copying it to the Clipboard and pasting it into the Clips pane or the timeline. If you want to experiment with different effects or cropping schemes, select the clip and choose Copy. Next, select another clip on the Clips pane and choose Paste. iMovie makes a copy of the clip and puts it on the Clips pane for you.

Moving Clips Faster

If you need to move a clip a significant distance—say, from the end of a project to the beginning—you could just drag it and let the clip viewer scroll automatically. But there's a faster way. Drag the clip from the clip viewer into any empty box on the Clips pane. Scroll through the clip viewer to the new destination, and then drag the clip from the Clips pane back into the clip viewer.

Multiple Clips at Once

Remember that iMovie now lets you select and manipulate multiple clips at once. You can apply the same effect, transition, or Ken Burns settings to several clips in one fell swoop. Just Shift-click to select a continuous range of clips, and ⌘-click to select clips that aren't next to each other.

Creating Color Clips

Want to create a text title with a background other than black? Here's how.

In the timeline viewer, drag any clip to the right to create a gap.

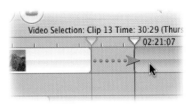

Next, position the playhead within this gap and choose Create Color Clip from the Advanced menu. iMovie turns the gap into a clip whose color is black.

To change the clip's color, double-click the clip, then click the Color swatch in the Clip Info dialog box. (While you're there, consider giving the clip a descriptive name, such as Blue Background.)

Now you can add a title to this clip. You can also use the previous tips to move the color clip to the Clips pane or make duplicates of it for use elsewhere in your project.

Freeze that Frame

On page 170, I mentioned creating a still frame in order to make Ken Burns do tricks he can't otherwise do.

That's just one way to use a still frame. Here's another. Say you've made a movie of Junior scoring the winning goal, and you've got a great close-up of his smiling face as his teammates hoist him up on their shoulders. If you create a still image of that shot, you can place the still at the end of your movie and add closing credits to it. When played back, the action will freeze on Junior's happy mug as the credits roll.

Here's a way to use still frames to provide the illusion of bringing an old photograph to life. First, create a still frame of the first frame of a video clip. Now create a duplicate of this frame using the tip on the opposite page. Add both frames to the timeline, positioning them just before the video clip, then apply the Sepia Tone effect to the first of the two frames.

Next, add a cross-dissolve between the sepia version and the non-sepia version. Finally, use direct trimming to adjust the length of the non-sepia version, making it as short as possible. (Snug it up against the right edge of the cross dissolve.)

When the footage plays back, your audience will see a sepia version of the scene turn into a full-color, full-motion version.

More Ways to Freeze

One way to create a still frame is to position the playhead at the spot that you want to freeze, then choose Create Still Frame from the Edit menu. Here's a shortcut: position the playhead at the desired spot, then Control-click on the playhead and choose Create Still Frame at Playhead from the shortcut menu.

You can also save a frame as a JPEG or PICT file for use in another program. Position the playhead at the frame you want to save, then choose Save Frame As from the File menu (⌘-F). In the Save dialog box, choose the JPEG or PICT format from the pop-up menu.

You can add JPEG frames to your iPhoto library and even make and order prints. However, the images are small—640 by 480 pixels—so don't expect to get high-quality prints in large sizes. You can email them, though, and that can be a fun way to share a few particularly good frames.

Navigation Tips

Control Your Clicks

Experienced Mac users make a habit of using those little shortcut menus that pop up when you Control-click on something (or right-click, if you have a two-button mouse or trackpad).

Earlier iMovie versions didn't provide Control-click shortcuts, but in iMovie 4, you can Control-click on just about anything to bring up a shortcut menu that lets you do relevant tasks. Try Control-clicking on a clip in the Clips pane, on the playhead, on the scrubber bar beneath the iMovie monitor, and on audio and video clips in the timeline.

Get Around Faster

Take advantage of iMovie's View menu to quickly navigate a large project. If you've scrolled a large distance and you want to jump back to the playhead's location, choose Scroll to Playhead (Option-⌘-P).

The Scroll to Selection command (Option-⌘-S) lets you quickly jump back to a selected clip. Zoom to Selection (Option-⌘-Z) zooms in on the selected clip or clips.

And if you're using bookmarks, remember that you can jump to the previous bookmark by pressing ⌘-[and to the next bookmark by pressing ⌘-].

Editing and Sharing Tips

Combining SFX with FX

In the movie world, *SFX* are sound effects, while *FX* are visual effects. As anyone who has watched a Hollywood blockbuster knows, they go together perfectly.

Many of iMovie's visual effects are candidates for sound effects, too. Pair the Fairy Dust effect with the Stardust sound effect. Combine the Electricity visual effect with the Electricity sound effect. And if you're adding a little tectonic action with the Earthquake effect, try using the Suspense sound effect along with it.

You get the idea: think about enhancing your visual effects with complementary sound effects to add impact.

Effects First, Markers Later

If you apply a visual effect to a clip that contains one or more iDVD chapter markers, you may lose the chapter markers. Apply the effect first, *then* add chapter markers.

Recording with iSight

If you have Apple's iSight camera, you can use it with iMovie 4. The iSight's video quality isn't as good as what you get from a miniDV camcorder, but may do in a pinch.

When an iSight camera is connected and turned on, you can record by switching into camera mode and then clicking the Record Using iSight button.

You can also use the iSight's microphone to record narration or ambient sound effects. Add the clip you recorded to the timeline, then Control-click on it and choose Extract Audio. Delete the video portion of the clip, then move the audio to the desired location on the timeline.

Exporting Your Movie's Sound

There may be occasions when you want to export part or all of the audio track of your project. Maybe you want to bring it into an audio-editing program, such as Spark ME or Amadeus, for fine-tuning. Or maybe you recorded a music recital and you'd like to bring the performance into iTunes.

To export your project's soundtrack, choose Share from the File menu, click QuickTime, choose Expert Settings, and click Share. In the Save dialog box that appears, choose Sound to AIFF from the Export pop-up menu. Click Options, then choose the desired audio settings.

If you'll be bringing your audio back into iMovie, use the default options. If you'll be importing the audio into iTunes, choose 44.100 from the Sample pop-up menu.

Burning Movies to CD and Video CD

If your Mac has a CD burner, you might want to burn your exported movie to a CD so you can share it with others. In the Share dialog box, click QuickTime, then choose the CD-ROM option. Next, insert a blank CD into your Mac's optical drive and copy the movie to the CD. The resulting CD will play on any Mac or Windows computer that has QuickTime installed.

If you have Roxio's Toast Titanium software, you can also create a Video CD. This video format is very popular in Asia, and somewhat obscure everywhere else. But most stand-alone DVD players can play Video CDs, as can all current personal computers. (To play Video CDs on a Mac, use Mireth Technology's MacVCD X software, available at www.mireth.com. And if you don't have Toast Titanium, you can also make Video CDs using Mireth Technology's iVCD.)

Video on a Video CD is compressed in MPEG-1 format. The image quality is a far cry from that of the MPEG-2 format used on DVDs; Video CD image quality is more akin to that of VHS videotape. One reason is because the video frame size is smaller—352 by 240 pixels, instead of DVD's 720 by 480. Another reason is that the video itself is compressed more heavily—about 90:1, compared to roughly 30:1 for MPEG-2. But on the plus side, a Video CD can shoehorn about an hour of video onto a CD-R disc.

A variation of the VideoCD format is called *Super Video CD*, or *SuperVCD*. On a SuperVCD, video is stored in MPEG-2 format, yielding better quality than a Video CD. The SuperVCD format also allows for many DVD-like features, such as alternate

Get links to iMovie add-ons.
www.macilife.com/imovie

GO TO WEB

language tracks. Its video quality still falls short of a DVD's, however.

Video CD and SuperVCD are second-best alternatives to DVDs, but if you don't have a SuperDrive, any alternative is better than none. For background on the Video CD and SuperVCD formats, see www.vcdhelp.com.

Adding On to iMovie

Several companies sell inexpensive add-ons that expand iMovie's repertoire of effects, titles, and transitions. Companies offering iMovie add-ons include Virtix, GeeThree, and Stupendous Software. Each of these companies also offers

free iMovie effect plug-ins. You'll find a selection of free iMovie plug-ins from GeeThree in the Extras folder of your DVD. For links to more plug-ins, see www.macilife.com/imovie.

Editing Like the Pros: Making the TV Connection

What a difference a check box makes. Activate iMovie's Play Video Through to Camera option (in the Preferences dialog box), and anything you play—a single video clip, a title or transition, or your entire project—plays back not only on the Mac's screen, but also on your camcorder.

What's so hot about that? Simply this: the video iMovie outputs to your camcorder plays at full resolution and full motion—it isn't the jittery, preview-quality video iMovie displays on the Mac. Pop out your DV camcorder's LCD monitor, and you can use it to get a far more accurate assessment of the video.

But don't stop there—connect your camcorder's video output to

a TV to view your work on a large screen. This is how video professionals edit, and once you try it you'll never settle for iMovie's preview-quality playback.

First, connect your DV camcorder to the Mac with a FireWire cable as usual.

Next, connect your camcorder's video output to the video input of a TV set. If your TV and your camcorder each have S-Video connections, you should use

them for the best video quality. If your TV lacks S-Video but has a composite video input (an RCA jack), use it. If your TV lacks video inputs, add an RF modulator between the camcorder and the TV set. You can buy the modulator at Radio Shack for about $30.

Once you've made the connections, choose Preferences from the iMovie menu and click the Play Video Through to Camera check box.

When this option is selected, your project's audio will not play back through your Mac's speakers. You can rely on your camcorder's tiny, built-in speaker for sound playback, but you might want to connect your camcorder's audio outputs to your TV's audio inputs, if it provides them; to a stereo system; or to a pair of external amplified speakers.

To make VHS dubs of your projects, connect a videocassette recorder between the camcorder and TV: connect the camcorder's outputs to the VCR's inputs, and the VCR's outputs to the TV's inputs.

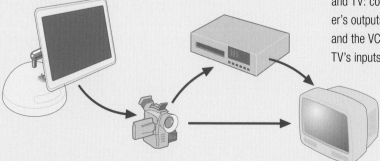

Tips for Making Better Movies

Editing takes more than software. You also need the right raw material. Advance planning will help ensure that you have the shots you need, and following some basic videography techniques will make for better results.

Plan Ahead

Planning a movie involves developing an outline—in Hollywood parlance, a *storyboard*—that lists the shots you'll need to tell your tale. Professional movie makers storyboard every scene and camera angle. You don't have to go that far, but you will tell a better story if you plan at least some shots.

Consider starting with an *establishing shot* that clues viewers in on where your story takes place—for example, the backyard swimming pool. To show the big picture, zoom out to your camcorder's wide-angle setting.

From there, you might cut to a medium shot that introduces your movie's subject: little Bobby preparing to belly flop off the diving board. Next, you might cut away to Mary tossing a beach ball. Cut back to Bobby struggling to stay afloat, and then finish with a long shot of the entire scene.

Keep in mind that you don't have to shoot scenes in chronological order—sequencing your shots is what iMovie is for. For example, get the shot of Mary's throw any time you like and edit it into the proper sequence using iMovie.

Steady Your Camera

Nausea-inducing camera work is a common flaw of amateur videos. Too many people mistake a video camera for a fire hose: they sweep across a scene, panning left and right and then back again. Or they ceaselessly zoom in and out, making viewers wonder whether they're coming or going.

A better practice is to stop recording, move to a different location or change your zoom setting, and then resume. Varying camera angles and zoom settings makes for a more interesting video. If you must pan—perhaps to capture a dramatic vista—do so slowly and steadily.

And, unless you're making an earthquake epic, hold the camera as steady as you can. If your camera has an image-stabilizing feature, use it. Better still, use a tripod or a monopod, or brace the camera against a rigid surface. Keeping the camera steady is especially critical for movies destined for the Internet—because of the way these videos are compressed, minimizing extraneous motion will yield sharper results.

Compose Carefully

The photographic composition tips on page 149 apply to movie making, too. Compose your shots carefully, paying close attention to the background. Get up close now and then—don't just shoot wide shots.

Record Some Ambient Sound

Try to shoot a couple of minutes of uninterrupted background sound: the waves on a beach, the birds in the forest, the revelers at a party. As I've mentioned previously, you can extract the sound from this footage and use it as an audio bed behind a series of shots. It doesn't matter what the camera is pointing at while you're shooting—you won't use the video anyway.

After importing the footage, use the Extract Audio command described on page 178 to separate the audio.

Shooting with Compression in Mind

If you know that you'll be distributing your movie via the Internet—either through a Web site or email—there are some steps you can take during the shooting phase to optimize quality. These steps also yield better results when you're compressing a movie for playback on a Bluetooth device, and they even help deliver better quality with iDVD.

First, minimize motion. The more motion you have in your movie, the worse it will look after being heavily compressed. That means using a tripod instead of hand-holding your camera, and minimizing panning and zooming. Also consider your background: a static, unchanging background is better than a busy traffic scene or rustling tree leaves.

Second, light well. If you're shooting indoors, consider investing in a set of video lights. A brighter picture compresses better than a poorly lit scene. To learn about lighting, read Ross Lowell's excellent book, *Matters of Light and Depth* (Lowel Light, 1999).

Vary Shot Lengths

Your movie will be more visually engaging if you vary the length of your shots. Use longer shots for complex scenes, such as a wide shot of a city street, and shorter shots for close-ups or reaction shots.

Be Prepared, Be Careful

Be sure your camcorder's batteries are charged; consider buying a second battery so you'll have a backup, and take along your charger and power adapter, too. Bring plenty of blank tape, and label your tapes immediately after ejecting them. To protect a tape against accidental reuse, slide the little locking tab on its spine.

Don't Skimp on Tape

Don't just get one version of a shot, get several. If you just shot a left-to-right pan across a scene, for example, shoot a right-to-left pan next. The more raw material you have to work with, the better.

Converting Analog Video and Movies

Somewhere in your closet is a full-sized VHS camcorder—the kind that rested on your shoulder like a rocket launcher. You have a FireWire-equipped Mac, and you want to get some of that old VHS video into it.

If you've since upgraded your artillery to a miniDV-format camcorder, connect it to your VHS camcorder or to a VCR and then record your VHS footage on DV tapes. Connect the video and audio output jacks on the VHS deck to your DV camcorder's video and audio input jacks. If your VHS deck and camcorder each provide S-video jacks, use them to get the best picture

quality. After you've made your DV dubs, connect your DV camera to the Mac and use iMovie to import the video.

An Analog-DV Converter

A faster way to get analog video into your Mac is through a converter, such as those sold by Formac Electronics, DataVideo, Sony, and others. These devices eliminate the time-consuming process of dubbing VHS tapes to DV format. Connect a converter to your Mac's FireWire jack, then connect your old VHS rocket launcher to the converter's video and audio inputs. Then, launch

iMovie and use its import features to bring in VHS video. Using iMovie's Share command, you can also blast edited video through the converter back to the VHS camcorder.

When importing VHS video, you may notice a thin band of flickering pixels at the bottom of the image. Don't worry: these artifacts won't appear when you view your finished video on a TV screen.

Converting Films

As for those old Super 8 film-based flicks, you'll need to send them to a lab that does film-to-

video transfers. Many camera stores can handle this for you. The lab will clean your films, fix bad splices, and return them along with videotapes whose contents you can bring into the Mac. If you have a DV camcorder, be sure to use a lab that will supply your converted movies on DV cassettes—you'll get much better image quality than VHS provides. Some labs also offer optional background music and titles, but you can add these yourself once you've brought the converted video into the Mac.

Creating Time-lapse Movies and Animation

Our minds are mesmerized by animation, whether it's a time-lapse movie of a brewing storm, some claymation that brings Play-Doh to life, or the hand-drawn artistry of a classic cartoon.

With some inexpensive software and a video camera, you can put your world into motion. The process is simple, if time consuming. For animation, shoot one frame of video at a time, moving objects or changing a drawing between each frame. Time-lapse movies are easier: point your camera at an interesting scene, then go to the mall while your software snaps a frame at whatever interval you like. When you play your final movie, toy cars will race, clouds will billow, and flowers will bloom—you get the idea.

A time-lapse or animation project can be a fun school or family endeavor. Here's a look at the tools you'll need, along with some tips and project ideas.

The Tools

To put your world in motion, you need a camera, a tripod, and some software. To get the best video quality, connect a miniDV camcorder to your Mac's FireWire jack. If you don't have a camcorder, an inexpensive Web cam, such as Apple's iSight, will also work.

As for software, if you have a DV camcorder, your first stop might be Gary Fielke's free DVTimeLapse. True to its name, DVTimeLapse creates time-lapse movies using miniDV-format cameras—it doesn't work with Web cams such as the iSight.

Boinx Software's iStopMotion (www.istopmotion.com) works with DV camcorders as well as Web cams. For details on it and other animation tools, see www.macilife.com/imovie.

The Techniques

Prepare your gear. Mount your camera on a tripod and plug the camera's power adapter into a wall outlet—batteries won't last long enough.

Many DV camcorders shut themselves off after a few minutes when you aren't recording to tape. You can usually bypass this auto-shutoff by taking the tape out of the camera. If your camera still insists on slumbering, try leaving its tape door open.

Connect the camcorder to your Mac, launch your software, and you're ready to go. Here are some possible destinations.

Toys in motion. For an easy stop-motion project, put some toys in motion: the Matchbox Car 500. For your animation stage, choose an area where the lighting is going to be fairly consistent over several hours. If you're relying on light from windows, try to shoot on a cloudy day. Dramatic variations in lighting from one frame to the next will ruin the illusion of motion.

See an example of time-lapse animation in the Extras folder.

GO TO DVD

For animators, patience isn't a virtue—it's a must. Move objects slowly and gradually—just a fraction of an inch between frames. And whatever you do, don't bump your tripod between frames.

To save time, try shooting two frames, instead of just one, between each move. Animators call this animating *on twos*, and it takes half the time but usually delivers fine results.

Kids in motion. For a variation on the previous theme, animate some kids: point the camera at the back yard, and have the kids take a small step between each frame. In the final movie, they'll appear to move without walking.

Time for time-lapse. Making time-lapse movies is much easier, since your subject does the moving on its own. All you have to do is set up your scene and start capturing.

What to shoot? A snowstorm, a rose, the clouds, a burning candle, a glass filled with ice, the shadows cast by a fence or set of window blinds. Anything that moves or changes shape slowly in the real world is a great candidate for time-lapse photography.

Sunsets and sunrises make spectacular time-lapse movies. To avoid damaging your camera, don't zoom in on the sun or point the camera directly at a midday sun.

How frequently should you capture a frame? That depends on how quickly your subject is changing and on how long you want your final clip to be. For a time-lapse of a rose blooming, I used a one-minute interval, which turned an hour of real time into one second of video. For some cloud scenes, I used a 15-second interval.

To calculate the ideal frame interval, begin by determining the duration of the real event, the desired duration of your final clip, and the number of frames per second you want the final clip to have (20 frames per second is a good starting point). Say a rose bud takes four hours to blossom, and you want the time-lapse clip to play for nine seconds. Multiplying nine seconds by 20 frames per second yields 180 frames. Finally, divide the duration of the real event by the number of frames you need. In this example, 240 minutes divided by 180 frames equals about 1.3 minutes—or about 80 seconds between frames.

Post-Production

After creating an animation, try enhancing it in iMovie.

Make a montage. When researching animation and time-lapse techniques, I shot a variety of time-lapse scenes, then edited them into a montage.

After shooting the clips and importing them into iMovie, I added a music track. I've always loved *Koyaanisqatsi,* a film comprised largely of beautiful time-lapse photography; its Philip Glass music score by is a perfect complement to time-lapse scenes. A quick search of the iTunes Music Store led to the soundtrack album, and 99 cents later, I had my movie's soundtrack. (Remember, you can't use copyrighted work in commercial projects.)

Next, I imported my time-lapse movies into iMovie and added them to the time-line, cropping each clip so that the scenes would change roughly in tempo with the music. Then I added a cross-dissolve transition between each scene.

Run it backwards. To put a different spin on a time-lapse clip, reverse it: see a rose close itself or a glass of water turn into a glass of ice. After adding the clip to iMovie's timeline, select it and choose Reverse Clip Direction from the Advanced menu.

Create a time-lapse title. Making a movie of your Hawaii vacation? Shoot a time-lapse clip while you're there, then use iMovie's Titles pane to superimpose text over it. Making a movie of the kid's birthday party? Create a stop-motion clip of the kids scooting around the back yard, and use it to close out the movie.

iDVD:
Putting it
All Together

The Macintosh
iLife '04

iDVD at a Glance

With Apple's SuperDrive DVD burner and iDVD software, you can go from being a viewer to a producer. iDVD lets you burn movies and photos to DVD-R media, complete with menus you can fully customize.

Designers and photographers can use iDVD to assemble digital portfolios that they can hand out like brochures. Filmmakers and advertising professionals can distribute rough cuts of movie scenes and commercials to clients and colleagues. Businesspeople can create in-house training discs and video archives of corporate meetings. Videographers can offer DVDs of weddings and other events. And home-movie buffs can preserve and share family videos and photographs.

Creating a DVD involves choosing and customizing a menu theme and adding the movies and photos you want to include on the DVD. You can perform these steps in any order and preview your work along the way. When you've finished, you can burn the final product to DVD-R media.

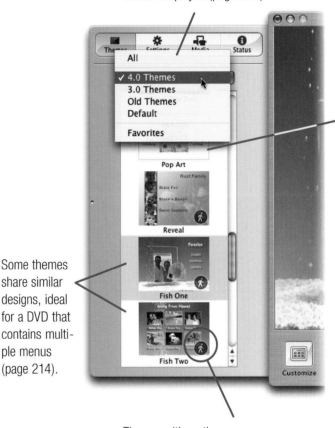

You can narrow down the list of themes displayed (page 206).

Some themes share similar designs, ideal for a DVD that contains multiple menus (page 214).

Themes with motion menus are indicated by the motion icon.

A Short Glossary of DVD Terms

authoring The process of creating menus and adding movies and images to a DVD.

button A clickable area that plays a movie or slide show, or takes the user to another menu.

DVD-R The blank media that you'll use most often when burning DVDs. A DVD-R blank can be burned just once.

DVD-RW A type of DVD media that you can erase and reuse.

menu A screen containing clickable buttons that enable users to access a DVD's contents.

motion menu A menu whose background image is an anima-

tion or movie, a menu that plays background audio, or both.

MPEG-2 The compression format used for video on a DVD. MPEG stands for *Moving Picture Experts Group*.

iDVD compresses movies you've added into MPEG-2 format. You can monitor the status of this process here.

iDVD provides several pre-designed menu templates, called *themes*, some of which provide motion menus and audio.

To create a custom menu background, drag an image from iPhoto or another program to the iDVD window (page 206).

Many themes have *drop zones*, special areas into which you can drag photos or a movie (page 207).

Each menu on your DVD has a title, whose position and formatting you can customize (page 217).

To add a movie to your DVD, drag it into iDVD's window. iDVD creates a button, whose appearance you can customize (page 217).

After you've customized a theme, you can save it for future use (page 224).

To show or hide the Customize drawer, click Customize.

A DVD can have multiple menus; to create an additional menu, click Folder (page 215).

You can create slide shows containing images from iPhoto and background music from iTunes (pages 210–211).

To preview and burn menus containing motion or background audio, click Motion.

Get the big picture (page 215) and add *AutoPlay* content (page 219).

To try out your DVD before burning it, click Preview (page 208).

To burn your finished DVD, click Burn (page 222).

Choosing and Customizing Themes

A big part of creating a DVD involves choosing which menu theme you want. iDVD includes menu themes for many types of occasions and subjects: weddings, parties, vacations, kids, and more. Many of these themes have motion menus containing beautiful animations and, with some themes, background music or sound effects.

Your design options don't end once you've chosen a theme. Many of iDVD's themes provide *drop zones*, special areas of the menu background into which you can drag photos or movies. Drop zones make it easy to customize a theme with your own imagery.

Most drop zones have special effects that iDVD applies to the photos or movies that you add to them. For example, the Road Trip One theme puts your imagery in a car's rear-view mirror. The Projector theme creates an old-movie appearance, complete with scratches. The Theater drop zone adds animated curtains—and if you look closely, you'll see the curtains even cast shadows on your imagery.

Some extremely sophisticated software engineering lies behind themes and drop zones. But who cares? What matters is that they let you create gorgeous DVD menus with a few mouse clicks.

Choosing a Theme

Step 1.

Click the Customize button to open the Customize drawer.

Step 2.

If the list of themes isn't visible, click the Themes button.

Step 3.

Choose the theme you want by clicking it.

Use the pop-up menu to access themes from older versions of iDVD.

Note: In order to see a theme's motion, you must have motion turned on. To turn motion on or off, click the Motion button. As you work on your DVD, you'll probably want to turn motion off since iDVD runs faster this way. Just remember to turn motion back on before burning your DVD.

Take a tour of iDVD's themes, and see how to customize them.
⊙ **Touring iDVD's Themes**
⊙ **Adding Items to a Drop Zone**

Adding Items to a Drop Zone

Step 1.

Click the Media button in the Customize drawer. Then, to access photos in your iPhoto library, choose Photos from the pop-up menu. To access movies, choose Movies.

Step 2.

In the iPhoto or iMovie media browser, select the item or items you want to add.

You can select multiple photos or an entire album. If you add multiple photos to a drop zone, iDVD displays them successively as the menu is displayed. You can add up to 30 photos to a drop zone. You can add only one movie to a drop zone.

Step 3.

Drag the selected items into the drop zone.

As you drag into a drop zone, a dotted line indicates the drop zone's boundaries.

Step 4.

To fine-tune an item's position within the drop zone, drag it using the hand pointer 🖐.

Tips for Working with Drop Zones

Drop Zones Aren't Buttons

It's important to understand the difference between drop zones and buttons. A drop zone is merely an area of imagery within a DVD menu—it isn't a clickable button that your DVD's viewers can use to watch your DVD. A drop zone is a piece of eye candy; a button is a navigation control that plays a movie or slide show or jumps to another menu.

How to Tell the Difference

As you drag items into the menu area, how can you tell whether you're dragging into a drop zone or creating a button? Easy: When you're dragging into a drop zone, a dotted-line pattern appears around the edges of the drop zone, as shown above. If you don't see this pattern, you aren't in the drop zone, and you'll end up creating a button.

Other Ways to Add Items

You can also add items to a drop zone by dragging them from the Finder: simply drag the items' icons into the drop zone. And you can drag photos from iPhoto directly into a drop zone.

If you don't like dragging and dropping, here's one more way to add items: Control-click within a drop zone, and choose the Import command from the pop-up shortcut menu that appears.

Removing Items

To remove the contents of a drop zone, drag the item out of the drop zone. When you release the mouse button, the item disappears in a puff of smoke. As an alternative to dragging, you can also Control-click within the drop zone and choose Clear from the shortcut menu.

Adding Movies to Your DVD

iDVD's job is to integrate and present assets from other programs. The assets you're most likely to add to your DVDs are movies you've created in iMovie or another video-editing program, such as Apple's Final Cut Express or Final Cut Pro.

You can add movies to your DVDs using a couple of techniques. Use the movie browser to access movies stored in specific locations on your hard drive. Or, simply drag a movie directly into the iDVD window.

As you add movies and other assets, remember that you can preview your DVD-in-progress at any time by clicking the Preview button. When previewing, use the remote control (below) to test your DVD.

Adding a Movie Using the Movie Browser

Step 1.
Click the Customize button to open the Customize drawer.

Step 2.
Click the Media button, then choose Movies from the pop-up menu.

iDVD lists movies contained in your Movies folder. To have iDVD list movies located elsewhere on your hard drive, choose Preferences from the iDVD menu, click the Movies button, and add additional folders to the list.

Available movies appear here.

Movies created using iMovie contain a small iMovie icon.

To preview a movie in the movie browser, select the movie and click this play button, or simply double-click the movie.

Use the Search box to locate a movie in the browser.

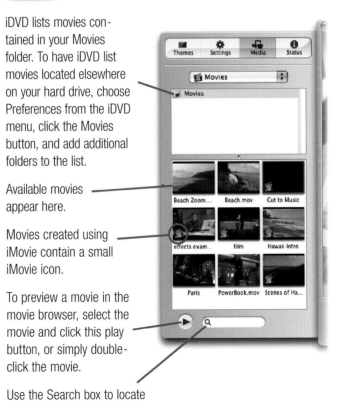

Displays a movie's menu.

Displays the top-most menu on DVDs containing multiple menus.

Turns preview mode off.

Jump to the previous or next chapter in a movie, or to the previous or next photo in a slide show.

Click the arrows to navigate. Click Enter to choose the highlighted menu button.

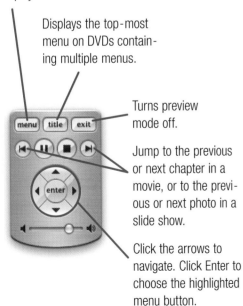

See how to add movies.
◉ **Adding a Movie**

Step 3.

Drag the desired movie into your DVD's menu area.

iDVD adds the movie to your DVD and creates a menu button for it.

Tip: Be sure you don't drag the movie into a drop zone; see "Tips for Working with Drop Zones" on page 207.

If the movie contains DVD chapter markers, iDVD creates two buttons: one named Play Movie and another named Scene Selection. If the movie lacks DVD chapters, iDVD simply creates one button, giving it the same name as the movie itself. To rename any button, select it and edit the name.

Other Ways to Add a Movie

You can also add a movie by dragging its icon from the Finder into the iDVD window. For example, if you have an iMovie project that isn't displayed in iDVD's Movie browser, open the iMovie project folder, locate the reference movie inside (it ends with .mov), and drag it into the iDVD window.

And finally, you can add a movie by choosing the Video command from the File menu's Import submenu.

Tips for DVD Movies

Encoder Settings

Video on a DVD is compressed, or *encoded*, into a format called MPEG-2. iDVD performs this encoding either as you work or after you click the Burn button.

In iDVD 4, you can have up to two hours of video on a disc. By adjusting iDVD's encoder settings, you can control how much video will fit as well as the quality of the video itself. Choose Preferences from the iDVD menu, click the General button, and cast your eyes on the Encoder Settings options.

The Very Best

If you have more than one hour of video—or you want the best quality iDVD is capable of—choose Best Quality. In this mode, iDVD puts on its thinking cap and analyzes your video, with the goal of compressing it as little as possible.

You get great quality and up to two hours on a disc, but be patient. Encoding upwards of two hours of video may take several hours on slower, single-processor G4 Macs.

The Very Fastest

If you have under an hour of video, consider the Best Performance option. The video still looks great and encoding is much faster. When you choose Best Performance, you have the option of allowing iDVD to encode while you work: click the Enable Background Encoding check box. If iDVD runs sluggishly, uncheck the box, and encoding will take place after you click Burn.

For more encoding insights, see page 227.

Using Movies from Final Cut

iDVD can also encode Final Cut Pro or Final Cut Express movies. Export the movie by choosing QuickTime Movie from the File menu's Export submenu. (In older Final Cut versions, this command is Final Cut Movie or Final Cut Pro Movie.) If the movie has chapter markers, be sure to choose the Chapter Markers option in the Markers pop-up menu of the Save dialog box.

Creating DVD Slide Shows

iDVD slide shows are a great way to share photos. Even low-resolution photos look spectacular on a television screen, and they can't easily be copied and redistributed—a plus for photographers creating portfolio discs. (You can, however, opt to include the originals on the disc, as described in "The DVD-ROM Zone" on page 220.)

iDVD provides a few ways to create a slide show. You can use iDVD's iPhoto browser to drag an entire photo album into the iDVD window. You can also use the iDVD button in iPhoto to send an album or a selection of photos to iDVD. And you can manually drag photos from iPhoto (or anywhere else) into iDVD's slide show editor.

You can give your slide shows background music from your iTunes library and fine-tune other aspects of their appearance. You can also choose to have a transition between each images; iDVD 4 gives you six transition styles from which to choose (see page 218).

A slide show can contain up to 99 images. Each image can be any size and orientation; however, vertically oriented images will have a black band on their left and right sides.

Creating a Slide Show Using the iPhoto Browser

Step 1.

In iPhoto, create an album containing the photos you want in the slide show, sequenced in the order you want them to appear (see page 102).

Step 2.

In iDVD, click the Customize button to open the Customize drawer.

Step 3.

Click the Media button, then choose Photos from the pop-up menu.

Your iPhoto library and its albums appear here. To display more photos or albums, drag the horizontal separator below the album list up or down.

The photos in your library or a selected album appear here.

To search for a photo based on its title, type part or all of its title here.

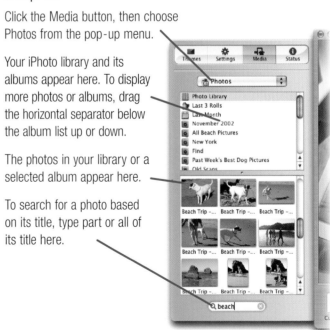

See techniques for creating DVD slide shows.
◉ **Creating a Slide Show**
◉ **Using iPhoto's iDVD Button**
◉ **Adding Music to a Slide Show**

Step 4.

Locate the desired album and drag it into the iDVD menu area.

Tip: Be sure you don't drag the album into a drop zone; see "Tips for Working with Drop Zones" on page 207.

iDVD creates the slide show as well as a menu button for displaying it. iDVD gives the button the same name as the album, but you can rename it to anything you like.

Creating a Slide Show Within iPhoto

When you're working in iPhoto, you can send an album or a selection of photos directly to iDVD, where they become a slide show.

Step 1.

Select the photos you want to include in the DVD slide show. To include an entire album or roll, select the album name or the roll name.

Step 2.

Click the iDVD button in iPhoto's Organize pane.

iPhoto sends the photos to iDVD, which creates a new slide show for them.

Creating a Slide Show from Scratch

You can also create a blank slide show and then manually add photos to it.
You might use this technique to add photos that aren't stored in your iPhoto library.

Step 1.

Click iDVD's Slideshow button.

iDVD adds a button named My Slideshow to the currently displayed menu. Rename this button as desired.

Step 2.

Double-click on the button that iDVD just created.

The slide show editor appears.

Step 3.

Drag photos (or a folder containing photos) into the slide show editor.

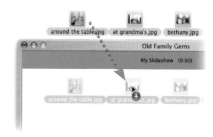

Refining a Slide Show

Regardless of how you create a slide show, you can fine-tune it by using the slide show editor. To display the editor, double-click on the menu button that corresponds to the slide show you want to edit.

To change playback order, drag images. You can select multiple images by Shift-clicking and ⌘-clicking.

Switch between list view and thumbnail view.

To have iDVD repeat the slide show over and over, check this box (see opposite page).

When checked, this box superimposes arrows over the images as a hint to viewers that they can move back and forth in the slide show using their DVD remote controls.

To have iDVD store the original images on the DVD, check this box. (For details, see "The DVD-ROM Zone" on page 220.)

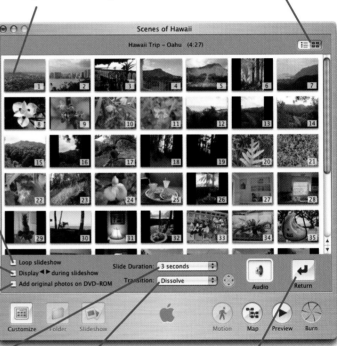

You can specify a duration for each image, or have the slide show timed to match its background audio. If the slide show has background audio, the Manual option isn't available.

You can have a transition between each photo. For some transition styles, you can also specify a direction, such as a left-to-right wipe.

Return to the menu that leads to this slide show.

Tip: To delete a photo from the slide show, select it and press the Delete key. This doesn't delete the photo from your hard drive, it just removes it from the slide show.

See techniques for refining a slide show.
◉ Adding Music to a Slide Show
◉ Refining a Slide Show

Adding Music to Slide Shows

You can add a music track to a slide show. One way to add music is by using the iTunes browser in iDVD. Open the Customize drawer, click the Media button, then choose Audio from the pop-up menu. Locate the song you want (use the search box if need be), then drag it to the Audio well. To add an entire playlist, drag

it to the Audio well. Don't like to drag? Select the song or playlist you want to add, then click the Apply button in the iTunes browser.

You can also drag a song directly from the iTunes window or, for that matter, from any folder on your hard

drive. And you don't even have to drag an audio file: if you drag a QuickTime movie to the Audio well, iDVD will assign its audio to your slide show.

If you create a slide show by clicking the iDVD button in iPhoto, the slide show will retain whatever song was assigned to it in iPhoto. (For details on assigning songs to albums, see page 116.)

How iDVD matches your soundtrack to your slides depends on the option you choose from the Slide Duration pop-up menu. If you choose a specific duration, such as five seconds per slide, iDVD repeats your soundtrack if its duration is shorter than the slide show's total duration. If the soundtrack is longer than the slide show, iDVD simply stops playing the soundtrack after the last slide displays. And if you choose the Fit to Audio option, iDVD times the interval between image changes to match the soundtrack's duration.

To remove a slide show's background music, drag the icon out of the Audio well. When you release the mouse button, the icon vanishes in a puff of smoke.

Slide Show Tips

TV-Safe Slide Shows

Normally, when you view a slide show on a TV screen, you don't see the outer edges of each photo. This is because TV screens typically crop off the outer edges of an image. If you want to see your images in their full, uncropped glory, choose iDVD's Preferences command, click the Slideshow button, and check the box labeled Always Scale Slides to TV-Safe Area. When this option is active, iDVD sizes images so they don't completely fill the frame—thus eliminating cropping.

Looping a Slide Show

Want to see that slide show again and again? Check the Loop Slideshow box, and the slide show will repeat until the cows come home—or at least until your DVD's viewer presses the Menu or Title button on his or her remote control.

You can also specify looping when you aren't in the slide show editor. Select the button that leads to a slide show (or select the slide show's icon in the Map), then choose Loop Slideshow from the Advanced menu.

Planning and Creating Menus

When creating a DVD, you're also designing a user interface. If your DVD contains a couple of movies and a slide show, the interface will be simple: just one menu containing a few buttons.

But if your DVD will contain a dozen movies and another half-dozen slide shows, it will need multiple menus. And that means that you'll need to think about how to structure a menu scheme that is logical and easy to navigate.

As you plan a complex DVD, consider how many buttons each menu should have. In iDVD 4, a menu can have up to twelve buttons. That's a lot—too many choices for a main menu. If you have several movies and slide shows to present, it's better to create a set of *submenus* that logically categorize your content.

It's a balancing act: create too few menus, and you present your viewers with a daunting number of choices. Create too many, and you make them spend time navigating instead of viewing.

Many of the themes in iDVD 4 are designed with submenus in mind. Examples include Road Trip One and Road Trip Two, and Wedding Silver One and Wedding Silver Two. You don't have to use these themes for projects containing submenus, but at least note their underlying philosophy: it's a good idea for a submenu to share some common design traits with the menus that lead to it.

Planning Your DVD

If your DVD will be presenting a large number of movies or slide shows, you need to plan how you will make that content available to the DVD's user. How many menus will you need? How will you categorize the content in each menu? This process is often called *information design*, and it involves mapping out the way you want to categorize and present your content.

A good way to map out a DVD's flow is to create a tree diagram depicting the organization of menus—much as a company's organizational chart depicts the pecking order of its management.

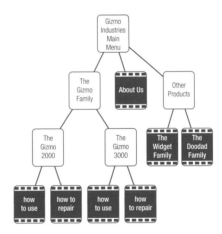

The chart shown here depicts the flow of a DVD a company might create to promote its new Gizmo product line. A main menu contains three buttons: two lead to other submenus, while the third plays a promotional movie about the company.

The submenu "The Gizmo Family" leads to two additional submenus, one for each Gizmo model. The "Other Products" submenu leads to two movies that promote other fine products.

See techniques for working with menus.
◉ **Creating a New Menu**
◉ **Navigating with the Map**

Creating Additional Menus

iDVD calls submenus *folders*. To create a folder, click the Folder button.

To design the new menu and add content to it, double-click its button. You can customize the look of each submenu independently of other menus.

Each submenu has a return button that, when clicked, returns the user to the menu that led to the submenu.

Finding Your Way with Map View

iDVD 4's map view lets you see the organization of your DVD project using a display that looks a lot like the organization chart depicted on the opposite page.

To switch to map view, click the Map button.

In map view, you can see at a glance how your project is organized. More to the point,

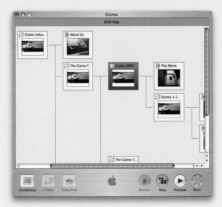

you can get around quickly. To jump to any menu, double-click it. To preview a slide show or movie, double-click it. Map view even creates a separate icon for each chapter in a movie, enabling you to quickly test your chapter markers.

Map view is about more than just viewing. You can use it to add looping to a slide show or movie, and to have a movie or slide show start automatically when your DVD is played. For details, see page 219.

To exit map view, click the Map button again or double-click an icon in the map view.

Customizing Menus

The design themes built into iDVD look great and, in some cases, sound great, too. But you might prefer to not use off-the-rack designs for your DVDs.

Maybe you'd like to have a custom background screen containing your company logo or a favorite vacation photo. You might like the background image of a particular iDVD theme, but not its music or its buttons' shape or typeface. Or maybe you'd just like to have the title of the menu at the left of the screen instead of centered.

You can customize nearly every aspect of your DVD's menus and navigation buttons. With the Settings pane of the Customize drawer, you can modify buttons, add and remove background audio, change a menu's background image, and more.

You can also create text labels—for example, some instructions for DVD newbies or a few lines of commentary about the DVD's subject.

Customizing Button Positions

Normally, iDVD positions buttons on a fixed grid. This keeps them lined up nicely, but there are times when you might want to manually specify a button's location—perhaps to line it up with a custom background image.

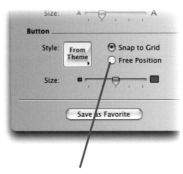

To manually control button position, select the Free Position option in the Button area of the Settings pane. Now you can drag buttons wherever you like.

Inserting a Line Break

You may want to create a button or title whose text spans more than one line. Easy: Just press the Return key to start a new line.

Adding Text

To add descriptive text, captions, or instructions to a menu, choose Add Text from the Project menu (⌘-K). A text area appears; drag it to the desired location, then click within that text area, and type. To start another line, press Return.

To format the text, use the Text area of the Settings pane; see the opposite page.

Kill the Watermark

iDVD displays the Apple logo watermark on each menu screen. To get rid of it, choose Preferences from the iDVD menu, click the General button, and then uncheck the Show Apple Logo Watermark box.

Staying TV Safe

TV sets omit the outer edges of a video frame—a phenomenon called *overscan*. To make sure buttons and other menu elements will be visible on TV sets, choose the Show TV Safe Area command in the Advanced menu, and avoid putting buttons or other elements in the shaded area.

See techniques for customizing a menu.
◉ **Customizing a Menu**
◉ **Staying in the TV Safe Area**

iDVD: Putting it All Together

Customizing Menus

Changing the Background Image

To change the background image of an iDVD menu, simply drag an image into the menu area. For the best results, be sure to use a photo whose proportions match the 4:3 aspect ratio of television. You can ensure these proportions when cropping in iPhoto: from the Constrain pop-up menu, choose 4 x 3 (DVD).

Tips: Some photos make better backgrounds if you reduce their brightness and contrast so the image doesn't overwhelm the buttons. In iPhoto, duplicate the image and then adjust the brightness and contrast of the duplicate.

If you replace the background on a theme that has a drop zone, the drop zone remains. To remove a drop zone when replacing a background, press ⌘ while dragging the image into the menu.

Want a plain white background? You'll find one in the Extras folder of the DVD. You can also make your own patterned or solid-colored backgrounds in a program like Photoshop Elements. Create a graphic with dimensions that are 640 by 480 pixels, save it as a JPEG image, and then drag it into iDVD.

If your project contains several menus, you can apply one menu's custom design to other menus in the project; see page 219.

And, if you decide you'd rather just have the theme's original background, simply drag the custom background's image thumbnail out of the Background well in the Settings pane.

Customizing Button Shapes

iDVD's design themes not only specify things such as background image and audio, they also determine the shape of each menu button. To change the shape of a menu's buttons, choose an option from the pop-up menu in the Button area.

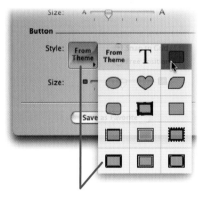

To use the button shape from the current theme, choose From Theme. For a text-only button, choose the T option.

Each button style has its own style of highlight, which appears when a user selects the button. To see the highlights for a button style, click iDVD's Preview button.

You can also control the size of the buttons: drag the Size slider.

Changing Button Text Labels

With the Text area of the Settings pane, you can change where a button's text labels appear in relation to the button's thumbnail image. You can also get rid of text and just have button images.

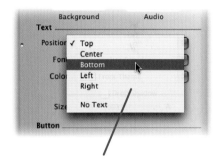

To customize button labels, choose an option from the Position pop-up menu.

To add a soft shadow to some text, select the button or label and click the Drop Shadow box.

You can also change the font, font color, and type size for button text and for the menu's title and any text you've added. If you don't like the results, choose the Undo command as many times as needed to get back to where you started.

Tip: To format all of a menu's buttons at once, select them all first: click on one button, then press ⌘-A. Similarly, to select every text item you've added, click one item and then press ⌘-A.

More Design Tips

Adding Menu Transitions

iDVD 4 added the ability to have a transition between menus. You can choose from six transition styles: cube, dissolve, droplet, mosaic, page flip, and wipe. For menu transitions, I like cube, page flip, or wipe—each conveys the notion of moving from one area to another. In my opinion, dissolve and droplet are better suited to slide shows. And mosaic is simply too busy for my tastes.

To add a transition to a menu, choose the desired transition from the Transition pop-up menu in the Settings pane. Some transitions, such as cube, also allow you to specify a direction—set this by clicking the little arrows next to the pop-up.

Avoid mixing multiple transition styles in a single DVD. It's just tacky.

Note: In iDVD 4, a menu transition is, unfortunately, a one-way street. That is, a transition appears only as you drill *down* into a DVD's menu structure. If you navigate from a submenu back to a main menu, you don't see a transition.

Moving Buttons Between Menus

To move a button from one menu to another, select the button and choose Cut. Next, move to a different menu (use map view to get there in a hurry), then paste.

As I demonstrate on the DVD, this trick can be handy when you add a slide show using the iDVD button in iPhoto. When you click the iDVD button in iPhoto, the slide show's button is placed on your DVD's main menu. To move it to a submenu, cut and paste it.

Creating Online Help

You can also *copy* a button instead of pasting it. You might do this to provide access to a piece of content from several different menus.

For example, say you've created a series of online help screens in the form of a slide show. To make the online help available from every menu in your DVD, copy its button and then paste it into each menu.

New Menu from Selection

After adding numerous items to a DVD, you realize that a particular menu has too many buttons. The solution: move some of those buttons to a new menu. But don't wear out your wrists cutting and pasting. Just select the buttons you want to move (Shift-click on them), then sprint

up to the Project menu and choose New Menu from Selection. iDVD removes the selected buttons and stashes them in a new menu.

Silencing Motion Menus

You might like the look of a motion menu, but maybe you don't want any music or sound effects to play. To silence a motion menu, click the little speaker icon in the Audio well of the Settings pane. If you change your mind, click the icon again. To silence the menu for good, drag the icon out of the Audio well, and it disappears in an animated puff of smoke.

Audio-Only Menus

Conversely, maybe you would like some background audio to play, but you don't want motion in your menus. First, choose a theme that lacks motion, or replace an existing motion theme's background with a static image. Next, drag an audio file, iTunes playlist, or QuickTime movie into the Settings pane's Audio well. Keep in mind that you must click iDVD's Motion button in order to hear (and burn) your menu's background audio.

In iDVD 4, a menu can play for up to 15 minutes—a big improvement over the 30-second limit of previous versions.

Motion Buttons

In many themes, iDVD also applies motion to your movie buttons: small, thumbnail versions of the movies play back when the menu is displayed.

See more DVD customizing techniques.
◉ **Replacing a Menu's Audio**
◉ **Moving Buttons Between Menus**
◉ **Specifying an AutoPlay Movie**

You can even specify which portion of the movie plays: just select its button and then drag the slider that appears above the movie.

To specify how much of a movie plays in a motion button, drag the Duration slider in the Settings pane.

There are times when you might not want a movie's button to be a thumbnail movie. Maybe the movie is dark, and its thumbnail version is illegible. Or maybe the movie thumbnail distracts from the motion menu's background. In any case, simply select the movie's button and then uncheck the Movie checkbox that appears above it. Now use the slider to choose a static thumbnail image for the movie.

If you're using a theme that has text-only buttons—for example, Montage—you can add motion or thumbnail buttons by choosing a different button style in the Button area of the Settings pane.

Copying Custom Menus

Your project contains several menus and you've customized one of them with a new background image or movie and maybe some customized fonts. Now you decide you'd like to apply your design to all the menus in your project. Easy: choose Apply Theme to Folders from the Advanced menu.

Conversely, if you've customized a folder menu and want to apply that design to the project's other menus, choose Apply Theme to Project.

More Map View Fun: Looping and AutoPlay

iDVD's map view is about more than just seeing the big picture. You can also use it to loop a piece of content and to specify that a movie or slide show will play automatically when someone begins playing your DVD.

Loopy. To have a movie or slide show loop, select its icon in map view and choose Loop from the Advanced menu. (You can also specify looping by selecting a movie's or slide show's menu button and choosing Loop.)

AutoPlay. On many DVDs, a movie appears when the DVD begins playing—an FBI warning, for example, or a movie-studio logo.

You can use map view to add *AutoPlay* content to your DVD. Simply drag a movie, a photo, a set of photos, or an entire iPhoto album to the project icon in the top-left corner of the map view.

If you drag photos to the project icon, you can double-click the project icon to open the slide show editor, where you can specify transitions and add background music (page 213).

Don't want an AutoPlay item after all? Just drag it out of the project icon.

Cute little AutoPlay movies are built into many of iDVD 4's themes, including Road Trip, Drive In, Montage, Kids Theater,

and Marquee. You can replace or delete these AutoPlay movies from your DVDs as you see fit.

Creating a kiosk DVD. Want a movie or slide show to play automatically and continuously? Drag it to the project icon and then, with the project icon still selected, choose Loop from the Advanced menu.

Adding DVD-ROM Content

One of the reasons why the DVD format is so versatile is that it can accommodate not only video, sound, and pictures, but also any disk files that you may want to distribute.

Here's the scoop on this aspect of DVD authoring, along with a peek under the hood to see how MPEG-2 compression manages to squeeze up to two hours of video onto a 4.7GB DVD.

The DVD-ROM Zone

A DVD can hold more than video and slide shows; it can also hold "computer files"—Microsoft Word documents, PDF files, JPEG images, and so on. You might take advantage of this to distribute files that relate to your DVD's content.

If you've created an in-house training DVD for new employees, you might want to include a PDF of the employee handbook. If you've created a DVD containing a couple of rough edits of a TV commercial, you might also include some PDFs that show the print versions of your ad campaign. If you've created a DVD promoting your band, you might include some audio files of your tunes.

When a DVD-Video disc also contains files intended to be used by a computer, it's said to have a *DVD-ROM* portion. If users play the DVD in a living-room DVD player, those files are invisible. However, if they use that same DVD with a personal computer, they can access the files.

Including Photos

iDVD makes it easy to take advantage of the versatility of DVDs. As described on page 210, when creating DVDs containing slide shows, you can have iDVD copy the original images to the DVD-ROM portion. In the slide show editor, simply check the box labeled Add Original Photos on DVD-ROM.

This option is ideal for photographers who want to distribute high-resolution versions of their images along with slide shows. You might also find it a useful way to back up a set of digital photos. The slide shows serve as a handy way of viewing the images, while the original, high-resolution files are archived in the DVD-ROM portion of the disc.

Tip: If you *always* want to include a slide show's original images on your DVD, choose Preferences from the iDVD menu, click the Slideshow button, then check the box labeled Always Add Original Slideshow Photos to DVD-ROM.

Managing DVD-ROM Content

To add other types of files to your DVD, choose Edit DVD-ROM Contents from the Advanced menu. Use the DVD-ROM Contents window to manage and organize the contents of the DVD-ROM folder.

Your DVD will contain a folder whose name is your project's name plus *DVD-ROM Contents*.

To add files to the DVD-ROM area, drag them into the DVD-ROM Contents window, or use the Add Files button. To delete a file from the DVD-ROM area, select it and press the Delete key.

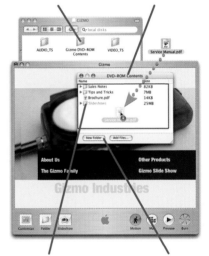

If you've added photos from one or more slide shows to the DVD-ROM area, they appear in a folder named Slideshows. You can't rename this folder or move it to another folder. To delete it, return to the slide show editor and uncheck its DVD-ROM box.

You can create additional folders within the DVD-ROM folder, and you can drag files or other folders into it.

MPEG: Compressing Space and Time

One of the jobs iDVD performs is to compress your movies into MPEG format, the standard method of storing video on DVD-Video discs. Like image and audio compression,

MPEG is a lossy format: the final product lacks some of the quality of the original. But as with image and audio compression, the amount of quality loss depends on the degree to

which the original material is compressed.

Like JPEG, MPEG performs spatial compression that reduces the storage requirements of

individual images. But video adds the dimension of time, and MPEG takes this into account by also performing temporal compression.

The key to temporal compression is to describe only those details that have changed since the previous video frame. In an MPEG video stream, some video frames contain the entire image; these are called *I-frames*. There are usually two I-frames per second.

 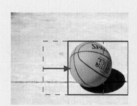

An I-frame describes an entire scene: "There's a basketball on a concrete driveway."

Sandwiched between those I-frames are much smaller frames that don't contain the entire image, but rather contain only those pixels that have changed since the previous frame.

"It's rolling toward the street."

To perform temporal compression, the video frame is divided into a grid of blocks, and each square is examined to see if anything has changed. Areas that haven't changed—such as the stationary background in this example— are simply repeated in the next frame.

This is why video with relatively little motion often tends to look better than video that contains a great deal of motion. When little changes from one frame to the next, the quality of each frame can be higher.

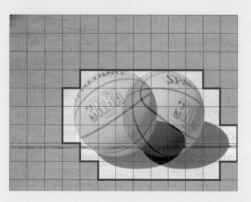

Burning Your DVD

You've massaged your media and made your menus. What's next? Burning the final product onto a DVD-R blank. Simply double-click iDVD's Burn button and insert a blank disc. But before you burn, read the following tips.

Preview First

Before you insert that pricey blank DVD-R, preview your work by clicking iDVD's Preview button. Use the iDVD remote control to step through your menus and spot-check your video, slide shows, and any menu transitions you've added. If your DVD contains motion menus or background menu audio, be sure to click the Motion button before previewing.

Update as Needed

Older SuperDrives can be damaged by 4x DVD-R media, which became widely available in late 2002. If you're using 4x DVD-R media and have an older SuperDrive—generally, one that predates August 2002—you may need to update the drive's internal firmware. To download the updater, see www.apple.com/hardware/superdrive. For more background on the issue, see www.macilife.com/superdrive.

On the other hand, if you're lucky enough to have a dual-processor G5 system, be sure you're using iDVD 4.0.1 or a later version, if available. iDVD 4.0 had a bug that could cause burn errors on dual G5 systems if you selected the Best Performance encoding preference.

Run Lean

When burning a DVD, avoid running complex programs that put a lot of demands on your system. Recording a track in GarageBand while also burning a DVD is not a good idea, for example. Also, consider turning off file sharing and quitting any disk-intensive programs.

Plus or Minus?

When shopping for blank DVD-R and -RW media, you're likely to see DVD+R and DVD+RW blanks, too. Avoid them—they use a different recording standard than most SuperDrives, and they won't work in them.

You can learn about the different standards that exist for DVD burning by reading Jim Taylor's superb DVD FAQ (www.dvddemystified.com).

Burning to DVD-RW Media

Apple doesn't publicize it, but the SuperDrive can read from—and write to—rewritable DVD media, called DVD-RW. A DVD-RW blank costs considerably more than a DVD-R blank, but you can erase and reuse it about a thousand times.

You can use -RW media to test your project before committing it to a write-once DVD-R blank—but you have to trick iDVD. Here's how. Double-click the Burn button as you normally would, and insert a DVD-R blank when iDVD tells you to. Next, when you see iDVD's "Preparing" status message, press your keyboard's

Eject key and replace the DVD-R with an erased DVD-RW. (To erase a DVD-RW, use Mac OS X's Disk Utility program.) iDVD will never know the difference.

But the DVD player in your living room probably will; as the tip on the following page describes, many DVD players can't read rewritable media.

After the Burn

If you're running low on disk space, you can reclaim up to 4GB after burning your DVD. In the General area of iDVD's Preferences dialog box, check the box labeled Delete Rendered Files On Closing a Project. When you quit iDVD or open a different project, iDVD deletes the MPEG-2 movie files that it created from your original videos. But note that if you want to burn another copy of the disc, iDVD will have to encode its video all over again.

You can burn multiple copies of a DVD using iDVD, but you might find the job easier with Roxio's Toast Titanium, which provides disc-duplication features. Insert the DVD you burned and then copy its Video_TS and Audio_TS folders to your hard drive. You can burn additional copies of the disc by dragging these folders into Toast.

Toasting Slowly

If you do use Toast to burn additional copies of your DVD, consider burning at a slow speed, such as 1x or 2x. Burning at a slow speed can yield discs that play more reliably, particularly on set-top DVD players.

Watch the DVD burning process.
◉ **Burning a DVD**

Will It Play?

You've burned a DVD-R disc and are ready to show it off to your boss. You pop the disc into the conference room DVD player and press the play button—and nothing happens.

Welcome to The Incompatibility Zone. The sad fact is, some DVD players and personal computer DVD drives are unable to read DVD-R or DVD-RW media. Generally, older DVD players and drives are most likely to have this problem, but you may encounter it in newer players, too.

Roughly 85 percent of DVD players can read DVD-R discs, and about 65 percent can read DVD-RW discs. Those are good numbers, although they won't be of much solace if your player—or your boss's—is in the minority.

If you're shopping for a new DVD player, be sure to verify compatibility with DVD-R (and, if you plan to use rewritable media, DVD-RW). And diplomatically inform your friends, family, and colleagues that if they have problems playing your DVD, the fault probably lies with their players.

Making More

If you need to have more than a few copies of a disc—for example, 2,000 training DVDs for a large company—you'll want to work with a replicator. Most replicators will now accept a burned DVD-R as a master.

Prices for replication vary widely and, as you might expect, go down as the quantity you order goes up. One excellent source for low-volume replication is CustomFlix (www.customflix.com), which also provides e-commerce and shipping services.

Archiving Projects for Burning Elsewhere

iDVD 4 introduced an archiving feature that saves a project and all of its assets in one self-contained file. You can move this file to another Mac to continue working on the project or to burn it.

Archiving enables you to author on one Mac, then burn on another. This is great for anyone who has multiple Macs but not multiple SuperDrives. If you have a PowerBook without a SuperDrive and a desktop Mac with one, you can still work on a DVD on a cross-country flight.

Just archive and transfer your project when you land.

To archive a project, choose Archive Project from the File menu.

If you created customized themes for the DVD—or if you want to be certain that your themes will be available in a future version of iDVD—check the Include Themes box. If you're using standard themes and you aren't obsessed about future compatibility, you can uncheck this box and your archive file will be a bit smaller.

If iDVD has already encoded the DVD's content, you can include those encoded files in the archive by checking the Include Encoded Files box. Doing so will make your archive file quite a bit larger, however.

After you specify archive settings and click Save, iDVD goes to work, copying everything in your project into a file. You can transfer this file to another Mac using a FireWire hard drive, a fast network, or the FireWire disk mode that laptop Macs provide.

iDVD Tips

Make It Last

DVD-R discs don't last forever. To improve their reliability and longevity, don't use peel-and-stick labels. If a label isn't perfectly centered, the DVD will be off-balance when it spins, and that could cause playback problems. Label discs with a Sharpie or other permanent marker. Write small and be brief—the solvents in permanent ink can damage a DVD's substrate over time.

If you want a flashy label on your DVDs, use one of the growing number of color inkjet printers that can print on CD and DVD media.

Keep burned DVDs in jewel cases, and store them in a cool, dark place.

More Themes

Want to go beyond the themes that are built into iDVD? Try out some of the themes from DVDThemePak (www.dvdthemepak.com). Each ThemePAK contains a eight or more themes, most with motion menus and drop zones. All of the themes are lovely, but there are some absolute gems in each set. Several of the company's free themes are included in the Extras folder of this book's DVD.

Other sources for iDVD themes include iDVDThemes (www.idvdthemes.com) and iDVD Themetastic (www.idvd-themetastic.com).

Burning Movies from a Digital Camera

Many digital cameras can shoot small movies, which you can transfer to your Mac using Mac OS X's Image Capture program or the Finder (page 143). You can include digital camera movies in an iDVD project—just drag them into the iDVD window.

Indeed, you can burn nearly any kind of QuickTime movie onto a DVD, including movies you've downloaded from the Web or copied from an old CD-ROM.

If a movie is smaller than the DVD standard of 720 by 480 pixels, iDVD enlarges it to fill the screen. This results in a loss of sharpness, but enlarged movies can still look good when viewed on a TV. It's better to have shared a blurry movie than never to have shared at all.

Reverting Your Project

You've made some modifications that you don't like. Many programs, including GarageBand, have a Revert command that lets you get back to the last version you saved. iDVD lacks a Revert command, but you can simulate one: just reopen the project by choosing its name from the Open Recent submenu in the File menu. Click Don't Save when iDVD asks you if you want to save changes before reopening the project.

Saving a Theme Design

You can save a customized theme as a "favorite" and apply it to future projects with one mouse click.

Click the Save as Favorite button at the bottom of the Customize pane.

If you have multiple user accounts on your computer, you can make the custom theme available to all users.

The new theme appears in the Themes pane. To see it, choose Favorites or All from the themes pop-up menu. On your hard drive, saved themes are stored in your home directory in the following path: Library > iDVD > Favorites. Shared themes are stored in the same path at the root level of the drive.

Project Management Tips

When you add a movie or set of images to iDVD, the program doesn't actually add those files to your project file. Rather, iDVD simply links to the existing files on your hard drive.

If you need to move a project from one Mac to another, create an archive of the project using the Archive Project command in the File menu. As described on page 223, this command copies all of the project's assets into one file.

If you copy just the project file—or if you delete an asset that you added to the project—iDVD displays broken-link icons for buttons whose assets are missing.

When you open a project containing broken links, iDVD displays an error message.

Broken link icon appears for missing assets.

You can avoid the hassle by not moving assets once you add them to a project, or by creating an archive of the project to gather all its assets in one place.

To get the big picture of a project, choose Project Info from the Project menu.

You can change the DVD's name here. This doesn't change the name of your project file; rather, it changes the name of the final DVD. The DVD specification doesn't permit a disc name to have spaces in it; iDVD replaces any spaces with underscores, as in HAWAII_SCENES.

If you've moved a file to a different folder or drive, you can aim iDVD in the right direction: click Find File, then locate and double-click the file.

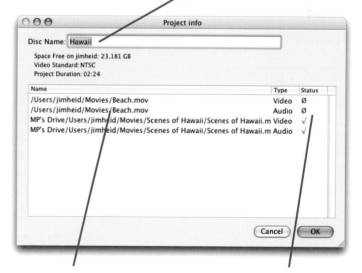

To reconnect to a missing file, double-click its entry, then locate the file and double-click its name.

The Project Info window displays a list of the project's assets; its Status column indicates if any assets are missing (Ø).

More iDVD Tips

Painless Pane Switching

You want to drag a movie, audio file, or image into the Settings pane, but the Media pane is currently visible. How do you get your media from here to there? Easy: just drag the media's icon *over* the Settings button and pause there for a moment—iDVD switches to the Settings pane. Now continue dragging into the Background or Audio well.

Hacking iDVD

The iDVD application is a *package*, a kind of sophisticated folder that stores iDVD's program code and other resources. By exploring the contents of the iDVD package, you can take an inside look at iDVD's themes, and even extract video and audio from them.

To open the iDVD package, Control-click on the iDVD application icon and choose Show Package Contents from the pop-up shortcut menu. The Finder displays a directory window showing the contents of the iDVD package. Double-click on the Contents folder, and then on the Resources folder.

Within the Resources folder, you'll find iDVD's themes (each ends with the text *.theme*). Each theme is also a package—to explore it, Control-click on its icon and choose Show Package Contents from the shortcut menu. Double-click the

Contents folder and then the Resources folder, and you'll find background movies and audio loops. To extract an item—for example, to grab the background audio from the Drive In One theme—press Option while dragging the item's icon out to the desktop. This makes a duplicate of the item, leaving the original theme unchanged.

Take care to not throw away or alter any resources whose purpose you don't understand, lest you have to reinstall the iDVD application.

From PDF to DVD

An iDVD slide show isn't restricted to the JPEG image format. A slide show can display numerous graphics formats, including PDF.

iDVD's PDF support means that you can display just about any document in a slide show. Want to put a Microsoft Word document or a Web page in a slide show? Create a PDF version of the document: choose Print from the File menu, then click the Save as PDF button. Drag the PDF into the iDVD slide show editor, and iDVD creates a slide containing the contents of the PDF's first page. (If you have a multi-page document, save each page as a separate PDF.)

Before making a PDF of a document, you might want to choose the Page Setup command and click the landscape-orientation button. That way, your PDF

will have the same horizontal orientation as a slide. If you make the PDF in portrait orientation, your slide will have black borders on either side of the page.

Think twice about using a PDF that contains lots of text, especially in font sizes below 14 point. Small text looks fuzzy on a TV screen.

Making Custom Motion Menus

You aren't limited to the motion menus that accompany iDVD. You can make any QuickTime movie a motion menu background: just drag the movie to the Background well in the Settings pane.

If your motion menu movie is smaller than full-screen, iDVD enlarges it to fit. For the best video quality, use a movie whose dimensions are 640 by 480 pixels or 720 by 480 pixels.

As for what to put in your own custom menu, that's up to you. If the star of your DVD is an iMovie production, you might use a two- or three-minute excerpt of your movie. (Select a few clips in the timeline, then click the Share Selected Clips Only option in iMovie's Share dialog box.) Open a new iMovie project, bring that footage in, then use iMovie's Brightness & Contrast effect to make the footage appear faint. That way, buttons and text labels will still be easy to read. Save your work, then drag the movie to the Background well in iDVD's Settings pane.

Smooth looping. A motion menu loops until a user chooses a menu option. To avoid a visually jarring loop point, try this: in iMovie, create a still frame of the very first frame of your menu movie. Add this still frame to the very end of the movie, and put a fairly lengthy (say, two-second) dissolve between the end of the movie and the still frame. Finally, use direct trimming to make the remainder of the still frame as short as possible. (Drag its right edge to the left until it's right next to the dissolve in the timeline.) Now, when your movie loops, its last frame will appear to gradually dissolve into its first frame.

If you're after something more abstract, you can buy royalty-free libraries of animated backgrounds that you can use as motion menus. Two sources are ArtBeats (www.artbeats.com) and Digital Juice

(www.digitaljuice.com). If you have Final Cut Pro, you can use its LiveType program to create rich animated textures.

A motion menu in iDVD 4 can be up to 15 minutes long. But keep in mind that menu video uses disc space just like any other video clip.

Automating iDVD

iDVD provides thorough support for AppleScript, the automation technology that's built into Mac OS X. iDVD's AppleScript support enables you to create scripts that automate the creation and layout of DVDs.

The ultimate example of iDVD's autopilot features is a free utility that Apple has created called iDVD Companion. iDVD Companion is a program that runs alongside iDVD, adding a window containing

three tabs that let you nudge buttons in single-pixel increments, align multiple buttons, and specify the exact pixel location of a menu's title—all things that iDVD alone can't do.

iDVD Companion also provides its own menus, and their commands do things iDVD can't do by itself. For example, iDVD Companion's Select Back Button selects the arrow-shaped back button that iDVD uses in menus and slide shows. Once that button is selected, you can use iDVD Companion's nudge features to change its position. To download iDVD Companion and other iDVD scripts, visit www.apple.com/applescript/idvd.

More iDVD Tips

Encoding Insights and Tips

You don't have to know how iDVD 4 encodes MPEG-2 video, but if you're curious, here are the details.

Best Quality. When you choose Best Quality in the Encoder Settings area of the Preferences dialog box, the bit rate depends in part on how much media is in your project. Data rates will vary from a low of 3.5 megabits per second (Mbps) to 7 Mbps. With

best-quality encoding, iDVD uses variable bit rate (VBR) encoding: the bit rate of a video stream changes according to the complexity of the scene. Motion-intensive scenes get a higher bit rate, while scenes containing little motion get a lower rate.

(For you compression gurus, iDVD uses single-pass variable bit rate encoding. Thus, iDVD still can't quite deliver the

degree of quality you can get from Apple's Compressor program, which supports two-pass VBR and provides additional quality-optimization settings.)

Best Performance. When you choose the Best Performance option, iDVD encodes at a fixed bit rate of 8 Mbps—as did previous versions of iDVD when your DVD had an hour or less of video.

Tip: If you've burned a DVD using best-quality encoding and you delete some content from the project, you may be able to improve the video quality of the remaining content by having iDVD encode it all over again. Choose Delete Encoded Assets from the Advanced menu, then burn the project again.

GarageBand: Making Your Own Music

GarageBand at a Glance

GarageBand turns your Mac into a musical instrument and a multitrack recording studio. Even if you aren't a musician, you can use GarageBand to create original songs.

If you've never played a note, start by exploring GarageBand's library of pre-recorded musical phrases, called *loops*. Assemble the loops you like into a tune. For extra credit, change the pitch of some loops by *transposing* them.

If you play the piano, plug a music keyboard into your Mac and go to town—GarageBand's *software instruments* enable your Mac to mimic instruments ranging from pianos to guitars to drums and beyond. Use loops to create a rhythm section, and then play along. Record your performances, then use GarageBand's editing features to make yourself sound better.

If you sing or play an instrument, connect a microphone, electric guitar, or other audio input to your Mac and hit the Record button. Create a three-part harmony by laying down vocal tracks one at a time. You'll save a fortune on backup singers.

As you compose, you may want to enhance certain tracks with *effects*. Add reverberation to create a concert hall sound, simulate old guitar amplifiers, or modify a software instrument to create a unique sound. Refine your mix as you go along by adjusting volume levels and stereo *panning*. When you're finished, export your song to your iTunes music library.

Here's how to become a one-Mac band.

The Loop Browser

GarageBand includes more than 1,000 loops, and you can add more. To locate and audition loops, use the loop browser. Find loops by clicking buttons or typing search terms, such as *conga* (page 237). Once you've narrowed your search, click a loop to hear it.

The Track Editor

Transpose loops and refine your performance using the track editor, whose appearance changes depending on which type of track you're editing.

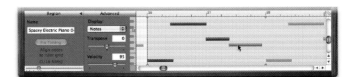

Editing notes. With the track editor for software instruments, you can edit individual notes (page 244).

Editing audio. With the track editor for real instruments, you can modify recordings (page 247).

See and hear GarageBand in action.
◉ **GarageBand: Making Your Own Music**

Each track is a member of your virtual ensemble (page 234). Each track has controls for muting and adjusting volume (page 250).

Adjust a track's overall volume and left-right stereo position in the Mixer (page 250).

By repeating and modifying loops in the *timeline*, you can assemble everything from rhythm sections to entire arrangements (page 236).

The moving playhead shows the current playback location; drag the playhead to move around within a song.

The *beat ruler* shows beats and measures. To move the playhead to a specific spot, click the ruler.

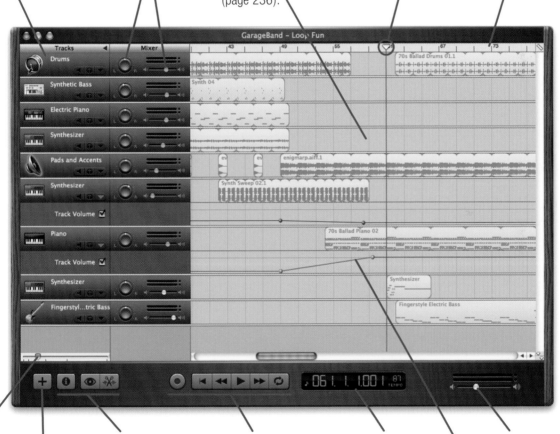

Drag the zoom slider to zoom in and out on the timeline.

Create a new track (pages 236, 242, and 246).

Display the Track Info window (pages 248 and 257), the loop browser (opposite page), and the track editor (opposite page).

Transport controls: record, play, rewind, and cycle playback (page 239).

The time display shows the playhead's exact position and the song's tempo. Drag the numbers to move the playhead and change the tempo.

Adjust the overall song volume.

To control volume over time, create *volume curves* (page 251).

How to Be a Songwriter

How you use GarageBand depends on your musical experience and your musical tastes. Here's a look at a few different paths you may take. And note that you aren't restricted to just one route—you might move from path to path as a song comes together.

Composing with Loops

Use the loop browser to locate a loop that sounds interesting (page 236).

Playing a Keyboard

Create a software instrument track and choose the desired software instrument (page 242).

If you like, customize the instrument to create a unique sound (pages 248 and 257).

Start a New Project

Specify the key, tempo, and time signature for your song. You can change any of these details later. You can even adjust tempo while your song is playing back.

Recording Audio

Create a real instrument track and choose the desired effect settings (page 246).

Adjust volume levels to get a loud, but not distorted, signal (page 247).

See how to get started in songwriting.
⊙ **Starting a New Project**

Drag the loop into the timeline to add it to your song; drag the loop pointer to repeat the loop as desired (page 236).

Refine the loop as desired: split and transpose it (page 240), edit it (pages 244 and 254), or change its effects (page 248).

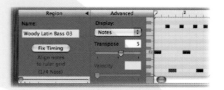

Record your performance, using GarageBand's Count In command and metronome to keep you in tempo (page 243).

Refine and arrange: modify and move regions (page 239), apply effects (page 248), and fix mistakes (page 244).

Mix

Adjust each track's volume levels and panning, optionally adding a set of final-mastering effects (page 252). When you're finished, export the song to your iTunes music library.

Record your performance, laying down multiple takes if you like (page 246).

Edit your recording—rearrange it, change its effects, or combine the best parts of several takes into a single track (page 247).

Two Types of Tracks

When you compose in GarageBand, you work with two very different types of tracks: *real instrument* tracks and *software instrument* tracks. The loops that GarageBand provides also fall into these two broad categories: loops with a blue icon are real instrument loops, and loops with a green icon are software instrument loops.

But what's the difference between a real instrument and a software instrument? The answer lies in the fact that today's Macs are powerful enough to generate sound using more than one technique. In fact, GarageBand is able to generate sound using multiple techniques *at once*.

Here's a look a how GarageBand makes its noise—and at what it all means to you.

Real Instruments: Prerecorded Sound

A real instrument track holds a digital audio recording—a riff played by a bass player, some strumming on an acoustic guitar, a phrase played by a string section, or a vocal that you record.

A real instrument track is blue, and a real instrument loop has a blue icon. Notice that the track and the icon depict a wave-form—a graphical picture of sound, similar to what we saw back on pages 26 and 176.

The purple variation. Audio that you record—a vocal, for example—is stored in a real instrument track. In the timeline, though, GarageBand uses purple color-coding to indicate these regions.

Software Instruments: Sound on the Fly

A software instrument track doesn't hold actual sound. Instead, it holds only *data* that says what notes to play and how to play them. The sounds you hear when you play a software instrument track are being generated by your Mac as the song plays back.

A software instrument track is a bit like the music rolls that a player piano uses—just as the holes in the music roll tell the piano which notes to play, the bits of data in a software instrument track tell your Mac which notes to generate.

A software instrument track is green, and a software instrument loop has a green icon. Instead of depicting a waveform, a software instrument region shows individual notes—why, it even looks a bit like an antique player piano roll (see photo, left).

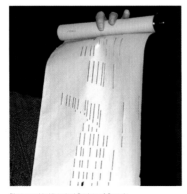

Photographic Historical Society of Canada

See an introduction to tracks.
⊙ **Two Types of Tracks**

GO TO DVD

Comparing Approaches

Each type of track has advantages and capabilities that the other lacks.

The real advantage. When it comes to realism, you can't beat real instrument tracks. Listen to the Orchestra Strings loops that come with GarageBand. They don't just sound like a string section—they *are* a string section. Compare their sound to that of the software instrument loop named 70s Ballad Strings 02.

Another advantage of real instrument tracks is that they can hold *your* digital audio. When you plug a microphone into your Mac and belt out *My Way,* your voice is stored in a real instrument track.

The software advantage. The primary advantage of software instrument tracks is versatility. Because software instrument tracks store individual note data, you can edit them in almost any way imaginable. You can even change the instrument entirely. Want to hear how your bass line would sound when played by a synthesizer instead of an electric bass? Just double-click on the software instrument track's header and choose a synth.

On the downside, software instrument tracks make your Mac work harder than real instrument tracks—it's harder to generate sound on the fly than it is to play back a recording.

Common ground. Although real instruments and software instruments work differently, you can do many of the same things with both types of tracks. You can loop regions within both types of tracks, and you can apply effects to both types. You can even transpose both types of tracks, although you can't transpose audio that you've recorded. Also, you can't transpose real instrument loops across as wide a range as you can software instruments—they'd sound too artificial.

By supporting audio recordings (real instruments) and also being able to generate sound on the fly (software instruments), GarageBand gives you the best of both worlds.

How Apple Loops Work

The loops that come with GarageBand are stored in *Apple Loop* format. If you've played with GarageBand, you've experienced the program's ability to adjust the pitch and tempo of loops to fit your song. Here's how that works.

Apple Loops contain more than just sound. They also contain *tags*—tidbits of data—that describe the sound, starting with

the key and the tempo in which the loop was originally recorded. The tags also contain information about the *transients* in the recording. A transient is a spike in volume—such as occurs when a drumstick slaps a drumhead. Transients denote where beats occur, and GarageBand uses this information when changing the playback tempo of an Apple Loop.

When GarageBand transposes an Apple Loop to a different key, it's performing a process called *pitch shifting.* When GarageBand changes a loop's tempo, it's *time stretching.*

Apple Loops also contain descriptive tags. These tags are what enable you to sift through loops by clicking on the buttons in the loop browser.

Finally, it's important to know that software instrument loops (the green ones) contain more than just "piano roll" note data. They also contain audio, just as real instrument loops do. This enables you to use them in real instrument tracks—and thus lighten the load on your Mac; see pages 253 and 258.

Working with Loops

For many GarageBand musicians (including yours truly), a song begins with some loops: a bass line, some percussion, a repeating synthesizer riff, or maybe all three.

The gateway to GarageBand's library of loops is the loop browser, whose buttons and search box let you quickly home in on loops of specific instruments or specific styles.

Once you find a loop that sounds interesting, you can add it to your song by dragging it into GarageBand's timeline. Once that's done, you can repeat the loop over and over, edit it, and transpose it.

As you can see in the GarageBand segment of the DVD that comes with this book, GarageBand lets you audition loops even as your song is playing back. This is a great way to hear how a particular loop will fit into the arrangement you're building.

Working with loops is as easy as clicking and dragging. But as you master GarageBand, there's a powerful subtlety behind loops that you may want to take advantage of. Specifically, you can use software instrument loops in real instrument tracks in order to lighten the load on your Mac's processor. If that makes no sense to you now, don't worry. When your arrangements become complex and you want to wring every bit of performance out of your Mac, you'll find all the details on page 258.

Adding a Loop to a Song

To display the loop browser, click its button () or use the ⌘-L keyboard shortcut. To add a loop to a song, drag the loop into the timeline.

Creating a New Track: When you drag a loop into an empty area of the timeline where there is no existing track, GarageBand creates a new track for the loop. The vertical bar indicates where the loop will begin playing. To move the loop after you've added it, drag it left or right (if the loop is too tiny to drag, zoom in).

Adding to an Existing Track: You can add a loop to an existing track. Mixing loops within a track can be one way to add variety to a song.

Tip: You can drag a software instrument loop into a real instrument track, but not vice-versa. For more details, see page 253.

See techniques for working with loops.

⊙ Browsing Loops

⊙ Adding and Repeating a Loop

⊙ Searching for Loops

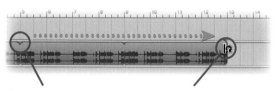

Looping a Region

When you add a loop to a track, you create a *region* that you can modify without changing the original loop. The most common kind of modification you'll perform is to loop a region so that it plays repeatedly.

The notches show the beginning and end of each repetition of the loop.

To loop a region, point to its upper-right corner and drag it to the right.

Using the Loop Browser

Resets the loop browser, clearing any search text and deactivating any keyword buttons you've clicked.

Click the keyword buttons to home in on specific instruments or styles.

To view all the loop keywords, enlarge the loop browser by dragging to the left of the Record button, or to the right of the tempo.

Tip: You can reorganize the buttons to match the way you use GarageBand: simply drag a button to a new location. To return to the original button layout, use the Preferences command.

Love that loop? Click the Fav check box to add it to your Favorites list. To display your favorites, click the Favorites button (it's under the Reset button).

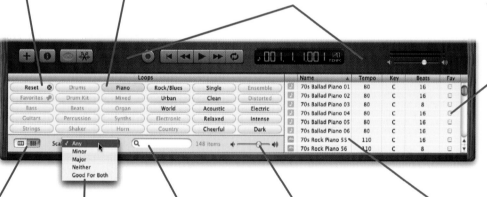

Switch between button view and column view.

Many loops use major or minor scales. You can use this menu to filter the list of loops to only those loops that complement your song.

To search by keyword, type some text and press Return. You can search for instruments (for example, *piano* or *guitar*) or styles (*jazz, funk*).

If you're auditioning a particular loop and it's overwhelming the rest of your arrangement, use this slider to turn down the loop browser's volume.

To audition a loop, click it. To hear how the loop sounds with the rest of your song, begin playing the song before you click the loop. You can also sort the list of loops by clicking column headings.

Working with Tracks

Tracks can be a lot easier to work with than musicians. Tracks never show up late for a gig, they always play in tune, their sense of timing is impeccable, and they never trash the hotel room.

Nonetheless, there are some important points to know about working with tracks and the regions that they hold. (A *region* is a set of notes or a snippet of sound. When you drag a loop into the timeline, the timeline or record a performance, you create a region.) For starters, when creating multitrack arrangements, you should rename tracks so that you can tell at a glance which parts they hold: the melody, a solo, an alternate take of a solo.

As you compose, you may want to silence, or *mute*, certain tracks. Maybe you've recorded several versions of a solo, each on its own track, and you want to audition each one to hear which sounds best.

On the other hand, there may be times when you want to *solo* a track—to mute all the other tracks and hear only one track. Soloing a track can be useful when you're fine-tuning a track's effects settings or editing a region in the track.

A big part of creating an arrangement involves copying regions within a track or from one track to another. And as you move regions around, you often have to work with the beat ruler at the top of GarageBand's timeline. By fine-tuning the ruler's *snapping* feature, you can have your regions snap into place on exactly the right beat.

Here's how to get along with the members of the band.

Renaming a Track

Normally, GarageBand names a track after the instrument you've assigned to it. But the music business is no place for normalcy. Besides, when you have multiple tracks that use the same instrument, it's hard to tell the tracks apart. Give your tracks descriptive names, such as *Vocal (Second Take)* or *Third Verse Strings.*

To rename a track, click its name in the track header, then type a new name. (This feature appeared in GarageBand 1.1. If you're using an earlier version, download the update from Apple's Web site.)

Soloing, Muting, and More

To solo and mute a track, use the controls in the track header.

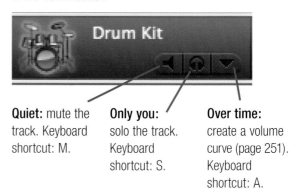

Quiet: mute the track. Keyboard shortcut: M.

Only you: solo the track. Keyboard shortcut: S.

Over time: create a volume curve (page 251). Keyboard shortcut: A.

Keeping Tracks Organized

Beginning with GarageBand 1.1, you can move tracks up and down by dragging their headers. To keep your arrangement organized, group related tracks together— put all your rhythm section tracks together, then all your solo tracks, and so on.

See techniques for working with tracks.

◉ **Renaming a Track**
◉ **Soloing a Track**
◉ **Copying Regions**

Play It Again: Cycling

When you're rehearsing, mixing, or recording, it's often useful to have part of a song play over and over. To do this, click the Cycle button (⊘) and then drag in the area just below the beat ruler to indicate the region that you want to repeat.

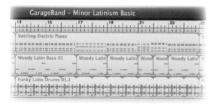

The yellow region repeats until time comes to an end or your parents pull the plug, whichever comes first. To resize the region, drag its left or right edge. To move the region, drag it left or right.

When cycling is on, playback always begins at the start of the cycle region.

Duplicating a Track

Beginning with GarageBand 1.1, you can make a duplicate of a track: a new, blank track with the same instrument and effect settings as the original. Select the track's header, then choose Duplicate from the Track menu (⌘-D).

Use the Duplicate command when you want to record multiple takes of a part, each in its own track. After you've laid down 12 takes, copy and paste the best parts into a single track.

Copying Regions

Copying a region is a common task, and GarageBand provides a couple of ways to accomplish it. You can copy and paste: select a region, choose Copy, move the playhead to the destination, and paste.

You can also use the technique I show on the DVD: press the Option key while dragging the region you want to copy.

Note: If you want to copy a region to a different track, the tracks must be of the same type. You can't copy a software instrument region to a real instrument track, or vice-versa.

Zooming tip: When you're moving regions over a large distance, use GarageBand's zoom slider to zoom out for a big-picture view. And use the keyboard shortcuts: Control-left arrow zooms out, while Control-right arrow zooms in.

Copying Versus Looping

You can repeat a region by either looping it or copying it. So which technique should you use? Looping is the fastest way to repeat a region over and over again: just drag the loop pointer as described on page 237.

The advantage of copying a region is that each copy is an independent region that you can edit without affecting other copies. With a repeating loop, if you edit one note in the loop, that edit is present in each repetition.

Snap to the Beat

When moving a region, you almost always want to move it to the exact beginning of a particular measure or beat. (There are exceptions to this rule; see page 241.) GarageBand's *timeline grid* supplies this precision: when the grid's snapping feature is active, GarageBand automatically snaps to beats and measures as you drag regions, move the playhead, drag loops to the timeline, and perform other tasks.

Normally, GarageBand adjusts the sensitivity of its grid to match the way you're viewing your song. If you're zoomed all the way out, GarageBand assumes you're performing fairly coarse adjustments, such as dragging a region from one part of a song to another. In this case, GarageBand's grid will snap to the start of each measure.

If you're zoomed all the way in, GarageBand figures you must be making precise adjustments, so it adjusts its grid to snap in thirty-second-note increments.

You can override GarageBand's automatic grid sensitivity: just choose the desired value from the grid menu.

Click the timeline grid button (▨) to display the grid menu.

The "swing" options delay every other grid point. This enables you to maintain a swing feel when dragging regions. The amount of delay is greater with the "Heavy" options.

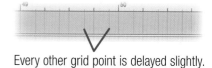

Every other grid point is delayed slightly.

Working with Regions

As I mentioned on the previous pages, you create a region any time you drag a loop into the timeline, record a few chords with a music keyboard, or record some audio.

You often need to do some work on the regions you create. If you're building an arrangement from loops, you can transpose those loops to create chord changes. While you're at it, you can edit individual loops to add variety and improve the way the loops fit into the song's chord changes, as I do on the DVD.

If you've recorded a performance using a music keyboard, you can edit individual notes to fix mistakes and improve expression. And if you've recorded a vocal or other real instrument track, you can duplicate it elsewhere in your song and perform other edits.

GarageBand highlights the region you've selected in the timeline.

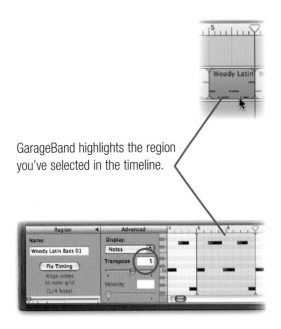

Building Chord Changes

Few of the loops included with GarageBand contain chord changes, but you can create chord changes by transposing loops.

You can "program" chord changes in a few ways. One particularly fast method is to repeat a loop for the entire duration of a verse (for example, 12 measures), split the loop at each point where you need a chord change, and then transpose the appropriate regions. As you can see on the DVD, this is a quick way to lay down a bass track.

If you'd like to follow along with the DVD, go to the Extras folder on your DVD, open the GarageBand folder, and locate the song named *Minor Latinism Bass.* Copy the song to your hard drive and then open it.

Step 1. Drag a loop into the timeline and use the loop pointer to drag it out to the desired length.

Step 2. Split the loop at the start of the change.

Drag the playhead to the beginning of the measure that needs to be transposed, then choose Split from the Edit menu (⌘-T).

Step 3. Split the loop at the end of the change.

Drag the playhead to the *end* of the measure that needs transposing, and choose Split again. You now have an independent region that you can transpose.

Step 4. Prepare to transpose.

Select the region you just created and open the track editor by clicking the track editor button (▦). Shortcut: Double-click the region to open it in the track editor.

Step 5. In the track editor, drag the Transpose slider or type a value in the box (left).

You can transpose in one-semitone increments. A *semitone* is one half step—for example, from C to C#. For the first chord change in the classic blues form, specify five semitones—for example, from C to F.

See techniques for working with regions.
- Splitting a Region
- Transposing a Region
- Editing a Region

Doubling a Track

As I show on the DVD, you can create a duet by duplicating a region in a different track. Create another track of the same type (software instrument or real instrument), then Option-drag the region into that track. (You can also use the Copy and Paste commands.) To start with the same instrument and effect settings, duplicate a track: select it and press ⌘-D.

Next, refine your duet. If it's a software instrument track, experiment with different instruments. You might also transpose one of the tracks to create a harmony (or put each part an octave apart, as I do on the DVD). If you're working with real instrument tracks, experiment with different effects settings. Finally, adjust each track's panning and volume (page 250.)

Tip: If you've doubled a real instrument region, one way to add richness to the duet is by very slightly offsetting the second track's region. Turn grid snapping off (choose Snap to Grid from the Control menu), zoom in on the region, then nudge it ever so slightly to the left or right. This way, the regions won't play back at exactly the same time, strengthening the illusion of multiple musicians.

Use the piano keyboard to help you locate the note you want.

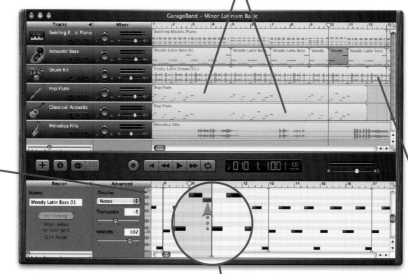

Working with Regions

Editing a Region to Fit the Changes

Building a bass line from software instrument loops? You can build a better bass line by editing regions so that they complement your chord changes. For example, if you're going from F to C, you might make the last note of the F measure a C# or a B. That way, the bass will "lead in" to the new chord change. Edits like these can also take some of the repetitiveness out of tracks built from loops.

First, double-click the region you want to edit. Then, in the track editor, drag the last note of the region up or down to the desired note. As you can see (and hear) on the DVD, GarageBand plays the note as you drag it, making it easy to determine where the note should be.

For more details on editing software instrument tracks, see the following pages.

Editing Real Instrument Regions

You can also transpose regions in real instrument tracks, provided that the regions were created from loops. (You can't transpose an audio recording that you made.) And although you can't change individual notes, you can perform some edits to regions in real instrument tracks; see page 247.

Recording Software Instruments

When you connect a music keyboard to your Mac, you unlock a symphony's worth of software instruments that you can play and record. There are pianos and keyboards and guitars of all kinds. There are synthesizers, strings, a flute, and some horns. And there are some drums you just can't beat.

As the following pages describe, you can edit your recordings and use effects to refine your tracks. You can even create completely new instruments of your own design.

If you don't have a music keyboard and don't want to spend a fortune on one, it's hard to beat the keyboard I use in the DVD: M-Audio's Keystation 49e, which sells for less than $100. This 49-key (four octave) keyboard plugs into the Mac's USB port. Its keyboard provides *velocity sensitivity*, which measures how hard each key is pressed, letting GarageBand capture the varied dynamics of your performance. It also has the essential controls you need for additional expression (see the sidebar on the opposite page).

You can also use a costlier keyboard that requires a separate MIDI interface. (MIDI stands for *Musical Instrument Digital Interface*, and is a standard for interconnecting electronic instruments and computers. Think of it as USB with a music degree.) Pricier keyboards often provide *weighted action*—their keys respond like a piano's instead of like an organ's, and thus feel more natural to experienced pianists. You'll also find more keys—up to 88 of them in a high-end keyboard like the Kurzweil PC88 I use.

Recording a Software Instrument

Step 1. Create a new track. Click the New Track button (⊞) or choose New Track from the Track menu (Option-⌘-N).

Step 2. Choose an instrument.

In the New Track dialog box, click Software Instrument, then choose your instrument.

Be sure Software Instrument is selected.

Select a category...

...and then select an instrument. You can use the up arrow and down arrow keys to move from one instrument to the next.

Optional: choose an icon to appear in the track header.

Tip: When the New Track dialog box is open, you can try out the selected instrument by playing keys on your music keyboard or by clicking the on-screen keys in GarageBand's Keyboard window (to show the keyboard, press ⌘-K).

C3 is equivalent to middle C on a piano.

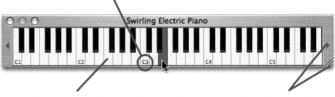

The keyboard is velocity sensitive, with a twist: the closer you click to the bottom edge of a key, the louder the note.

Scroll and resize the keyboard to access low and high notes.

See and hear some software instruments.
◉ Creating a New Track
◉ Choosing a Software Instrument
◉ Recording a Performance

GO TO DVD

Step 3. Get ready.

Position the playhead a few measures before where you want to begin recording. If you're starting at the beginning of the song, give yourself time to get ready by choosing Count In from the Control menu.

Step 4. Hit it.

Click the Record button (◉) or press the R key. To stop recording, press the spacebar or click the Play button (▶).

As you record, GarageBand displays the new region (and its notes, in piano-roll style) in the timeline.

Swirling Electric Piano

Anatomy of a Music Keyboard

Like many keyboards, M-Audio's Keystation 49e contains no sound-generating circuitry—it can't make noise any more than your Mac's keyboard can. When you play, the keyboard transmits MIDI data that describes which keys you pressed, how hard, and for how long. GarageBand takes that data and uses it to play software instruments.

Keyboards that lack sound-generating circuitry are often called *controllers*. Keyboards containing their own sound circuitry are generally called *synthesizers* or *samplers,* depending on how they produce their sound.

On the Keystation 49e, the volume slider controls the volume of the currently selected software instrument track.

Whether they can generate their own sound or not, all music keyboards provide two controls that allow for more creative expression when you play.

A *pitch bend wheel* lets you do something no acoustic piano permits: bend notes the way guitar players do. The pitch bend wheel pairs up well with guitar and synthesizer instruments.

A *modulation wheel,* or *mod wheel,* lets you vary the sound of an instrument, usually by adding a vibrato-type effect.

Most keyboards, including the Keystation 49e, can accept an optional foot pedal that plugs into the back of the keyboard and acts like a piano's sustain pedal. If you frequently play piano software instruments, you'll want a pedal.

Editing Software Instrument Tracks

After you've recorded some software instrument tracks, you can edit them using the track editor. There's almost no end to the kinds of changes you can make to MIDI data, and unlike when you're onstage, you can always undo any disasters.

Selecting Multiple Notes

You often need to select multiple notes—for example, prior to duplicating them or adjusting their velocity. You can Shift-click on notes to select more than one, and you can drag a selection rectangle around the notes you want to select.

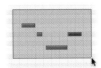

Fixing Wrong Notes

To fix a wrong note, drag it up or down until it becomes the right note. (If the note is very high or low, scroll the track editor or make it taller by dragging the area to the left of the Record button.)

If you fumbled and accidentally hit two keys when you meant to hit just one, delete the extra wrong note: select it and press the Delete key.

Moving a Note in Time

To move a note backward or forward in time, drag it left or right. You may have to zoom in on the track editor to get the precision you need; just drag the track editor's zoom slider to the right. You may also want to adjust the track editor's grid sensitivity by using its grid ruler button. Or turn the grid off entirely (⌘-G).

Improving expression. By editing the velocity values of some notes, you can improve expression and realism. This is especially true for software instruments, such as Classical Acoustic, that change dramatically depending on how hard you play a note.

To edit a note's velocity, select it and then specify the desired velocity in the Advanced area of the track editor. To change the velocity of a range of notes, select the notes first.

Velocity values can range from 1 (quiet as a hoarse mouse) to 127 (way loud). To give you a visual hint at a note's velocity, GarageBand uses shading:

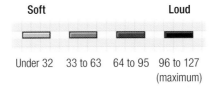

Soft			Loud
Under 32	33 to 63	64 to 95	96 to 127 (maximum)

Changing a note's duration. To make a note longer or shorter, drag its right edge to the right or to the left.

Drawing a new note. To draw a new note, press ⌘ and then drag within the track editor's grid, using the little vertical piano key legend to guide you to the right pitch.

Chords in a hurry. You can create chords by duplicating notes: press the Option key, click on a note, and then drag up or down by the desired note interval. This also works on a range of notes: select the notes, then Option-drag them.

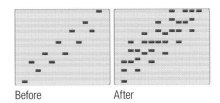

Before   After

Tip: Want to create a cinematic string section? Record a series of single notes, then duplicate them and drag the duplicate up seven semitones (a musical fifth). For some heavy metal action, try this with the Big Electric Lead guitar instrument. Just warn me first.

Fixing Timing Problems

With the track editor's Fix Timing button, you can have GarageBand *quantize* a region—move its notes so that they fall exactly on the beats in the beat ruler.

Before quantizing a region, use the track editor's beat ruler menu to choose the desired grid resolution. If you're quantizing a walking bass line in 4/4 time, use the quarter note (1/4) resolution. If you're quantizing a more nuanced performance, use a higher resolution. For jazz or other syncopated styles, try one of the swing settings.

After you've chosen a resolution, select the region you want to quantize and then click Fix Timing. Play it back and undo if necessary.

Beginning with GarageBand 1.1, you can quantize individual notes within a region: just select the notes, then click Fix Timing.

Quantizing can be a mixed bag; it works well with extremely mechanistic music styles (such as dance and even some classical), but expect disappointing results when quantizing a jazz piano solo or any musical form that plays somewhat fast and loose with beats. Fortunately, the Undo command will get you out of any quantizing quagmires.

Editing Controller Information

Not all MIDI data deals with notes. A keyboard's pitch and modulation wheels also generate data, as does a sustain pedal. You can edit and create this *controller data* in the track editor, too.

Editing controller data involves working *control points* similar to those of volume curves (page 251, and demonstrated on the DVD). By adjusting this data, you can change the expressiveness applied by a pitch or mod wheel, or adjust your pedal work.

Say you have a software instrument whose sound timbre "sweeps" when you move the modulation wheel (examples include Star Sweeper, Aquatic Sunbeam, Cloud Break, and Falling Star). If you want that sweep to change over a specific number of measures, create a *modulation curve*.

To create controller data from scratch, choose the contoller type from the Display pop-up menu in the Track editor. ⌘-click to create control points, then drag them as needed.

You'll find an example of this in the Extras folder of the DVD. Check out the GarageBand project named Modulate Me. It contains two regions, each playing the identical note. But in the second region, I drew a modulation curve to create a precisely timed sweep.

As for editing sustain data, you can clean up sloppy pedal work by fine-tuning the

position of the control points that represent each pedal push: just drag the control points left or right.

Pedal is pressed (sustain is on).   Pedal isn't pressed (sustain is off).

And if you don't have a sustain pedal, you can draw your own sustain data. Check out the project named Add Sustain in the Extras folder of the DVD. I recorded the first region without using my sustain pedal. Then I duplicated the region and added sustain data to the duplicate.

Press the pedal: ⌘-click to create a control point.

Release: ⌘-click where you want the pedal release, then drag down to the bottom of the grid. Drag control points left and right as needed to fine-tune timing.

I wouldn't want to draw in sustain data for a Billy Joel ballad, but for the occasional sustained arpeggio, it works.

Recording an Audio Source

If you sing or play an instrument—sax, guitar, kazoo, or, ahem, melodica—GarageBand provides yet another dimension to explore. Connect a microphone or other sound source to your Mac, and you can record a performance in a real instrument track.

If your Mac has an audio input jack, you can plug a microphone, guitar, or bass into it and start making noise. Note that the Mac's audio input jack works best with mikes that produce a fairly loud, *line-level* signal. Many mikes do not, and if yours is among them, you won't get a loud enough signal for the Mac. No problem—products aplenty await your wallet. On the DVD, I use M-Audio's MobilePre interface, which connects to the Mac's USB port. The MobilePre's two inputs can accommodate a stereo or mono sound source, including instruments and balanced or unbalanced microphones (described on page 174).

GarageBand lets you apply effects to audio that you record. You can even have GarageBand simulate the sound of a vintage guitar amplifier. But your audio is always recorded and saved with no effects—unprocessed, or *dry*. GarageBand applies its effects as your music plays back, so you can experiment with effects settings.

Before recording a real instrument track, be sure your audio hardware is properly configured. You may need to visit the Sound system preference and GarageBand's Preferences dialog box to ensure that the audio input is set to the hardware you plan to use. And be sure you have plenty of free disk space before you start—your recording will use 10MB per minute for a stereo track.

Preparing to Record

Create a real instrument track and choose effects for it.

Step 1. Create a new track. Click the New Track button (⊞) or choose New Track from the Track menu (Option-⌘-N).

Step 2. Click the Real Instrument tab and choose an instrument.

When you select an instrument, you aren't choosing what sound your instrument will make—you're choosing a set of effects that GarageBand will apply when playing back the track. You can change this setting later if you like.

Select a category, then select an instrument within the category. Don't want to apply any effects to the track? Select No Effects.

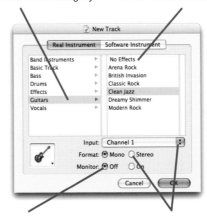

When monitoring is on, you can hear your instrument or microphone even when you aren't recording. This can be great if you're recording a guitar or bass, but with a mike, you're likely to get loud feedback when monitoring is on. This is why monitoring is turned off by default. If you're using a mike, you might want to plug headphones into your Mac when monitoring.

If you've connected a stereo microphone or device, click Stereo and be sure the Input pop-up reads Channel 1/2. Otherwise, click Mono.

Tip: To quickly create a real instrument track with no effects, choose New Basic Track from the Track menu. A basic track is set to record in stereo; double-click the track's header to change audio settings.

See and hear the audio-recording process.
⊙ **Recording an Audio Performance**
⊙ **Creating a Real Instrument Track**
⊙ **Changing a Track's Effects**

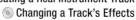

Step 3. Adjust recording levels.

Be sure the track you just created is selected in the timeline (click its header if necessary), then sing or play some notes with the same gusto and verve you plan to use when recording. Adjust the volume levels to get a strong signal, but not one loud enough to cause *clipping*, a horrific-sounding form of distortion.

The volume meters should illuminate fully during loud passages, but the two clipping indicators (the tiny circles) shouldn't light. If they do, lower the recording level. **Tip:** When the clipping indicators light, they stay lit until you click them again. This is GarageBand's way of letting you know that clipping occurred while your eyes were closed and you were blowin' that horn.

To adjust the recording level, drag the slider. If your audio hardware has a volume control and clipping indicator, check it to be sure it isn't clipping, too.

Step 4. Get ready.

Position the playhead a few measures before where you want to begin recording, or use the Control menu's Count In command to give yourself time to get ready.

Step 5. Hit it. Press Record (●) and make us all proud.

Tip: If you're using a mike, wear headphones while recording. That way, you won't record the sound of other tracks playing back. (During the DVD shoot, I lowered the playback volume of the other tracks to eliminate the need for hair-mussing headphones.)

Working with Recorded Regions

You can edit and manipulate regions containing audio that you've recorded. You can't transpose regions or change their tempo, but you can loop them. You can also duplicate them, either by copying and pasting or by Option-dragging. Duplicating a lengthy region doesn't use any additional disk space.

Digital splicing. You can also perform some rudimentary editing. Maybe you belted out a *yeah* that sounded more like Howard Dean than James Brown.

Double-click on the region to open it in the track editor.

Next, drag across the offending utterance (zoom in and turn off grid snapping for more precision), then hit the Delete key.

You can also copy and paste part of a region: select it in the track editor, then choose Copy. Move the playhead to a new location, then paste. You can also paste the recording into a different real instrument track. To "double" a vocal and add a richer, chorus sound, offset the duplicate slightly using the technique described on page 241. Don't forget to pan each member of your chorus to a different left/right position (see page 251).

Refining Your Sound with Effects

Effects can be just as important to your final arrangement as the notes you play. With effects, you can add richness to a track—or brain-liquefying distortion, if that's your idea of fun. You can add some spice to a track, or change it beyond recognition.

Effects alter the "color" of sound. Some effects simulate real-world phenomena, such as reverberation and echo. Other effects let you sculpt your sound to enhance certain frequencies, much like the equalizer in iTunes. Still other effects process (and sometimes mangle) audio in ways that could only exist in the digital world.

Recording studios have racks of hardware effects boxes. GarageBand's effects exist in software: by applying complex math to your sound, GarageBand can simulate the reverb of a concert hall, the characteristics of an old guitar amplifier, and much more. Best of all, you can customize GarageBand's effects in a limitless number of ways to create sounds that are yours alone.

You can apply GarageBand's effects to software and real instrument tracks alike. And as I've said previously, GarageBand never alters your original audio; effects are applied as your song plays. This lets you experiment with effects until you arrive at just the right amount of sonic seasoning.

Here's a look at how GarageBand applies its effects and how you can customize them.

Effects Basics

All of GarageBand's software instruments employ effects to some degree. Similarly, when you create a real instrument track and choose an instrument, GarageBand assigns a collection of effects to that track (page 246). And as I describe on page 252, a song's master track can apply effects to your entire song.

To examine and change a track's effects settings, double-click the track header, then click the Details button in the Track Info window.

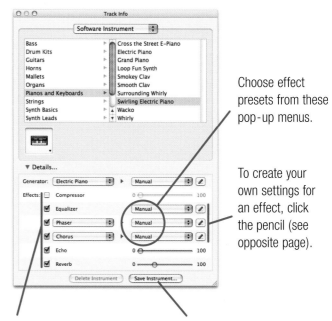

Choose effect presets from these pop-up menus.

To create your own settings for an effect, click the pencil (see opposite page).

For software instruments, standard effects include Compressor, Equalizer, Echo, and Reverb. (Real instrument tracks provide these same effects, and they add a *noise gate* effect, which removes noise from silent portions of a recording.) You can choose two additional effects by using the two pop-up menus.

Like what you've come up with? You can save the customized version of the instrument and use it again in future songs.

The Fab Four

Compressor, Equalizer, Echo, and Reverb are mainstay effects, the salt and pepper of sonic seasoning.

Compressor. A compressor is a kind of automatic volume control that adjusts volume thousands of times per second. Most popular music is heavily compressed, and FM radio stations often compress it even more. Compression can add punch to drum tracks and vocals, but too much compression can add an annoying "pumping" quality to sound.

Note that this form of compression differs from the kind that iTunes applies when encoding music.

Equalizer. As an iTunes veteran, you know all about EQ—it's a fancy set of bass and treble controls. GarageBand provides 16 EQ *presets*—factory settings—that you can apply and customize. Want to beef up that drum track? Try the Big Drum preset.

Echo. Also called *delay,* the echo effect simulates evenly timed sound reflections. **Tip:** GarageBand's echo repeats at a rate that matches your song's tempo. Try applying echo to vocal or

synthesizer "stabs" in a dance, electronica, or hip-hop tune. And beginning with GarageBand 1.1, you can use the Track Echo effect to have different echo rhythms on each track.

Reverb. A distant cousin to echo, reverb consists of thousands of randomly timed sound reflections. Reverb simulates the sound of an acoustic space: a concert hall, a small lounge, a stadium. In GarageBand, reverb is controlled in part by the song's master track (page 252).

Customizing Effects

You can customize effects in several ways.

Turn them off. Maybe you love GarageBand's Arena Run synth, but you don't like the way it echoes every note. Just turn off the Echo effect by unchecking its box.

Turn them on. Some of GarageBand's most aurally intriguing effects lurk within the two pop-up menus in the Effects area. Want to add a rich, swirling texture to a track? Try Flanger, Phaser, or both. Want to liquefy your listeners? Unleash Distortion, Bitcrusher, or Amp Simulation. Want a track to continuously

pan between the left and right channel? Try the tremolo effect's Circular Structure setting.

Important: Some settings can produce speaker-damaging volume levels. Lower the volume when experimenting. This is particularly prudent if you're experimenting with the Distortion, Bitcrusher, and Amp Simulation effects, or adjusting the Resonance slider in effects that provide one.

Try different presets. Many of GarageBand's effects have an assortment of presets that you can apply with a click.

Create your own presets. Click the little pencil (✎) next to an effect's Preset pop-up menu, and a dialog box appears where you can adjust the effect's parameters.

To create a new preset containing the current settings, open the pop-up menu and choose New Preset.

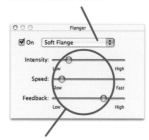

Each effect has a unique set of parameters that you can adjust.

Saving Instruments

When you customize a software instrument's effects, you're customizing the way GarageBand has defined that instrument. If you switch to a different instrument or effect preset, GarageBand asks if you want to save the changed instrument before switching.

If you click Don't Save (or just press Return), GarageBand discards your settings. If you think you'll want to use them again, click Save before switching to a different instrument or effect setting.

If you like tinkering with effect settings and you don't want GarageBand pestering you about saving them all the time, check the Never Ask Again box. You can also use GarageBand's Preferences command to control this paranoia mode.

For more details on creating instruments, see page 257.

Refining the Mix: Volume and Panning

A good song has a pleasing mix of melody, chord changes, and maybe lyrics. A good *recording* of a song has a pleasing mix between instruments. It's possible to have a poorly mixed version of a great song, and as a spin of the radio dial will confirm, it's possible to have a well-mixed version of a lousy song.

As a GarageBand-based recording engineer, the job of mixing is yours. Adjust each track's volume so all the tracks mesh—no single instrument should overwhelm the others, but important instruments or voices should be louder than less important ones.

And to create a rich stereo field, pan some instruments toward the left channel and others toward the right. You'll find some tips for panning on the opposite page.

Adjusting Volume and Panning

To adjust a track's playback volume level and panning position, use the Mixer area of GarageBand's window.

Note: If the Mixer isn't visible, display it by clicking the little triangle at the top of the Tracks area or by choosing Show Track Mixer from the Track menu (⌘-Y).

To pan a track, drag the knob to turn it clockwise (toward the left speaker) or counterclockwise (toward the right).

To adjust a track's playback volume, drag the slider. Watch the clipping indicators to avoid distortion.

Note: If you've edited the track's volume curve, you can't drag the slider. Instead, make volume adjustments to the curve.

See and hear mixing techniques.
⊙ Panning a Track
GO TO DVD

Editing a Volume Curve

To create fades or mute a track for part of a song, edit the track's volume curve.

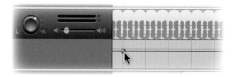

Step 1. Display the track's volume curve.

Select the track's header and then click the volume curve button or press the A key.

Step 2. Click the Track Volume check box.

Step 3. The horizontal line represents the track's volume. Click the line to create a control point where you want the volume change to begin.

Step 4. Click to create a second control point, then drag it down to lower the volume, or up to raise it.

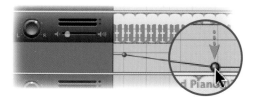

Fine-tuning curves. To adjust a control point's location in time, drag it left or right. If grid snapping is turned on, the control point snaps to the nearest position in the grid. To delete a control point, click it and press the Delete key. To work with multiple controls points at once, select them by Shift-clicking or drawing a selection rectangle around them.

Mixing Tips: Panning

By sweating the details of your stereo mix, you can make your song more aurally interesting. Two ears, two speakers—take advantage of them.

Sit right. Your position relative to your speakers will affect how you hear a stereo mix. When refining your track panning, sit directly between your speakers. Test your mix with headphones if you like, but don't rely exclusively on them—your listeners won't.

Panning hard. Think twice about panning tracks *completely* to the left or right. In the real world, sound reaches both ears even when a musician is at the far side of the stage. Of course, some songs have little to do with the real world, so feel free to bend this rule.

Panning for realism. If you're after a realistic stereo mix, visualize your ensemble and pan accordingly. In a jazz combo, the drums might be slightly to the left, bass in the middle, piano slightly to the right, and sax further right.

Panning a duet. If your song contains a vocal duet or two instruments that trade solos, pan one of the vocalists or instruments somewhat left (about 10 o'clock on the pan wheel) and the other somewhat right.

To simulate backup singers, record each part on a separate track and pan the tracks near each other on one side of the stage—for example, one track at 9 o'clock and the other at 10 o'clock.

Panning similar instruments. If your song contains multiple instruments that have a similar frequency range—for example, a solo guitar and a rhythm guitar—pan each instrument to the opposite side of center. The 10 o'clock and 2 o'clock positions are good starting points.

Consider your effects. If you've applied an effect that enhances a track's stereo—for example, Chorus, Flanger, or Tremolo—think twice about panning that track heavily to one channel. You'll lose many of the benefits of the effect.

Panning percussion. If you've built up a drum kit by recording different drums and cymbals on different tracks, pan the tracks to increase realism. Put the snare and kick drum dead center. Pan the hi-hat slightly right, and the ride and crash cymbals slightly left. If you're using tom-toms, pan them according to their pitch: high-pitched toms slightly right, low-pitched toms slightly left. This layout mirrors the typical layout of a drum kit: the hi-hat is on the drummer's left and the floor tom is on his or her right.

Creating the Final Mix

When you've refined each track, turn your attention to the big picture: display the song's Master Track to apply final-mastering effects and optionally to create a fade-out at the end of the tune.

Once you've polished your song until it glitters like a platinum record, you can export it to your iTunes music library, where you can burn it to an audio CD, transfer it to your iPod, and use it in the other iLife programs.

Echo Presets

Reverb Presets

Working with the Master Track

GarageBand's *master track* is a special kind of track that doesn't hold notes or regions, but instead controls certain aspects of your entire mix. Specifically, you can apply effects to the master track and create a volume curve to have your song fade in or fade out.

To show the master track, choose Show Master Track from the Track menu (⌘-B.)

Applying effects. Apple has created dozens of final-mastering effects settings for common musical genres. Explore and apply them by double-clicking the master track's header. And, of course, you can customize them and create your own final-mix effects using the techniques I've described on previous pages.

Creating a fade. As I show on the DVD, to fade a song, create a volume curve for it in the master track. **Tip:** To create a musically appealing fade, edit the volume curve so that the fade *ends* at the very beginning of a verse or measure. Don't have a fade end in the middle of a measure—it feels abrupt.

Customizing reverb and echo. In GarageBand, reverb and echo effects are controlled by the master track. As described on page 249, you can adjust *how much* echo and reverb you want on a specific track, but to adjust the actual echo and reverb parameters that GarageBand uses, use the master track's Track Info window.

GarageBand's dozens of reverb and echo settings (shown at left) are worth exploring. The reverb presets are spectacular—everything from a living room to a large cathedral, with some offbeat stops in between. Explore them to add just the right sonic ambience to your track. And if you're into dance and electronic music, you can while away a weekend trying out and customizing GarageBand's echo presets.

Exporting to iTunes

When you've polished your song to perfection, add it to your iTunes music library by choosing Export to iTunes from the File menu. GarageBand mixes your tracks down to two stereo channels and saves the song as an AIFF file.

GarageBand saves files in full CD-quality form: 44KHz, 16-bit. To convert a song into AAC, MP3, or Apple Lossless format, configure iTunes for the format you want to use (page 22), then select your song and choose Convert from the Advanced menu. iTunes won't replace the AIFF version of

your song, so if you want to free up space in your iTunes library (and iPod), use the Show Song File command to move the AIFF file out of your music library.

Exporting an excerpt. At times, you may want to export only part of a song. Maybe you want to email it to a collaborator or mix it down in order to bring it back into GarageBand (see page 259). To export a portion of a song, turn on cycling and then resize the yellow cycling region in the beat ruler to indicate the portion you want to export.

Preserving effect tails. If your song has reverb or echo effects that last well beyond the last note, you may find that these *effect tails* are cut off after you export to iTunes. To fix this, turn cycling on and then resize the yellow cycling region so that it extends beyond the point where the effects die off. Now export the song again.

Customizing tags. To customize how your song is categorized in iTunes—artist name, album name, and so on—use the Export portion of GarageBand's Preferences dialog box.

A Closer Look at Software Instrument Loops

On page 235, I mentioned that software instrument loops contain more than just piano-roll MIDI notes—they also contain audio. To see this for yourself, drag a green loop into a real instrument track—instead of the usual piano-roll notation within a green region, you'll see a waveform display within a blue region.

Two in one. How does this work? A software instrument loop is really two loops in one. It contains not only the MIDI note data that can be used by a software instrument track, but also a *rendered* version of the loop—an actual audio recording, complete with effects.

Here's another way to see this for yourself. Use the Finder's Find command to locate a software instrument loop, such as Southern Rock Guitar 01. You'll notice the loop's file name ends in .AIF—it's an audio file in AIFF format. You can open and play this file using QuickTime Player or iTunes. You can even drag it into iMovie or iDVD. But embedded within the AIFF file is MIDI note data that GarageBand can use.

The fact that software instrument loops also contain audio data has an important ramification: As I mention on page 258, if you plan to use a software

instrument loop as-is, you can lighten the load on your Mac's processor by using the loop in a real instrument track.

If you haven't yet created the track for the loop, take advantage of the following shortcut that Apple added to GarageBand 1.1: press the Option key while dragging a green loop into the timeline, and GarageBand creates a real instrument track for it.

If you frequently use software instrument loops without changing them, you can use GarageBand's Preferences dialog box to have the program *always* create real instrument

tracks when you drag green loops into the timeline.

The downsides. There are some downsides to using a green loop in a real instrument track. You can't edit individual notes or change instrument or effect assignments, since all these things are part of the audio recording. Also, you can't transpose an audio region over as large a range. But for those times when you want to use a green loop as-is, adding it to a real instrument track is a great way to improve GarageBand's performance.

Arranging Tips

More Ways to Work with Regions

I've already discussed the most common tasks you're likely to perform with regions: looping them, moving and copying them, splitting them, transposing them, and editing them.

There's more. Here are a few additional ways you might work with regions.

Resizing a region. To extend a region—make it longer—point to its lower-right corner and drag to the right.

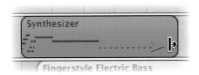

Why extend a region? Say you recorded a riff that you want to loop. If your recorded region doesn't end at the proper measure boundary, the region won't loop properly. By extending the region, you can have it loop.

Another reason to extend a region is to be able to draw in additional notes or controller data using the track editor. Yet another is to add some silence before a region's loop repeats.

To make the region shorter, drag its lower-right corner to the left. You might shorten a region in order to "crop out" some unwanted notes—possibly as a prelude to rerecording them. When you shorten a region, you don't delete the notes in the hidden portion of the region. To restore the notes, lengthen the region.

You can also resize a region from its beginning by dragging its lower *left* corner. This enables you to add silence to the beginning of a region (drag to the left) or to crop out audio from the beginning of a real instrument recording (drag to the right).

Joining regions. You've transposed a set of loops using the Split technique from page 240, and now you want to transpose the entire verse to a different key. Select all the loops and choose Join Selected from the Edit menu (⌘-J). GarageBand turns all the regions into one region that you can transpose.

Note: When you join real instrument regions that you've recorded, GarageBand combines those regions into a single audio file. GarageBand asks if you want to create a new audio file. Click Create, and GarageBand merges the real instrument regions into a new audio file.

Adding Variety

When you're working with loops, it's easy to create overly repetitious arrangements. Fortunately, it's also easy to add variety and make your loop-based songs sound less repetitious.

Vary loops. Many of the bass and drum loops that come with GarageBand and GarageBand Jam Pack have variations that sound similar but not identical. Rather than relying on just one loop for a bass or drum track, switch between some different but similar-sounding ones. (The Drums on Demand loops on your DVD are designed for exactly this.)

Edit some loops. Make your own loop variations. Make a copy of a software instrument loop and edit it—delete a few notes or transpose others. For real instrument loops, select part of the loop, copy it, and then paste it elsewhere.

Another way to edit loops is to change the instrument played by a software instrument loop. Try assigning an electric piano or clav to a bass loop.

Record your own bass track. Use bass loops to sketch out an arrangement and choose instruments, then replace the loops with your own bass line.

Take breaks. Add a *drum break* now and then—silence your drums for last beat or two of a measure or for an entire measure. You can split the region and then delete part of it. Or you can edit the region if it's a software instrument drum track. Or leave the region alone and create a volume curve that plunges the track's volume down all the way, then brings it back up.

Add fills. Don't want to edit a drum loop? Create a new track that uses a software instrument drum kit. Use this track to hold drum fills, such as an occasional cymbal crash or tom-tom fill. Want a kick drum to mark the beat during a drum break? Put it in this track.

Vary the percussion. Add one or more percussion tracks to some verses—shakers, tambourines, claves, congas, bongos. Click the loop browser's Percussion button to explore.

See techniques for arranging and recording.
◉ Staggering Loops
◉ Editing a Loop
◉ Recording at a Slower Tempo

Add a pad. A *pad* is a note, a series of notes, or a chord that forms a sonic background for a song. It's often a lush string section or an atmospheric synthesizer that plays the root note or a fifth (for example, G in a song written in C). One way to add variety to an arrangement is to have a pad play throughout one verse. Stop the pad at the start of the next verse, or add another track with a pad that uses a different instrument.

Hijacking GarageBand

If you've played with the settings in GarageBand's software instrument generators, you may have noticed something: by moving a setting's slider while simultaneously playing some notes, you can create some incredible sounds. You might have even found yourself wishing you could record those sounds—after all, one big advantage of a real synthesizer is those knobs that you can twiddle to alter the sound as you play.

GarageBand doesn't let you record the twiddling of its sliders, at least not yet. But there is a way. It's a bit awkward, but it works: by using Rogue Amoeba's Audio Hijack software (a trial version of which is included on your DVD), you can record yourself twiddling GarageBand settings.

Simply set up Audio Hijack to hijack GarageBand, and then start playing and twiddling. You can also record the panning of a track from one channel to the other—another feat GarageBand doesn't permit. When you've finished, drag the Audio Hijack recording into a real instrument track and continue building your song.

Changing Effects

Want to apply an effect, such as echo, to only part of a track? You can use the hijacking technique, but here's an easier method. Duplicate the track, then move the region to which you want to apply the new effect to the duplicate track. Now apply the effect to the duplicate track. To create a smooth transition between the two tracks, create volume curves for each track.

GarageBand Accessories

Here are a few software and hardware goodies that make my time with GarageBand more enjoyable.

MIDI Keys. Don't have a music keyboard? Use Chris Reed's MIDI Keys. This free program provides an on-screen keyboard similar to GarageBand's. But MIDI Keys goes further: you can play notes and even chords by hitting keys on your Mac's keyboard. I wouldn't want to use MIDI Keys to record *Flight of the Bumblebee*, but it's great for knocking out a few chords or experimenting with a melody while you wait for the in-flight movie to start.

SimpleChord. Another free gem, Dan Grover's SimpleChord is a great way to learn chords. Choose a chord from its pop-up menu, and SimpleChord plays the chord and highlights its notes.

The Bluetooth accompanist. If your music keyboard isn't directly next to your Mac, you may find yourself doing some uncomfortable stretching to switch between your Mac and your axe. For me, the answer was Apple's Bluetooth wireless keyboard and mouse, which have a range of about 30 feet. When I'm recording or practicing, I set them atop my Kurzweil keyboard and control GarageBand without contortions.

PowerMate. Griffin Technology's PowerMate is a big, smooth-turning metal knob—almost two inches in diameter—that connects to your USB port. So? It's a great way to navigate through a GarageBand project: twirl the knob to scroll, then press down on the knob to begin playback. The PowerMate is also a great tool for getting around in the iMovie timeline.

Adding On to GarageBand

You aren't limited to the instruments and loops that come with GarageBand—not by a long shot. You can expand your musical repertoire in several ways.

Adding Loops

Tired of the same old 1,000 loops? Go beyond them.

GarageBand Jam Pack. Apple's GarageBand Jam Pack gives you another 2,000 Apple Loops, more than 100 new software instruments, and 100 new audio effects presets. It should be one of the first stops in your search for more sonic options.

Third-party Apple Loops. Many companies sell collections of loops in Apple Loop format. Many also offer free loop collections. You'll find some in the Extras folder of this book's DVD, and I've linked to more on macilife.com.

Drums on Demand takes an innovative approach to building drum tracks. Rather than providing one or two loops for a particular type of song, Drums on Demand provides numerous loops, organized into what the company calls *Sound Sets*. Try the samples on the DVD.

You'll also find some Apple Loops from Bitshift Audio in the Extras folder. You dance DJs will love them. (While you're there, don't miss the trial version of iDrum, a software drum machine that runs within GarageBand.)

Third-party non-Apple Loops. Computer-savvy musicians have been relying on loops for years, and there are

thousands of loop CDs available. Many are in *ACID* format; ACID is a pioneering loop-based music program that debuted on Windows computers back in 1998.

You can convert ACID loops into Apple Loop format using Apple's Soundtrack Loop Utility program, which you can download free from Apple's developer Web site (http://developer.apple.com/sdk/). Look for the link named *Apple Loops SDK*. (I've also linked to it from the GarageBand page on macilife.com.)

You don't *have* to convert an ACID loop into Apple Loop format, but doing so enables you to transpose the loop and change its tempo. And the process isn't difficult. The free Soundtrack Loop Utility program includes full documentation.

Using loops. You can usually install loops that are in Apple Loop format by dragging them to the loop browser. When you do, GarageBand indexes the loops, making them available through the search box and buttons.

To use a non-Apple Loop—or any AIFF, WAV, or MP3 file—simply drag it into the GarageBand timeline to create a track for it and import it.

Adding Audio Unit Instruments and Effects

You can expand GarageBand's sound-generating and effects capabilities with software plug-ins called *Audio Units.* Some absolutely stunning software instruments are available in Audio Unit format. My favorite is Native Instruments'

B4, which mimics the legendary Hammond B3 organ with frightening realism. And yes, it runs within GarageBand.

I'm also a big fan of Pluggo from Cycling '74 (www.cycling74.com). Pluggo is a collection of more than 100 synthesizers and effects, and it enables you to run software instruments that use other plug-in formats, such as the popular VST format.

High-end software instruments like B4 cost several times what iLife '04 costs. If you don't want to spend that much, there are some great-sounding Audio Unit instruments and effects that don't cost a dime. To explore what's available, go to www.audio-units.com and www.osxaudio.com. Don't expect to get any work done for a while.

Where they live. Commercial Audio Unit plug-ins usually include an installer program that puts things where they belong, but some free Audio Units don't. So for the record, Audio Units are stored in Library > Audio > Plug-Ins > Components. They can also reside in your home directory, in the same path.

Expand your band with the
loops in the Extras folder.

GO TO DVD

Creating Your Own Instruments

In GarageBand, a software instrument is based on a foundation called a *generator*, and every generator has settings that you can tweak. You can create your own software instrument by picking a generator and then adjusting its settings.

For example, say you want to create an instrument that has a funky electronic synthesizer sound. Here's one way you might approach the task.

Step 1. Create a new software instrument track, and pick an instrument—any instrument.

Step 2. Double-click the track's header and examine the Generator pop-up menu.

Some generators are based on short recorded *samples* of actual instruments, such as piano and guitar.

Other generators create their sound "from scratch" based on sound synthesis techniques.

Step 3. Choose a generator.

Step 4. Examine the generator's presets. Try them out—you might find one you like.

Step 5. Click the pencil to the right of the generator's preset pop-up menu. This displays the settings that apply to the generator you chose.

Many generators let you customize what's often called the *ADSR envelope*. You can dramatically change a sound's percussive qualities by changing its envelope.

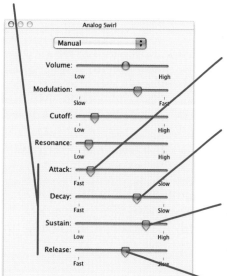

Tip: To get a feel for the kinds of settings each generator provides, drag the settings window so that you can see it and the Track Info window at the same time. Then paw through the generators and their presets, and watch the settings window change.

Step 6. Play with the settings until you arrive at a sound you like. While you're at it, adjust effects as desired—they're stored along with the generator settings.

Step 7. Click the Save Instrument button in the Track Info window and type a name for the new instrument. GarageBand saves the instrument settings on your hard drive (see the sidebar on page 259).

How quickly should the note sound when a key is pressed? A piano has a fast, or *sharp*, attack (as the hammers hit the strings). A flute has a slower attack.

How quickly should the sound volume fade or drop to the sustain level?

Should the sound sustain when a note is pressed and held down? A piano note decays over time; an organ note doesn't.

What happens when the key is released? With a fast release, the sound ends immediately. With a slower release, the sound fades gradually after the key is released.

Optimizing GarageBand's Performance

With apologies to the great James Brown, GarageBand is the hardest-working program in show business. It synthesizes sound, plays back audio tracks, generates effects—and never skips a beat.

Of course, this assumes that your Mac is fast enough. On slower Macs—for example, G3 systems and older PowerBooks—GarageBand can stumble and display an error message if it isn't able to perform its duties. GarageBand works hard to avoid stopping the music. For instance, if your Mac starts working up a sweat during playback, GarageBand defers scrolling the screen and updating its time readout.

To let you know how hard it's working, GarageBand changes the color of its playhead: from white (don't worry, be happy) to yellow (I will survive) to orange (the thrill is gone) to red (the sound of silence). If you see the red playhead, anticipate an error message—GarageBand is on the verge of maxing out your Mac.

But as I tell my guitar player friends, don't fret. You can do a lot to bring the music back—besides buying a faster Mac.

Performance Tips

Add memory. A memory upgrade will improve your Mac's overall performance.

Quit other programs. Let your Mac devote all its attention to GarageBand.

Quit and relaunch. Clear GarageBand's head: quit the program and then launch it again.

Use the audio in software instrument loops. If you plan to use a software instrument loop as-is (that is, you aren't going to edit the loop or change its instrument or effects assignments), you can lighten the load on your Mac by dragging the loop into a real instrument track. For more details, see the sidebar on page 253.

Tweak preferences. Choose GarageBand's Preferences command and click the Advanced button. There you can examine and change settings that GarageBand normally makes automatically. Try reducing the number of voices per instrument. Note that this restricts the number of simultaneous notes you can play.

Simplify your song. Mute some tracks and turn off some effects. The Amp Simulation effects are particularly power-hungry. You *can* greatly lighten GarageBand's burden by unchecking Reverb and Echo in the Master Track's Track Info window, but doing so will eliminate the ability to use these effects in your song. Still, you might find this a worthwhile price to pay for extra tracks. You can always transfer your song to a faster Mac to get that polish that good reverb provides.

Use an external drive. A high-performance external FireWire hard drive may be able to keep up with multiple real instrument tracks better than your Mac's built-in drive, especially if you have a PowerBook.

Optimize PowerBook performance. If you're using a PowerBook, open the Energy Saver system preference and choose Highest Performance from the Optimize Energy Settings pop-up menu.

Turn off FileVault. Mac OS X's FileVault feature can dramatically slow the reading of data from the Home directory of your hard drive. Turn off FileVault using the Security system preference, or store your songs outside your Home directory.

Bouncing to Disk

If the measures I've described here don't do it for you, there's still hope: an update of a technique that us old fogies—people who grew up with analog multitrack recording—know about all too well.

Back in the analog multitrack days, when you approached the limit of your four-track cassette deck, you would mix down the three tracks you had already recorded and put them on the fourth track. After the mix-down, you could erase and re-use the original three tracks.

This technique was often called *bouncing*, as in "I need to bounce those tracks if I want to record any more." It wasn't a perfect solution—once you bounced those original tracks, you couldn't change their relative volumes, for example—but it did let you keep on tracking.

Bouncing is alive and well in GarageBand. Say you've laid down a sweet rhythm

section groove—some drums, some bass, and maybe a keyboard or synthesizer pad. You want to play a synth solo over this, but your PowerBook doesn't have the power.

Solution: bounce your song-in-progress to a single track, then bring that track into a new GarageBand project.

Fine-tune your mix. Adjust every setting—panning, volume, effects, everything—until your mix sounds exactly as you want it. Save your project.

Export to iTunes. Choose Export to iTunes from the File menu. GarageBand creates a stereo mixdown of your tune and adds it to your iTunes music library.

Start over. Start a new GarageBand project. Be sure to set the key signature and tempo to match your song's settings. Locate your song in iTunes, and drag it

into GarageBand. You've just added your mixdown to your new song.

Add tracks and have fun. Because your rhythm groove is now one audio track—not a whole bunch of different, system-taxing tracks—your Mac can devote its energy to the new tracks.

Making changes. In the analog world, once you bounced a few tracks and then erased the originals, you were stuck with the mixdown that you created. The digital world is a better place. If you decide to change your rhythm groove, just open up your original project, make your changes, and export to iTunes again. Then open your second song, delete the rhythm track, and add the new mixdown to it.

How GarageBand Stores Instruments

GarageBand stores a software instrument as a file whose name ends with .cst—for example, if you named your instrument *Wacko*, its file will be Wacko.cst. GarageBand stores its instrument files deep inside your hard drive's Library folder.

Tip: To put your custom instrument in a different category in GarageBand's Track Info window, move its file into the appropriate category folder. For example, to move an instrument from the Synth Leads category to the Bass category, move its file from the Synth Leads folder to the Bass folder.

- Bass
- Choir
- Drum Kits
- Guitars
- Horns
- Mallets
- Organs
- Pianos and Keyboards
- Strings
- Synth Basics
- Synth Leads
- Synth Pads
- Woodwinds

Index

Index

Index

H

hard drives, 12, 78, 79, 156
hardware
    accessories/add-ons, 12–15
    connecting, 10–11
Harmon Kardon, 13
harmonics, 47
headphones, 11
Hewlett-Packard, 140
Hi-8 format, 155
Hijack/Hijack Pro, 58–59, 255
Home Media Option (TiVO), 62
HomePage, 120–121, 191
HTML, 122
hubs, FireWire, 13
Huffman compression, 27
HyperText Markup Language, 122

I

iBook, 124
iCal, 34, 86–87
iCalShare, 87
ICE, Digital, 140
Ice-Link, 81
iChat AV, 58
iDVD, 204–227
    adding movies to DVDs with, 208–209
    and Apple logo watermark, 216
    AppleScripts for, 227
    archiving feature, 223
    automating, 227
    burning DVDs in, 222–223
    buttons/controls, 204–205
    choosing/customizing themes in, 206–207
    creating chapter markers for, 188–189
    creating slide shows in, 210–213
    dragging media between panes in, 226
    encoder settings, 209, 227
    and Final Cut Express/Pro, 209
    hacking, 226
    managing projects in, 225
    and PDF format, 226

planning/creating menus in, 214–219, 226–227
    purpose of, 6, 204
    switching panes in, 226
iDVD Companion, 227
iDVD pane (iMovie), 152
iDVD Themetastic, 224
iDVDThemes, 224
iLife
    combining media with, 8–9
    dragging items between programs, 8
    purpose of, 6–7
    upgrading Mac for, 12–15
    vs. Windows alternatives, 6
    Web site, 54
iMac, 12
Image Capture program (Mac OS X), 142, 143, 144, 224
image-editing programs, 111, 131
images. *See* photos
imaging technology, 2–3
iMic, 60
iMix playlists, 19, 39
iMovie, 152–201
    add-ons, 197
    adding audio to movies in, 172–173
    adding clips to movies in, 160–161
    adding photos to movies in, 166–167
    adding special effects in, 184–185
    adding transitions in, 180–181
    advanced timeline techniques, 162–163
    buttons/controls, 152–153
    creating cutaways in, 164–165
    creating iDVD chapter markers in, 188–189
    creating titles in, 182–183
    emailing movies from, 190
    emptying trash for, 159
    enhancing animations in, 201
    exporting QuickTime movies from, 192
    exporting to Bluetooth devices from, 193
    exporting to tape from, 186–187
    importing video into, 156–157
    Ken Burns effect, 141, 166–171
    making better movies with, 198–199
    and movie-making process, 154–155

navigation tips, 195
Play Video Through to Camera option, 197
publishing movies to .Mac HomePage with, 191
purpose of, 6, 152
recording narration in, 173
scene-detection feature, 157
and time-lapse movies, 201
timeline-snapping feature, 163
working with audio tracks in, 176–179
working with clips in, 158–159, 194–195
iMovie 4 Visual QuickStart Guide, 192
Import button (iTunes), 20
Import command (iMovie), 167
importing
    changing iTunes settings for, 22–23
    defined, 20
    photos, 94–95, 141, 143, 145, 167
    playlists, 67
    video, 156–157
in points, clip, 162
Inbar, Yoel, 53
information design, DVD, 214
inkjet photo printers, 126, 129, 130
instrument tracks (GarageBand), 234–235.
    See also specific types
Internet
    photofinishers, 93, 130
    radio, 18, 56–59
    sharing photos via, 118–123
iPhoto, 90–145
    and Apple HomePage feature, 120–121
    AppleScripts for, 142
    assigning keywords to photos in, 100–101
    batch-changing photos in, 96, 105, 145
    burning CDs/DVDs in, 136–137
    buttons/controls, 90–91
    creating albums in, 102–105
    creating books in, 132–133
    creating/managing photo libraries in, 95, 138–139
    cropping photos in, 107, 131, 148
    customizing view in, 98
    dealing with duplicate photos in, 142

Index

Index

Index

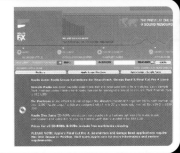

In addition to all great Apple Loops DVDs and CDs, there are Apple Loops Sample Packs at the **Apple Zone**. These downloadable construction kits cover all kinds of styles and instruments that kick-start inspiration to help you get composing quickly.

Visti **www.powerfx.com/applezone** for more info, and to listen to demos.

PowerFX is a leading sound development innovator and content provider specializing in sampling products and sound effects for today's sound production projects. PowerFX licensors include Apple, Sonic Foundry, Cakewalk, Ableton Live, MOTU, Propellerheads, Steinberg, Sounds Good, Bias, Denon, IK Multimedia Visiosonic,Voice Crystal, TC Electronics and Nokia. PowerFX sounds have been used in countless music, film and commercial productions.

Rock and Pop Trio: A huge and well recorded collection of acoustic drums, electric bass, and guitar riffs, rhythms and leads in a straight up rock style.

Street Stylin: An urban themed collection of loops in R&B/Hip Hop/Down Tempo flavors with synth basses, funky guitars, keys, FX and booming beats.

Studio Percussion: A broad and indispensable collection of clean and beautifully recorded percussion loops that can be used in almost any genre. It includes traditional percussion plus congas, bongos, shakers, timbales and bells.

Invincible Dance: A fresh collection of Club & Dance oriented loops featuring everything from bass & drum loops to synth pads and FX loops.

NuJazz House: Authentic acoustic & electric instrument samples in the Jazz vein that include drums, bass, electric piano, minor 7th chords & much more.

Electro Clashmatic: A Neo-Retro combination of classic Vocoder & Electro style beats & bass as well as modern synth & FX one shots.

ProScore DVDs are premier music composition and sound effect libraries created for use with Apple's Final Cut Pro 4 and Soundtrack. Each DVD contains over 2 200 diverse, pre-formatted Apple Loops that provide film, video and audio professionals with a creative advantage that's economical and efficient.

DV Composer's Toolkit is a complete musical composition arsenal with everything from urban and cinematic themes to Asian and Indian flavours. It features Soundtrack arrangements, ambiance textures and hundreds of asorted instument loops. **Massive FX** has everything you need to create authentic audio backdrops.

How GarageBand Gets Its Groove On.

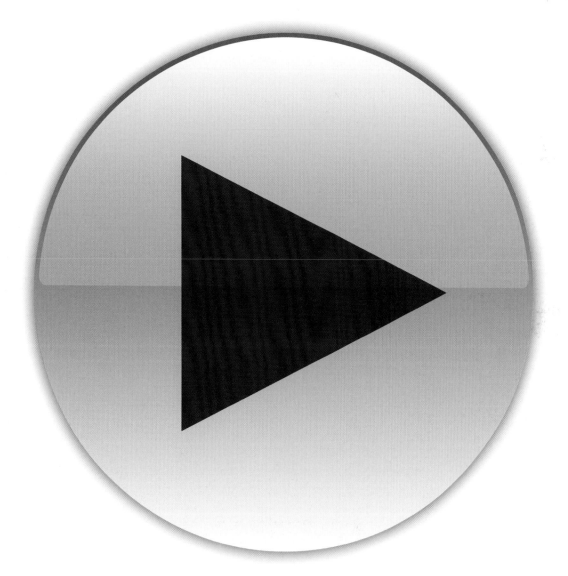

iDrum The Drum Machine For Mac OS X

www.glaresoft.com

FREE Digital Photography Tips DVD Featuring Jim Heid

How do you use iLife?

Help us make our books, seminars, and videos better–and get **a free* training DVD featuring Jim Heid!**

Fill out our short online survey at **www.macilife.com/survey** and we'll send you a special discount code that will allow you to order Avondale Media's "Go Digital" DVD without incurring the standard $19.95 charge. While you're there, check out the latest news, articles, tips and updates to the iLife suite of digital media applications.

DVD VIDEO

Avondale Media's "Go Digital" DVD

With "Go Digital," Jim Heid will teach you the essential tips for using digital cameras and digital video cameras. Along the way, you'll see how Apple's iLife programs–iTunes, iPhoto, iMovie, and iDVD–make it easier than ever to work with digital photos and movies.

Avondale
MEDIA

Visit our Web site to learn about our full array of DVD courses:

www.avondalemedia.com

* The standard $19.95 DVD cost will be waived; only the standard shipping and handling charge will apply. S&H costs are $6.95 for delivery within the U.S. Supply is limited; the survey will be posted on the site only until inventory is exhausted.